ITALY

from NAPOLEON to MUSSOLINI

ITALY

from NAPOLEON

to MUSSOLINI

René Albrecht-Carrié

COLUMBIA UNIVERSITY PRESS

NEW YORK and LONDON

To the Memory of My Father

PREFACE

A LITTLE over four years ago we celebrated with relief the end of the Second World War, first in Europe, shortly thereafter in Japan. There was, in America especially, a widespread feeling that a job had been finished, and the understandable urge to resume the interrupted and "normal" (meaning pre-war) course of existence found expression in the precipitateness with which we brought the boys back home and dismantled our war machine. We are, at present, very exercised—departing, in some ways, with resentment born of frustration, from the canons of calm judgment—about what appears to many an attempt on the part of Soviet Russia comparable to that of the Rome-Berlin-Tokyo triangle to organize the world in accordance with its designs. The latter attempt has undoubtedly failed, but, in a sense, this failure, and our victory, represent an essentially negative accomplishment, for the following reason.

On the level of power, Germany, Italy, and Japan were seeking certain definite and concrete acquisitions and advantages. But this is only part, in some respects not the major part, of the story. For, in connection with their attempt, cause as well as effect of it, there emerged the assertion of a wholly new set of values and view of life—new at least in the sense that they represented a departure from what we had come to regard as the established trend of social and political evolution since the beginning of the nineteenth century.

Like all historical phenomena, this one is complex, and our proximity to it, even discounting the part of emotions, preconceptions, and established patterns of thought, makes it difficult to appraise the factors involved at their true value. There is one view which would consider the phenomenon of Fascism and Nazism as a mere extension of the past. Nazi Germany is shown to have its roots in Bismarck, Frederick, and Luther. Mussolini is but the logical heir of Machiavelli and Sorel. These roots undoubtedly exist and it is useful to trace them. But as a complete explanation, this is one that, because of its limitations, amounts to gross distortion. At the other extreme, Nazism and Fascism are viewed as novel and momentary aberrations, which, once defeated in their native habitats, can be forgotten as dead things. This is equally incomplete and misleading.

Fascism-Nazism, and the war which they precipitated, were symptoms of a malady far more fundamental than the mere contest for power of rival nations or groups of nations. The social maladjustments of which the Axis phenomenon was a manifestation were not cured by the war, for, if the military force of the German and Italian nations has been broken, the social dislocations which gave Fascism and Nazism their appeal, and which the war itself served to accentuate, have not been resolved.

Nazism and Fascism are responses to problems that cut across national boundaries. But our world is a world of nations. That is where the complexity and the confusion arise. We have to deal with social and economic problems that cut across national lines in the framework of national units. The framework cannot be ignored or suddenly discarded.

That the successful conclusion of the war was by no means synonymous with effective organization of peace is hardly an original statement to make in 1949. The defeat of the triangle removed the force that had cemented the adventitious alliance of East and West. In the postwar task of reorganizing the world, of finding a practicable remedy for its political and economic ills, we and the Russians offer incompatible solutions. Our own task is to prove workable a solution that will reconcile the conflict between freedom and organization. In this attempt, rejecting the totalitarian solution of Russian Communism, we find that the forces and ideas which came to hold power in Germany and in Italy are still alive and in our very midst, however much disguised their presentation and parentage.

Bearing the foregoing considerations in mind, the purpose of this book is not to offer yet another blueprint for world organization, nor again to be a history in the ordinary sense of the word. It is rather to present an analysis and interpretation of certain forces and developments, the understanding of which is a necessary prerequisite to the organization of the future. Analysis and interpretation will be applied to Italy, used as an illustration and case study of a wider phenomenon.

In many ways, the case of Italy is a particularly interesting one. The rapidity with which Italy has been accepted by her enemies of yesterday, climaxed in her participation in the Atlantic Pact, is in itself remarkable. In this we must see two things: the degree of Italian power, and Italian diplomatic skill, both of which have roots in a long past. For reasons of relative power, popular attention was focused on Germany and developments in that country, while corresponding happenings in Italy were looked upon either as of little significance for the outside world or even with a certain condescending and sympathetic benevolence.

This was the mistake—a mistake peculiarly, though by no means exclusively, British—of thinking in terms of power only. It is true that Italy alone, on the basis of her own resources, could never have been a serious threat to the rest of the world. But it is well to remember that, of Nazism and Fascism, the latter was the elder twin.

To a considerable extent, Fascism came to be what it was as the result of an opportunistic adaptation to circumstances and conditions which are the fundamental realities, economic and political, of our time, as these appeared on the Italian scene. In the course of this process of adaptation, Fascism may be said to have come of age, evolving meanwhile a political philosophy, a technique of government, a whole *Weltanschauung,* which in turn became an active force in its own right. Thus it was that, having secured control of the power of the Italian nation, Fascism, driven by its inner logic, became a prime mover in setting in motion the train of events that precipitated the final explosion and set off the second world conflagration within a quarter of a century.

In any case, however, the episode of Fascism proper is evidently history—history which, though recent, we are beginning to see with a certain perspective—and what this essay proposes to do is to give an interpretative survey of the development of Italy from the beginning of the nineteenth century, leading to the climax of Fascism, with the question in mind: how and why did it happen?

Not with any preconceived deterministic approach, uncongenial to the writer, but rather with the simple advantages of hindsight and perspective (is not the first task of the historian that of performing post mortems?) to account for the course of the past. The result is interpretive and selective use of the material of Italian history, rather than chronological recital, and the conclusion the undramatic one that, in view of background and circumstances, the phenomenon of Fascism was by no means inevitable, but that it was "logical," "natural," or "understandable"—and the caution that it is just as likely to arise wherever and whenever suitable conditions may obtain.

There is a common temptation to look into the past for lessons for the future. Aside from the belief that the past is of sufficient interest to merit study for its own sake, on the issue of whether its study holds useful and applicable lessons for present and future conduct, the author is inclined to skepticism. The course of human events is too laden with complexities for the historian to venture on the path of the prophet. But of the value of understanding there can be little question; and to the understanding of a past which bears upon our future this may perhaps hope to be some contribution.

The author wishes to express his indebtedness to the Carnegie Endowment for International Peace for the material assistance which made possible the writing of the present book. He wishes it clearly understood, however, that he assumes sole and full responsibility for any of the statements and opinions which appear in it. To Dr. James T. Shotwell he is particularly grateful for the time given to a careful reading and criticism of the entire manuscript, to friendly debates on the nature of Fascism and on the history of Italy, and for numerous valuable suggestions.

ALGONQUIN PARK, ONTARIO   *René Albrecht-Carrié*
JUNE 21, 1949

CONTENTS

Part III. THE FASCIST EPISODE

Part I

INTRODUCTION

Chapter I · THE BACKGROUND OF MODERN ITALY

The citizens of a certain town [Siena seems to be meant] had once an officer in their service who had freed them from foreign aggression; daily they took counsel how to recompense him, and concluded that no reward in their power was great enough, not even if they made him lord of the city. At last one of them rose and said, "Let us kill him and then worship him as our patron saint." And so they did.

In our change-loving Italy, where nothing stands firm, and where no ancient dynasty exists, a servant can easily become a king. [Aeneas Sylvius, Pope Pius II]

(From Jakob Burckhardt, THE CIVILIZATION OF THE RENAISSANCE IN ITALY)

THE TRADITIONS OF ITALY

If one looks at the political map of Europe over the past four centuries, a contrast appears at once which reveals a long-developing trend. The main units of the west have changed little: Spain and Portugal hardly at all; England and Scotland have joined, making one the island of Britain politically as well as in fact; France has expanded her northern and eastern borders. These units as shown in solid blocks of color remain always identifiable and relatively constant. But outside of the western countries, the map presents to the eye the spectacle of many and varied changes. A Poland stretching into the depths of the Ukraine undergoes the most drastic readjustments, disappears altogether for over a century, to reemerge again in our time, but with still widely fluctuating borders. Within the relatively stable boundaries of an increasingly anachronistic Holy Roman Empire, the myriad changes that occur are a burden on both memory and attention. In the southeast, the rising Ottoman power, which at one time threatened the very heart of the Habsburg domain, eventually began to recede, making room for Habsburg expansion first, later for the emergence of individual Balkan peoples, some of whom, the Turk once eliminated, recoiled on these same Habsburgs. The appanage of the imperial title, later the presidency of the Germanic Confederation, also involved that house in all the internecine quarrels of the Germanic world, until scores were settled by a conclusive Prussian victory. The segments of the Italian peninsula, while less numerous and more stable than those of the Empire, have been the football of many dynasties and rulers, some local, but mainly Bourbon and Habsburg.

In the light of historic retrospect, the greater stability of the west is seen to come from the earlier identification of the state with a national unit. For good or evil, what we have come to accept, or even glorify, as nationalism, or the principle of the self-determination of peoples, has been one of the great driving forces of history. Appropriately, the First World War made it one of its slogans. There are other forces; nor would it be correct to speak of nationalism, in the sixteenth or seventeenth centuries, in fact before the French Revolution, as we understand the term today. But nationalism, in its simplest form the desire of a people to constitute itself into a self-governing political unit, is after all rooted in the existence of distinct peoples, a very old fact indeed.

Among the peoples of Europe none is older than the Italian in the consciousness of its existence as a distinct unit. If we consider language, that first and obviously simplest bond of cultural and national unity, Italian as a language is also among the oldest of living tongues; certainly the Italian of the Divine Comedy is closer to that of today than is either Shakespeare's English or fourteenth century French to the English and French of our time. If we think of the other aspects of culture and civilization—commerce and the various arts—here also the Italians were well ahead of the rest of Europe.

So the query comes naturally to mind, why is it that Italy did not emerge as a national state until 1870 (or 1861); why did she not do so for example at the same time as the western national monarchies, at the beginning of what has generally come to be called the modern period of history? To that question it may be profitable to turn our attention for a while, for the answer to it can throw light on many aspects of the development of a later Italy. Whether one cherish or abhor the thought, there is no gainsaying that the hand of the past lies heavy on the present and the future.

When considering the development of Italy, clearly the first factor to bear in mind is the inheritance of Rome. Interestingly enough, that inheritance, in so far as it still retained vitality at the beginning of the modern epoch, was rather a hindrance than a help to the formation of national unity in the modern sense. To be sure, as early as the beginning of the Christian era, Augustan Italy had achieved a shape very closely resembling that of the Italy that we know, a fact often stressed by present-day Italian nationalists as an argument in frontier revindications. However, Rome did not stand for Italy but for the much wider territory and concept of empire. Romanized Gaul, for instance, was as Roman as Rome herself, in some respects, after a time, even more so. The earlier and highly exclusive Greek concept of "barbarian" had been narrowed to apply to those peoples actually without the pale of civilization, and the word Roman came to include the great diversity of lands and peoples that acknowledged the sway of Roman rule and law. The Empire, in this respect at least, was a magnificent creation, the duration of which made it possible for the idea to strike deep roots that it was right, proper, and *normal* that all civilized mankind, at least, should constitute a single political unit. Our blundering and clumsy gropings toward *One World* were once reality. There was pride in the phrase *civis romanus sum,* but not nationalistic pride. The language, too, was a uniting medium; for, if the more civilized eastern part of the Empire clung to its Hellenistic culture, the new lands of the west adopted the Latin tongue. And it may be recalled in passing that the first line of political cleavage— a cleavage the effects of which may be seen to this day in a country like Yugoslavia—was along the line of division between the Latin and Hellenic cultural influences.

In time the Empire fell to pieces. The proper concomitance of internal weakness and external pressures brought this result about. The barbarians poured across the frontiers and, while the new Rome of Constantine managed to hold them off for another millennium, old Rome fell to them like the provinces. It took long for the process of disintegration to reach its nadir, and longer still for the slow painful process of rebuilding to produce viable political units. That is the story of the Middle Ages and the basis of the variegated European family of nations with which we are familiar. As it turned out, the old unity could not be recovered, but the idea of it survived long after the possibility must be irrevocably abandoned. On Christmas day of the year 800, the imperial crown was set upon the head of Charlemagne. The gesture was a tribute to the potency of the Roman idea but the expression of no existing reality. The able but unlettered barbarian could, while he lived, hold substantial territories together, even though they represented but a fragment of the old Empire. The profound decadence of all those elements that hold society together—towns, commerce, communications and administration—showed his structure to have been but a flash in a long and still deepening night. Anarchy returned. But still the imperial idea of universality lived on. The western lands, however, were definitely lost to it, and the subsequent Holy Roman Empire of the German nation is one of the more curious specimens of the museum of history. It was neither universal nor national, and the long connection between its chief component parts, Germanic and Italian, redounded on the whole to the greater disadvantage of both. In so far as it survived, the Roman ideal of universality was a block in the way of the formation of Italian national unity.

But there was more. When Charlemagne took the imperial title— whether the Pope actually set the crown upon his head or whether he did this himself is a point on which the annals are at variance—there is no question that the deed had ecclesiastical sanction. The divergent accounts of the event are an omen of the subsequent prolonged struggle for primacy between Pope and Emperor; but, however they may have quarreled, both were heirs to the Roman idea, the Pope in the more real sense for the Church did encompass the allegiance of all (western) mankind, and after the Eastern schism and the Moslem conquests, at least of western European mankind, a claim no emperor could make good after Charlemagne. The struggle was bitter, with many ups and downs. The papacy fell upon evil days and was at times the prize, not even of the Emperor, but of mere rival factions in the city of Rome. Then again, the German Henry IV went to Canossa, King John of England made over his country into a fief of Innocent III. Was not the spiritual above the temporal, hence could not the Pope depose any ruler? Later still, Philip the Fair of France could imprison a Pope. In the end, the papal claim to supremacy could not be made good and, while the peoples and rulers still owed allegiance to the Church of Rome, that allegiance was increasingly restricted to the spiritual field. The case of France is a good illustration; one of the reasons that country remained in the fold of Rome in the sixteenth century is to be found in the extensive rights which the Concordat of Francis I granted the crown in the affairs of the Church of France.

At the time of which we are speaking, Rome herself was no longer within the Empire. Instead of that, simultaneously with the weakening of the more far-reaching papal claim to supremacy, the temporal power of the Popes became more firmly established within Rome herself. The old claim, based on the spurious Donation of Constantine and the more authentic one of Pippin, had been made good. The States of the Church, stretching across the middle third of the Italian peninsula, were one among the European states. The justification for this state of affairs lay in the theory—formally still maintained—that the untrammeled exercise of the Pope's spiritual function required his possession of territorial sovereignty as well. The reality, at the beginning of the sixteenth century, was simpler and less grandiose. To all intents and purposes, the States of the Church were one among the Italian states, like Florence, Venice or Naples, and the Pope acted primarily as the sovereign of such a state, mainly engrossed in that capacity in the intricate politics of the peninsula, his personal advantage and that of his kin. The Italian states were all equally jealous of their independence and as a consequence all constituted obstacles to unity, but the papal claim to territorial sovereignty had a peculiar, and stronger, basis than any other. In the last resort, the Pope could appeal to all Christendom for protection against encroachment. In fact he did. Eventually, in the nineteenth century, it was French power, and even more concretely French bayonets, that kept Rome from being absorbed in the rest of Italy which that city—save for the small Venetian irredenta—was the last to join. To the very last, in his dual capacity of petty Italian sovereign and representative of a universal idea, the Pope was a particularly stubborn obstacle to the formation of Italian unity.

There was a third obstacle to Italian unity in the sixteenth century. We are apt to think of the earlier national integration of the west as a sign of more advanced political development. In a way this view is correct, and there is no denying that Italy—like Germany—with a considerable time lag followed eventually the pattern of the west. Yet the very advancement of Italy at the time of the Renaissance delayed the process. In the anarchy that engulfed all Europe at one time Italy had been no exception; one of the most concrete manifestations of decline was the virtual disappearance of town life, a phenomenon of which no more sensational illustration may be given than that of the city of Rome herself: estimated to be in the order of 1,000,000 in the days of Imperial Rome, the population had dwindled to some 30,000 in the fifteenth century. But as early as the eleventh century the widespread process of decline had begun to give way to the first signs of rehabilitation. Trade and towns began a slow revival, despite setbacks, uninterrupted to our day. Other cities benefited more than Rome from the change and grew to be considerably larger, but to a greater extent than anywhere in Europe those cities were Italian. The basis of their newborn strength was trade, local sometimes, but more important, foreign.

The Mediterranean became the highway of commerce *par excellence* and the Italians the great middlemen of Europe, whither they brought the luxuries and spices of the East, both Near and Far. The Crusades gave a boost to Mediterranean traffic. The leadership of the movement, military and political, was mainly French—or Frankish—and the medium of communication in the Levant became known as *lingua franca;* but the greatest economic advantage was diverted to Italian hands in shrewd, if not always overscrupulous, ways. Venice had ships that would transport crusaders to the Holy Land—for a price. And if the obligation could not be met in good hard coin it might be discharged by helping capture rival Zara for Venice, for example. Or again, the crusaders might be induced to stop off at Byzantium. Barbarians that they were, they could satiate their greed in the plunder of the imperial city, and a Latin kingdom might even be set up in it for a time. Venice was quite content with the less spectacular, but more profitable, guarantee of trade privileges.

Venice is the most striking case of commercial success, though by no means the only one. Her bitter rival Genoa and many others likewise grew and prospered by trade. In the twelfth century, the cities of the Lombard plain were strong enough in league to stand up to and defeat the Emperor. But, more often, these numerous cities were deadly competitors and the story is long and intricate of their everlasting feuds. In time, some of them emerged as dominant, when able to subdue a number of their neighbors and thus establish their rule over a larger territory. During the course of this development, and with the exception of the south, as Italian life was becoming more urbanized, the feudal system rooted in an agrarian economy was greatly weakened, and the towns achieved a large degree of autonomy of which they were very jealous. The process was not exclusively Italian—communes appeared in Flanders also, for example, and there also as an accompaniment to thriving trade—but it is fair to say that it was more marked and advanced in Italy as a whole than anywhere else in Europe.

The communal tradition struck deep roots in Italy; it became in fact a much more real and strong, because living, force than the remote and embalmed influence of old Rome herself, save in the manner earlier described. But precisely because this was a force of such vitality and one that commanded intense loyalty, it led after a while to a process of crystallization that prevented the grasping of the broader horizon of a larger unity. Old Rome, the papacy, and most of all the communes, determined the shape of Italy at the very time when new forces were stirring in the consciousness of Europe—nowhere more actively than in Italy herself—forces that were to produce that extraordinary outburst of expansion and to initiate the process which has been aptly described as the conquest of the world by Europe. We must pause to look a little more closely at the precise shape of this Italy and examine the reasons that prevented these forces from effecting the same change in the peninsula as in the western part of Europe.

THE STATE AS A WORK OF ART

With rashness perhaps, and allowing for differences, the temptation is yet strong to establish a parallel between the Europe of our day, taken as a whole, and the totality of the Italian peninsula some four hundred years ago. Italy, then, in her multiplicity, offered the spectacle of a self-contained microcosm, consisting of great powers and lesser states. Much the largest of these units, in the territorial sense at least, was the Kingdom of the Two Sicilies which accounted for a third of the whole. While this state was inevitably involved in the politics of Italy, it stood nevertheless in a position somewhat apart from the rest. Its geographical position was the reason for its having been subjected to outside influences which had touched the middle and the north to a lesser degree: the old Greek substratum, and more recently the Mohammedan tenure of Sicily on which the curious episode of the Norman conquest had been superimposed, gave that section a character, ethnic and cultural, which to this day have stamped it as unique and distinct from the rest of Italy. Moreover, the vicissitudes of history had finally put the land in the hands of the House of Aragon. With the merger of Aragon and Castile, the Neapolitan kingdom became an outpost of Spanish power and may be said to have been the first to enter that limbo where all Italy was shortly destined to fall and of which we shall speak presently.

At the opposite extremity from the Two Sicilies stood the Republic of Venice. The *Serenissima* was wedded to the sea as the picturesque annual ceremony appropriately recalled. The position and policy of Venice call to mind later Britain. For both, the bases of power were the related factors of sea-borne trade and naval strength. Venice was *the* naval power of the day, not only by Italian but by European standards as well. As late as 1570, the chief contribution to the battle of Lepanto was Venetian, and a measure of the degree of Venetian power may be gathered from the fact that at one time Emperor, Pope, and King of France, to say nothing of other Italian states, were in league against her. Venice was injured, but the combination of her own strength and her diplomacy soon restored her. Because of her power, Venice, like later Britain, although her interests were far flung, was inclined toward aloofness and splendid isolation. Even though she had been led to expand on the mainland, where she had come to control a territory which by Italian standards may be called extensive, Venice was above all imperial. Her galleys went as far as Britain, but her preserve was the eastern Mediterranean where she long held her own against the advancing Ottoman power. Venice was also the mother of diplomacy in the modern sense, the reports of her envoys still standing as the earliest monument of their nature.

Situated on the outskirts of Latinity at the meeting point of the three great ethnic groups of Europe—Latin, German and Slav—the Alpine bounds of the Venetian mainland have always been one of the pressure points of Europe. They are still so, as contemporary struggles remind us. For a while, even the Moslem power reaching overland was destined to be a threat. Contact with and the influence of Byzantium were very pronounced in Venice, as the great edifice of St. Mark's and local architecture witness. The business of managing the state was cultivated with assiduity. Though a republic, Venice was no democracy but rather the most tightly controlled autocracy, yet not subject to one-man rule. The famed and feared Council of Ten decided upon all matters of state beyond appeal. Yet her rule was efficient and sane and neither oppressive nor capricious, as is shown by the acceptance of it by her mainland conquests. If the preservation of law and order were the highest endeavor of statecraft, then the Venetian constitution would be a model one. Many indeed thought so. There were no revolutions in Venice; plots and conspiracies were quietly and effectively disposed of.

The position, tradition, and culture of Venice all went to give her the stamp of a very marked and strong individuality. Both Naples and Venice were Italian, yet one could hardly find a greater contrast than between the two, or between either and the rest of the Italian states, among whom one may discern a larger common denominator of ways and institutions.

Of the Papal State and its peculiar nature we have spoken. Its unique character derived from the unique nature of the papacy, but unlike Naples or Venice, there was no element of aloofness in its policy. The Popes were Italians. The experiment of a non-Italian Pope in the person of Adrian of Utrecht, in the early part of the sixteenth century, was by common consent a failure. Adrian was a good and well-meaning man, but unhappy and bewildered in the unfamiliar atmosphere and intrigues of the Roman Curia. The experiment was not repeated and his successors, like his predecessors, were well versed in the intricacies of Italian state and family politics in which they took a most active and earnest interest.

Next door to Venice, and second to her in wealth, was Milan, or Lombardy, astride the middle reaches of the fertile plain of the Po. Centrally situated in the vast semicircle formed by the Alps around the north of Italy, Milan was a logical entrepôt for transalpine trade, and the foundation of her power was, like Venice's, commercial wealth.

Milan was torn by strife between the rival claimants to her rule, Visconti and Sforza. Milan was also, though more in name than fact, a fief of the Empire and, in addition, a French claim derived from marital alliances made her the first pretext for those foreign incursions as the result of which nearly all Italy was soon to lose her independence.

The states that have been mentioned and Florence—of which more in a moment—were the great powers. There were other units of varying degrees of size, importance, and strength. The Savoyard Duchy, astride the Alps, was comparable in extent, though not in significance, with the larger units. One half of it, Savoy, was in fact not Italian, and not until the nineteenth century was Savoy destined to play a major role in Italian politics. Of more account was smaller Genoa, the basis of whose strength was similar to Venice's. Genoa was still wealthy, but in the harsh competition with her maritime rival she had definitely lost out and was no longer in the same category of power. Mantua, Modena, Ferrara, and some other minor units would complete the list.

As just mentioned, this survey has omitted Florence. If Venice recalls nineteenth century Britain, Florence brings to mind France in the same period. Gifted and seemingly mercurial, she was a perfect illustration of the quotation of Pope Pius II at the head of this chapter. The people, the Medici, even that strange phenomenon, Savonarola, dominated the state in quick succession near the turn from the fifteenth to the sixteenth century. No stability of acceptance here, but a turmoil of questioning debate and agitation. Florence was still expanding and with great effort finally succeeded in subduing rival Pisa, later absorbing Siena to give Tuscany her final shape. Florence may be regarded as the quintessence of the Italian microcosm. Like that of the other states, her power derived from commercial wealth. The house of Medici, whose coat of arms recalls their origin, is perhaps the best single instance of this accumulation of wealth. The Medici were bankers, a calling developed in Italy earlier than in England and other parts of Europe, whither the Italians introduced it (witness London's Lombard street). In itself, the existence of banking as a profession betokens the importance that the transactions of commerce had in time assumed. Florence may be regarded as the summation of Italy mainly in two respects, in culture and in thought.

Dante was Florentine. He, with Petrarch and Boccaccio who shortly followed him, is usually credited with making the dialect of their city into the Italian tongue. This happened in the fourteenth century. Dante's masterwork is a synthesis of the late medieval outlook, but Petrarch, born while Dante was still living, is called the father of humanism. There may be humor in the fact, of which Petrarch himself is a perfect illustration, that the humanists were so awed by the glory of the Ancients, or at least by their idea of the Ancients, and succeeded so well in restoring Cicero's Latin, that they made it into the dead language it has become. Petrarch's casual and incidental (in his own estimation) Sonnets to Laura, written in the vernacular, are now far more alive than the polished orations and epistles in which he took such care and pride. But whatever fancied notions the humanists may have entertained of antiquity, what counted was the fact that the worship of it was a convenient club with which to belabor the hitherto accepted ideas of the role and destiny of man. Even though there was no religious break in Italy, the fundamental tenet of Renaissance humanism, when reduced to its barest essentials, is the implied acceptance of the worth of earthly existence for its own sake. In that broad sense, the spirit of the Renaissance represents a deep-rooted revolt against the outlook of medieval Christianity; and, in that sense also, the outburst of exploring activity which caused Europeans to go to the far corners of the earth, the northern Reformation, the beginnings of modern science, are all aspects of the same deep stirring that went on in the minds of men at this time. Italy was the home of the Renaissance from which it spread abroad; and within Italy, where it found its highest expression, Florence was the capital and heart of the movement.

The connection between wealth and the arts has been too often expounded—and oversimplified—to need repetition. There was great wealth in Italy and there were enlightened patrons of the arts, none more outstanding than the Florentine Medici themselves. But it was most especially in Florence that there occurred that phenomenon which wealth alone cannot conjure, the existence of a galaxy of men who produced art of the highest order. The interest in art was by no means exclusive to that city. Da Vinci spent much time in Milan and even ended his days at the court of Francis I of France. The Popes were as great and discerning patrons of the arts as any, but it was Florentine Michelangelo whom they called to Rome. This is not the place to retail a long list of familiar accomplishments; suffice it to point out that artistic development was the chief form that the Renaissance took in Italy.

The phrase "artistic development," should not, however, be taken in the narrow sense of manifestations restricted to the plastic and pictorial arts alone, but in the broader meaning which makes it applicable to all aspects of the activity of man, including the organization of society. Living, in all its phases, too, is art. To quote from Burckhardt's justly famed work on the Renaissance in Italy:

As the majority of the Italian states were in their internal constitution works of art, that is, the fruit of reflection and careful adaptation, so was their relation to one another and to foreign countries also a work of art. That nearly all of them were the result of recent usurpations, was a fact that exercised as fatal an influence in their origin as in their internal policy. Not one of them recognized another without reserve; the same play of chance which had helped to found and consolidate one dynasty might upset another. Nor was it always a matter of choice with the despot whether to keep quiet or not. The necessity of movement and aggrandizement is common to all illegitimate powers. Thus Italy became the scene of a "foreign policy" which gradually, as in other countries also, acquired the position of a recognized system of public law. The purely objective treatment of international affairs, as free from prejudice as from moral scruples, attained a perfection which sometimes is not without a certain beauty and grandeur of its own.

It was in most Italian Florence that Machiavelli saw the light of day. Always interested in government and the affairs of state, his share in them was not such as to have warranted for him a conspicuous place in history. It is rather the fact that, associated as he was with the period when the Medici were in exile, their return coincided with his fall from favor, and the consequent retirement to which he was condemned gave him enforced leisure in which to set down the results of his experience, his meditations, and his reading. The *Discourses on Livy* and the *Prince* are the chief bases of his controversial fame. Machiavelli had a keen mind, though apparently not a very sensitive nature, and may perhaps be cited as an illustration of the shortcomings of intelligence alone.

One measure of his influence may be seen in the fact that his name has provided the language with the adjective "machiavellian." The wholly unfavorable connotations of this epithet do not do justice to the man, yet they are understandable. Was not the model for his Prince supposed to be that most unsavory character Caesar Borgia, son of Pope Alexander VI, bent upon carving for himself a state through the resort to any and all means, barring none? Machiavelli admired Caesar Borgia, though his admiration was not due to a liking for evil and unscrupulousness as such. The point is that Machiavelli's thought operated on a different level. His concern was with the question, How organize the state in order to preserve it? Bemoaning the condition of the Italy of his time, he thought to see in Caesar a force that could solve the problem of disunity. Considering such an outcome desirable, he was wholly indifferent to the methods by which it could be brought about.

Machiavelli has often been praised for having brought a scientific approach to the problem of the state and, to a point, this praise is warranted. The typical approach of scientific endeavor, especially in the fields of exact or pure science, where it has been most successful, has been the analytic method which isolates a small sector of nature or experience, divorcing it from its surroundings and ultimate significance in the larger scheme of things. Using the results of his analysis of matter, the chemist may be able to manufacture an explosive; he will be satisfied with the result in proportion to its *effectiveness:* a more powerful explosive is *better* than a weaker one. But this has no relation to the question whether a bomb is good or whether we want bombs. To the chemist *as chemist* the question has no meaning.

So Machiavelli, the political scientist, with the problem of the state. That state is good which is effective or efficient. As with the chemist and his explosive, the broader issue of the ultimate function and purpose of the state is left out as extraneous. In that realm, the philosopher, the moralist may operate, if they so wish; to the "practically" minded man their endeavors are largely futile. On this level, then, Machiavelli may be granted the scientific turn of mind, and it is on this level that his title to fame and his subsequent importance rest. For what his contribution amounts to is an acute analysis of the nature of power and of the manner in which it could be used in the light of the conditions of his day. In this context *can* and *should* become equated. It is difficult to conceive of Machiavelli becoming exercised over such an issue as that of freedom of expression for example, for that would imply a value judgment extraneous to his approach. For him the question would rather pose itself in this form: does such freedom enhance or impede the smooth functioning of the body politic? If we admit that the fundamentals of politics as practiced in actuality have changed little in the course of time, then we can understand Machiavelli's importance and his reputation. And this makes it also possible to understand why Machiavelli was eagerly adopted by Fascism—nothing is easier than to read into him a glorification of violence—while at the same time the liberal Croce does not repudiate him.

What has been said so far may serve to explain why the controversy over Machiavelli has raged so long and will doubtless continue to prosper. At this point, further clarification may be useful. The illustration of the chemist was used advisedly. For, as stated before, the scientist of that type may and does proceed without reference to ultimate purpose and meaning; he is, in fact, often impatient with, if not resentful of, the intrusion of such "time wasting" tangents. But the political scientist may not operate in this fashion, isolating a discrete segment of experience; for what can be the value of speculating on the organization of the state unless we have some clear idea of its ultimate function and purpose? It is impossible, in fact, even to begin the inquiry without some fundamental assumptions both about this purpose and about the nature of the ultimate component of society, Man. Nor can Machiavelli escape this. And it appears at this point that his view is the fundamentally pessimistic one that considers the human animal as essentially evil, or at least weak. From this view derive at once conclusions as to the nature of the stimuli to which this being will respond. But this is an assumption of which the least that can be said is that it is an oversimplified view. For the fact is that the nature of man is infinitely complex, and without entering upon a controversy about the precise proportions of the varied components of this nature, it is only willful blindness that will deny the existence of human aspirations and the capacity for human sacrifice. Therein lies Machiavelli's shortcoming: of that side of man's nature he remains totally unaware, or at least he considers it so unimportant as not to warrant taking into consideration.

And here lies also the difficulty of the political scientist, the organizer of society: unlike the exact scientist, he has to deal with a reality the complexity of which cannot be resolved by examining its separate aspects in discrete and unrelated fashion.

It was no accident that the analysis of Machiavelli should appear in Italy, but a reflection of the fact that the arts of politics and government were more advanced and better cultivated in that land. It is precisely because of this greater advancement of Italy over the rest of Europe, because of the vitality of the different parts, the existence of powerful and numerous conflicting interests, together with the highly developed consciousness of distinction, that the resistance was all the greater to any drawing together of the separate fragments. But the very vitality of these various units was to be at the same time a great source of weakness, for a new age was being molded to which these forces of the past were unable to adapt themselves. It was therefore necessary that they should first be destroyed before fruitful development could be resumed. Here in brief is summed up the story of three centuries of Italian history.

SOJOURN IN LIMBO

The above quotation from Burckhardt is followed by this further sentence: "But as a whole it [the state of relations among the Italian states] gives us the impression of a bottomless abyss." Machiavelli was conscious of the weaknesses of the existing structure and, if he so admired the ruthless Borgia, it was not out of sheer perversity but because he thought he saw in him the possibility of salvation. The internecine wars of the Italian states were conducted according to the highly developed rules of a fine art—or perhaps we should say a game. This was good for the professional soldiery and their *condottieri,* for casualties in battle were trifling; greater results could be achieved from subtly spun intrigues and treacheries that would dispose of the proper individuals. Such a system, like the whole system of Italian statecraft, could operate successfully only so long as it was self-contained and undisturbed by some effective, if perhaps crude, external innovations.

And this is precisely what was about to happen. Beyond the Alps, the fifteenth century had witnessed the consolidation of the Kingdom of France. The French crown had long had connections and interests in the Italian peninsula, more particularly, through marital alliances, in Naples and Milan. The shrewd Louis XI found better things to do nearer home than waste his substance on Italian adventures, but just because of the effectiveness of his consolidation at home his successors were freer to look farther afield. It was this danger that Machiavelli had perceived, but the Italian states never thought of the possibility of united resistance to outside intervention. Wrapped up as they were in their rival politics, such intervention was considered by them as a mere additional factor to be used in the calculations of Italian power combinations. Moreover, if it should come to the actual use of force instead of diplomacy, the French king had armies of his own. Foreigners he did use, Swiss and German *landsknechte,* but the bulk of his force was native. French, Swiss, and German soldiery might be uncouth barbarians in the eyes of Italians accustomed to greater amenities, but they were an effective force, not a motley collection in the tow of mercenary *condottieri.*

Beyond the sea, Spain likewise had finally taken her modern shape. Spain achieved unity at the same time that she expelled the Moors from their last European stronghold; she was, as a result, full of crusading and expanding energy. Much of that energy went into the new lands of the west brought to her notice in the same year 1492, when the Moors left Granada. But Spain was already involved, through Aragon, in Naples, and she was besides destined soon to become a part of the Habsburg domain. The Habsburgs did not rule over united lands; the imperial title meant more glory than power, but their resources were substantial from the possessions which they held in their own direct right. Charles V of Habsburg, before he became Emperor in 1519, had already inherited the rule of these direct Habsburg possessions and in addition the Spanish crown (with all that went with it) as well as the Netherlands. As a result, France was virtually encircled, and a conflict between the French (Valois, then Bourbon) and the Habsburg houses was inevitable, especially as overlapping claims to specific territories furnished ready occasion for a clash.

The same year 1492 not only witnessed in Italy the almost simultaneous deaths of Lorenzo de Medici and of the Pope (whose successor was the Spanish Alexander VI), but also produced an intensification of peninsular political activity. Within two years, the French appeared upon the scene. As it turned out, there was to be little profit for the French kings in Italy; their activity in that land soon merged into the broader, and for them far more vital, struggle with the Habsburg house. From the point of view of Italy, this meant being the battleground of greater rivals. With the sole exception of Venice, which long held her own and retained her independence, the power of the new national monarchies was in a category different from that of the Italian states.

There is no cause to go into the details of these wars. By the middle of the century, all French claims in Italy had been abandoned, in fact as well as in theory, never to be asserted again. Long before his death in 1558, Charles V had complete control of Italy and, with the division of his domain into Austrian and Spanish parts, as Salvatorelli puts it, "Italy ceased to be a factor of European history; even those states which had remained independent now counted for very little in the sphere of international politics, or in the general destinies of the peninsula, which was now subjected to the direct rule or the preponderant influence of Spain." Italy had entered into the limbo of history from which she was not to emerge for some three centuries.

As mentioned before, the temptation is strong to draw a parallel between sixteenth century Italy in Europe and present Europe in the world at large. Like Europe now, Italy then consisted of a number of separate units of varying dimensions and power. These units were the seat of much wealth; in culture and in the art of politics they were more advanced than the rest of Europe, just as the Europe of our time has contained the greatest concentration of skills. The Italian states also possessed long separate traditions which thwarted the possibility of submerging their differences for the sake of their single and common good. President Truman made reference some time ago to "the folly of a nationalism so extreme as to block cooperative economic planning among nations"—not to mention any sort of political union. The folly of the European nationalisms of our time is quite comparable to the folly of the Italian states, which blinded them to the true significance of the rising national monarchies of the west. Similarly, at the present time, there have appeared units of a different order of magnitude from the purely European, against which the European units cannot singly hold their own. That Italy should have declined in power, even if she had been or become a unit, was inevitable in any event. The overseas discoveries alone would have had that effect, for the shift of the centers of trade, wealth, and power from the Mediterranean to the Atlantic could not be prevented. Even in that expansion Italy, a country of mariners, took no share, save in the form of supplying the skill of individual Italians in the service of the western monarchs, Spanish, English, and French. But despite her inevitable decline, Italy as a whole could still have been an important factor in Europe; instead of that she became a complete political cipher, save again for a qualification in the case of Venice. Even in the fields which had been preeminently her own, commercial skills, the arts and culture, the leadership was eventually to pass into other hands. Modern Italians of a united Italy, like Germans in a comparable situation, have developed an underlying sense of grievance from the effects of this historical injury to their respective nations.

Beyond this point, however, the parallel may not be extended. The eclipse of Italy is history; the future of Europe is prophecy. Granting that the same causes produce the same effects, the course of human affairs is too complex for us to be aware with certainty of the multiplicity of forces at work and to grasp with accuracy the relative weight and interaction of these forces, even when we are conscious of their existence. Politics, unlike physics, is not an exact science; we should indeed still describe it as art.

The vicissitudes of the Italian states during their long sojourn in limbo need not detain us either. Spanish influence continued to be paramount throughout the seventeenth century, until the issue of the Spanish succession brought about a major readjustment in the European alignment. In order to maintain the balance of power and to compensate for the accession of the Bourbon line to the Spanish throne, Spanish influence was largely replaced by Austrian Habsburg in the peninsula. Savoy was also recompensed with the island of Sicily, soon to be exchanged for Sardinia, whence her ruling house, which had meanwhile assumed the royal title, took its official name. Despite the reappearance of the Bourbons in Naples and in Parma near the middle of the century,

Habsburg influence remained the most important during the eighteenth century.

As that century was drawing to a close, and as again beyond the Alps great forces were stirring which were to affect profoundly the course of Italian affairs, the main divisions of the peninsula presented a picture not very different from that of the sixteenth century. Naples stood in the south as before, and next to it the papal realm. Tuscany accounted for the rest of the middle region. In the north also, we find the same units, decadent Venice, Milan in the center, and a somewhat more important Piedmont, or Kingdom of Sardinia, next to the Genoese Republic by whom the island of Corsica had been sold to France. But the whole vegetated in a state of relative torpor, for the centers of active life had long ago deserted it.

As in the earlier instance of French invasions which had initiated the process of subjection, French armies were soon again to cross the Alps in their renewed quarrel with the House of Habsburg. But these armies now carried ideas as well as weapons in their baggage. Napoleon, no respecter of tradition, toppled over the whole Italian structure. At first a number of republics appeared upon the map. Later on, much of Italy was merely incorporated into the French Empire while a Kingdom of Italy was created. The Napoleonic structure did not last, but neither could the old structure ever recover fully from the shock it had received. Under these auspices Italy entered the nineteenth century whither we shall now follow her.

Part II

UNITED ITALY

Chapter II · ITALY BECOMES A
NATIONAL STATE

Eppur si muove (*Reported comment of Galileo at his trial*)

ITALY IN 1815

Whether one thinks of Napoleon as primarily the carrier or the betrayer of the Revolution, the quarter of a century from 1789 to 1815 constitutes a unit in the history of Europe, for this period signalized an irretrievable break with the past. So it appears in retrospect at least; but we can also perceive from our distance of time that the effects of the changes initiated in 1789, if irretrievable, were to be gradual. The coalition that fought and finally defeated Napoleon's France was held together by two forces, distinct aspects of the same danger in its eyes: the threat to the actual possessions of the rulers, and that to the old order of society. The length and magnitude of the effort which it had been necessary to exert in order to defeat Napoleon served to emphasize, in the eyes of the victors, the need of complete obliteration of what he had stood for. It was only fitting therefore that Metternich should preside at the Congress of Vienna and remain the guiding hand of the continent in the years that were to follow. We can see that the attempt was doomed, but it took a third of a century before he himself had to relinquish office.

To all outward appearances, the effects of the French Revolution and the French conquests were thoroughly undone in Italy. There was in fact no such thing as Italy in 1815, save as a "geographical expression." To a degree, Italian unity, on the cultural level at least, had never ceased to exist; but on the political level, it was rather a memory than a hope. As seen in 1815, the effect of Napoleon's arbitrary arrangements had been less to promote directly the cause of unification than to shake the structure of the past. This in itself, however, was a necessary and useful preliminary step. But the development of the communes and city states had given rise to a tradition with deeper roots than the memory of Roman unity. The long and proud history of Genoa caused it to evince little enthusiasm at its union with Piedmont in 1815: this seemed more in the nature of an old-fashioned dynastic annexation on the part of the House of Savoy than a step on the road to national consolidation—and was meant as such. The Kingdom of Sardinia was not backward in its endeavors to restore the *status quo ante;* with humorless consistency, Victor Emmanuel I consulted the court almanac of 1798 in order to ascertain the rightful (if still living) holders of positions in the state.

To be sure, the ideas that had presided over the Great Revolution, the whole background of eighteenth century Enlightenment, were familiar in Italy, as in other lands. But these ideas were the patrimony of a very restricted class. For Italy was backward, by comparison with Britain and France at least, both politically and economically. In these two countries, the problem of national unification had long been solved, with the result that the issues which were paramount in the life of the state were now of a different nature. For both it may be true to say that matters economic were coming to assume growing, perhaps dominant, importance—despite the fact that the discovery was not made until later that economics at *all* times determines the course of history. England came first in this development. One of the chief results of the revolutions which she underwent during the seventeenth century had been to open the avenues of power to the commercial class. England became the "nation of shopkeepers," and if the description was meant to be derogatory—and in that sense unwarranted—it was true in the sense that she did become the leading commercial state of the world. The ruling class of England has known how to adapt itself to changing circumstances, thus giving rise to the belief, or myth, in a peculiar English political genius. At any rate, ever since the Glorious Revolution, the tradition of evolutionary, as against revolutionary, change has taken deep root in England. Her internal organization was little touched by the storm that broke loose in 1789. During the same period, in France, the monarchy which formed the state degenerated into a despotism tempered by corruption. This, and the tenacity with which the ruling class clung to privilege for which no compensating service was any longer rendered, precipitated the explosion. When the smoke of battle had cleared, the result was seen to be the creation of a state of affairs not incomparable to the English: the bourgeoisie were the chief gainers from the Revolution.

England and France had meanwhile become the leading states of Europe in economic development. This fact, combined with political unity over a relatively large territory, made them the strongest states, after Spain and Holland, contenders for a time, had fallen behind in the race. Ever since the Age of Discovery, the "westward course of empire" had shifted the centers of power and brought them to the shores of the English Channel. This state of affairs continued for the major part of the nineteenth century. If Italy, therefore, were to participate in the dominant trend of the times, she—like Germany—must commence by becoming a unitary state. The lack of political unity was an impediment to economic progress, which, once initiated, would in turn foster greater unity. This backwardness, economic and political, constituted a vicious circle, while the long period of subjection to foreign rule had served to dry up the springs of cultural life. During the seventeenth and eighteenth centuries, Italy had lost to others, to France in particular, the cultural leadership which had been hers during the flowering of the Renaissance. The active centers of life, political, economic, and cultural, had moved to the north, and it is essentially correct to say that despite notable exceptions and accomplishments Italy was in the main a passive recipient of outside influences.

In the economic field, the dominant factor, which has since continued to color all other developments, was the advent of industry. Here, also, England was the leader and France the next (omitting little Belgium which in no circumstances could lay claim to great power status) to adopt the new developments. The rise of industry meant greater wealth on the one hand, and, on the other, the appearance of new social problems. Therein lay the live sources of political thinking in the nineteenth century. In so far as thinking of this nature had an impact upon Italy, in this case also it was largely an imported product. Here again, political unification was a prerequisite to full participation in the active currents of contemporary life.

This backwardness, or lag, of Italy behind the western countries is a factor of capital importance, the effects of which can be observed long after she became one nation. The process of unification and the manner in which it took place are worth examining. There would be little point in a mere detailed recounting of the sequence of events which finally brought unity to the peninsula during the half-century following the settlement of the Congress of Vienna. What we rather wish to do is to examine some of these events as illustrating the forces at work during the process, with an eye to following the influence and continuity of certain trends in a later period.

THE ACHIEVEMENT OF UNIFICATION

The unrest which never ceased to agitate the peninsula had two chief foci: the demand for internal reforms of a liberal nature within the various Italian states, and a growing desire for amalgamation of the distinct units. Inasmuch as Metternich's Austria represented at the same time a foreign and a retrograde influence, the two tendencies could unite in opposition to her: in the end, unity was essentially achieved in connection with wars against Austria. The papacy was also an obstacle, of a relatively minor nature, and depended on foreign support rather than upon intrinsic strength.

As early as 1820–21, a mere five years after the settlement of Vienna, there were risings in the Kingdoms of Naples and of Sardinia which induced the grants of liberal constitutions in those states. But the episode ended in dismal failure: the King of Naples, appearing before the Congress of Laibach, claimed to have acted under coercion and was glad to withdraw his concessions—with the backing of Austrian force. In Turin, likewise, Charles Felix, succeeding his brother Victor Emmanuel, disavowed the constitution granted by the temporary regent Charles Albert.[1] During the severe repression that followed in both states,

---

[1] A word should be said to clarify the role of Charles Albert in these and subsequent events.

Victor Emmanuel's brother Charles Felix had no male issue; thus the heir presumptive of the House of Savoy was Prince Charles Albert of the junior branch of Carignano.

Victor Emmanuel abdicated in March, following a military coup, and appointed Charles Albert regent in Turin pending the arrival of his brother Charles Felix, who was in Modena at the time.

Charles Albert seems to have sympathized with the revolutionary liberals and even made a show of resistance to the wishes of Charles Felix. But his hesitant

Austria intervened in the provinces of Lombardy and Venetia, which were under her immediate rule. This is the time when Silvio Pellico was sent in captivity to the Spielberg fortress, a typical illustration of the nature of the liberal agitation, of the individuals who promoted it, and of the methods used to combat it. Typical also, the product of this imprisonment, Pellico's little book, *Le mie prigioni,* which served well the cause of liberation. In Italian, as in other European nationalisms of the first part of the nineteenth century when the movement was idealistic and liberal, the contribution of the literati was both important and effective.

This category of people, middle class intellectuals for the most part, continued their agitation. Within ten years, under the impact of the July revolution in Paris which overthrew Charles X, there were new risings, in central Italy this time. Their fate was the same as that of the earlier attempts in Naples and Piedmont. Again Austria intervened, and the cautious government of Louis-Philippe, on whom some Italians had counted, ended by merely sending a French force to Ancona in order to redress the balance of Austrian influence. Some minor reforms in the Papal States, notoriously maladministered, were all that there was to show in the end. Metternich's ideas of the right order of things for Italy seemed to be firmly established in control.

The impact of these failures stimulated a critical reexamination of methods among those interested in reform and unification and helped the growth of a moderate party which came to look to Piedmont as the most likely rallying center. Backward as it was, the Kingdom of Sardinia

character led him at the last moment to obey the orders of Charles Felix and to withdraw to Tuscany, with the result that the constitutionalists he had encouraged were left in the position of rebels and, in the failure of hoped-for outside assistance, the movement collapsed, leaving Charles Felix in control and the Piedmontese situation unchanged.

Thereafter, Charles Albert seems to have been bent upon obtaining forgiveness for his liberal dabblings. In 1823 he was required to sign what amounted to a pledge of good behavior, meaning adherence to Metternichian principles of government. His conversion to reaction proved to be genuine. He mounted the Sardinian throne in 1831, in the midst of the liberal agitation evoked in central Italy by the Paris revolution of 1830, but he gave no encouragement to his former supporters, becoming instead an instrument of their suppression.

He did once more return to his liberal leanings, but not until 1846. His role in 1848 is discussed below.

was the most progressive of the Italian states and the only truly independent one. Charles Albert, its king, although he had sought to
gain forgiveness for his earlier liberal flirtings by serving in the French
army that had intervened in Spain in 1823, as the Austrian had intervened in Naples, showed signs of returning to his earlier affections.

For a brief moment there was a diversion. Pope Pius IX, succeeding
Gregory XVI in 1846, had the reputation of a liberal, a reputation which
the reforms instituted at the outset of his reign seemed to confirm.
This had the value of an example for the rest of the Italian rulers and
gave a temporary boost to the movement that advocated unity through
federation under the presidency of the Pope. But the hope was short-
lived, for the events of 1848–49 frightened the reforming Pope away
from his liberalism, and he eventually became the champion of the
fight against all tendencies tinged with the brush of modernism.

The earthquake of 1848 shook Italy like the rest of Europe. At the
two political poles of the continent, Paris and Vienna, the Republic
was for the second time established in the former place, while in the
other, Metternich himself thought he could no longer withstand the
forces of change and resigned his office. Hope ran high throughout
Italy. Milan rose against the Austrians, Radetzky had to withdraw to
the shelter of the Lombard Quadrilateral fortresses, Charles Albert declared war, volunteers for the fight against Austria began to gather, with
or without the consent of the rulers in the various states.

But the fever was of short duration. Delays and bungling gave the
Austrians a chance to retrieve themselves, making skillful use of the
rivalries among the various nationalisms which they held in subjection.[2]
Piedmont negotiated an armistice in August. The convulsion, however,
did not quite end with this. At the end of 1848 and the beginning of
the following year, the Grand Duke of Tuscany and the Pope were
both refugees in Gaeta while a republic presided in Rome.

Charles Albert resumed hostilities in March. Soon defeated in the
field at Novara, a new armistice was followed by his abdication. By
midyear the movement had thoroughly collapsed; not without irony,

---

[2] The use of Slav contingents in Italy became one of the sources of the Italian dislike for the Croats and was often recalled at the time of the dispute between Italy
and Yugoslavia during and after the First World War.

it was an army of the Second French Republic that entered Rome in June: Catholic influence at home and the politics of balance in the foreign field were responsible for this anticlimax. All that seemed to remain was the Piedmontese *Statuto* or constitution of March, 1848, which Victor Emmanuel II, successor to Charles Albert, refused to withdraw.

Yet, as it turned out, 1848 was a decisive turning point for Italy. While there was discouragement in many quarters, the situation had in some respects been clarified. Hope in leadership from the papacy must be abandoned; reliance on popular risings had shown their ineffectiveness, which is perhaps not surprising in view of the fact that the ideology of liberalism and national union had so far not penetrated deeply into the masses. Increasingly, therefore, advocates of these methods became reconciled to the third solution: a rallying round the Piedmontese Kingdom and dynasty, as a core to which the rest of the peninsula could aggregate itself. And from this time the stream flowed uninterrupted and clear. The goal was reached under the steady guidance of one man, Cavour. Within ten years of the collapse of 1849, he engineered a successful war with Austria, as the result of which the political structure of Italy collapsed. If the result is surprising in view of the failure of 1849, it must be remembered that in their indifferent passivity the broad masses of the people, if they would not actively fight against oppressive regimes, felt no love for or loyalty to these regimes and were quite content to see them disappear. By 1861, save for Venetia and a much reduced papal domain, Italy was one. Venetia was acquired in 1866, Rome brought within the fold in 1870.

Such, in brief outline, are the events that made Italy one. Cavour's activity will have to be examined more closely, for the inheritance of it was heavy upon the new Italy. But before doing this we must look at the influence of another personality.

THE ROLE OF IDEAS: MAZZINI, THE APOSTLE

The achievement of Italian unity is often credited to the triumvirate of Cavour, Mazzini, and Garibaldi. In so far as personalities stand out as guiding stars in the historic firmament, distinct from the more obscure but deeper forces that leaven the great unvocal masses of the people, the picture is correct. But the three stars are of unequal brightness. Among them, Garibaldi, undoubtedly the most picturesque personality, was the least important. A courageous and sincere man, selfless knight of the cause of liberty wherever it might need defending, his stature as statesman or thinker is not high. His dash, even flamboyance, dramatized the cause of Italian independence and provided the needed color not altogether free of a touch of bombast—a not infrequent ingredient of the Italian scene. He was at the time and has since remained the perfect symbol around which the tribute of popular patriotic fervor could rally.

The role of Mazzini was altogether different; it has in fact been much misunderstood. Even among his own countrymen, as Professor Salvemini expresses it, "it is undeniable that a great many, nearly all the so-called Italian Mazzinians, have been in complete ignorance of who Mazzini was." This surprising state of affairs is due to the fact that, because Mazzini was in truth vitally interested in the achievement of Italian unity, the successful attainment of this goal has served to focus attention on that aspect of his activity and thought, at the expense of the other and wider interests that motivated the man. As a consequence, if his place in Italian history is warranted, the picture of him in that niche is too narrow and largely false. It is perhaps not wholly an accident that the Italian state has undertaken an elaborate edition of his writings, but that there is no adequate biography of him in Italian, while there are several studies in English.

The man and his work were consistent, psychologically consistent at least. A sickly and precocious child, he soon showed signs of extreme, almost abnormal, sensitivity. At the age of sixteen, the sight of refugees from the persecutions that followed the abortive attempts of 1821 caused him to don the black suit of mourning for Italy's misfortunes that was to be his garb for the rest of his life. A small incident in itself, yet revealing; no more expressive contrast could be conceived than this against Garibaldi's red shirt. His mother, first friend and confidante until her death, may have passed on to him the Jansenistic tinge of her own religion, a strain not usually associated with the Italian character. Yet Italy has produced her quota of saints and ascetics who, if not numerous or representative, nevertheless are an important part of her tradition and have exerted on her development an influence out of proportion to their numbers. St. Francis, Dante, and Savonarola, dissimilar as they are, all have characteristics in common with Mazzini. His sensitivity, a high sense of justice qualified by an austere feeling for duty, could not but throw him into the ranks of the liberals. Of the eighteenth century writers, which he had read extensively, he rejected much, but the humanitarian side of their theories made a lasting impression upon him. His connection with the *Carbonari* earned him in 1831, at the age of twenty-six, a short imprisonment in Savona. Characteristically, it was while in prison that he suddenly and definitely became conscious of his mission, and equally in character was his refusal to accept forgiveness in exchange for a promise on his part to stay away from his native Genoa. Instead, he elected exile abroad where he spent the remaining forty-odd years of his life, in Switzerland, in France, and in England. Thus Mazzini became in many ways a stranger to his native country; in liberal England, rather than in nearer Catholic or Jacobin France, he found a congenial spiritual home. In England also he found the people who understood him best, and incidentally contributed not a little to the establishment of the nineteenth century English tradition of friendliness and sympathy for Italian aspirations.

This long exile was an equally long conspiracy, and in terms of relative amounts of time and energy the bulk of it was spent in working for the creation of a free and united Italy. So far as one could observe at the time, and from Mazzini's own point of view, the result of all this tireless effort was one colossal failure, or rather a series of failures, which could not even be called magnificent, made up as they were in equal parts of tragedy, meanness, and ridicule. Such were, for instance, the abortive attempt to invade Savoy from Switzerland in 1834 and the dismal failure of 1853 in Milan. The high hope roused in him by the acclaim of Milan after the expulsion of the Austrians in 1848, and again a few months later when he presided as chief triumvir of the Roman Republic, was soon to be dashed. Bitterest of all defeats was the gradual desertion of his most faithful adherents. Even his mistress grew tired of the chilly fare of his austere devotion to the cause. For Mazzini would not compromise. Unification was to him secondary to the kind of Italy that would be created as a result of it. He was willing to accept the leadership of Charles Albert or of Pius IX for the attainment of his goal, but only if they in turn adhered to his program for the new Italy. To both, upon their accession, he wrote letters outlining their duties. Their failure to respond and their subsequent acts merely confirmed his belief that a republic alone would offer a satisfactory solution. Little wonder that he came to be looked upon as a visionary utopian and that his followers in growing numbers rallied to the less lofty but more realizable ideal which Cavour pursued and achieved. Sensitive as he was, he grew at times profoundly discouraged, and his very strong sense of obligation alone induced him to persevere in the furtherance of his self-appointed mission. To the very last he refused to accept the Italy that finally emerged in 1870 or even the forgiveness which this Italy (he stood under sentence of death in Piedmont since 1857), grateful for the ideal which he had upheld through the dark days, yet misunderstanding, was anxious to grant. It was fitting, historically fitting at least, that he should die in Pisa, through which he was passing surreptitiously (although the government elected to wink at his presence in the country) under an assumed English name.

Yet all this tireless activity is only part of the story. For if Mazzini was earnestly interested in the unification of Italy—may, in fact, be truly said to have been a martyr to this cause—this cause was but a part, and a small part, of the far greater ideal which animated him. As a thinker, Mazzini does not rank highly, any more than as a writer or a statesman. His complete misunderstanding of the Crimean episode from the Sardinian point of view is a case in point. But Metternich's fear of him, for all the paucity of results he achieved, was instinctively sound, for Mazzini's real goal was no less than the bringing about of a new era of mankind, the Age of Association as he conceived it. For the Church of Rome he had little but contempt. To him, that institution had betrayed its trust. Yet his outlook was fundamentally religious and his vision of the good society verged on the theocratic. A good deal of his social thinking can be traced to the influence of the utopian socialism that flourished in France during the first half of the century, but for the socialism of Marx he had no use. Its materialism repelled him and he became a violent opponent of socialism during his later years, a fact which subsequently tended to weaken his influence among the working class of Italy.

In his writings he proceeded by definite assertions rather than rational argument or logical analysis, but the strength of his ideal enabled him to fight through temporary doubt and continued failure. For all his distrust of the slogan of liberty, equality, fraternity, and his dislike of the Rights of Man, in place of which he stressed the Duties of Man, the doctrinaire quality of his thinking was in some respects akin to the intransigeance of a Robespierre. "God and the people" became his slogan, and through the people the voice of God would be heard. A doctrine with dangerous implications, for it is capable of degenerating into the suppression of the minority by the majority, which is inevitably the voice of the people, and in another step becomes the suppression of all opposition to the representatives or representative, perhaps self-appointed, of this majority. This is a minor component in Mazzini's thought, but in view of later developments in Italy it deserves mention as the link through which he could be annexed by a system which has stood for all that he would have abhorred in practice.

Mazzini was interested in humanity at large, though like many lovers of humanity he found little attraction in most individual representatives of the species. In his broad vision, the various nations, fundamental realities as they were, were destined to be free; once free, their peoples would work in harmonious association. Self-determination was to him a self-evident good. Italy, oldest of nations and territorially defined by nature with exceptional clarity, ought of course to be united. But the foregoing will show how small a part this unification of Italy had in Mazzini's grandiose scheme. Good patriot that he was, he assigned to this united Italy, whose Rome had twice been the center of world unity (Mazzini's world did not extend beyond Europe), politically first, spiritually later, the unique and splendid mission of leading once more the world in the path of fruitful and peaceful association. This Messianic thinking, abstruse, remote, unrealistic, far from free of contradictions, led to no concrete results in the practical domain; but its very quality made it a most excellent leaven—propaganda as we should call it—and an indispensable adjunct to the work of more practical men. It was therefore fitting and fundamentally sound that, even though on the basis of misunderstanding, Mazzini should acquire the aura of prophet and saint of the *Risorgimento*. From the point of view of Italian history, Cavour and Mazzini, much as they disliked and fought each other, were complementary and perhaps equally necessary. To quote Professor Salvemini again, "To Mazzini belongs the glory of having imposed upon Italian public life an idea-force to which all others . . . have had to become subordinate and tributary." Because of the importance of this strain, echoes of which we still find in our time (in the thought of Don Sturzo for example), the importance of the Mazzinian legacy must be stressed.

THE TRIUMPH OF REALITY: CAVOUR, THE WIELDER OF POWER

But, as pointed out before, in terms of practical results, Mazzini's activity was at best a noble failure. To this, the life, personality, and career of Cavour present the sharpest contrast. Perhaps the chief impression that one gathers from studying the man is that of normality. Born to the upper class, five years later than Mazzini, he evinced none of the romantic stress of his contemporary. A younger son, he was normally destined for a career in the army, but his ambition and liberal ideas caused him to give up what seemed an umpromising prospect. His interests were broad, and while he thought he might have made a mark in the exact sciences he felt that the age of mathematics was past, giving way to that of the moral (social as we should call them) sciences—a correct surmise to the extent that, if scientific progress has continued at an accelerated pace since Cavour's time, the thought of the nineteenth century has been dominated by the social effects of scientific and technical development rather than by the outlook represented by the eighteenth century Newtonian World Machine. This judgment of Cavour's is a measure of the keenness of his perception. Cavour was nothing if not modern; he recognized, and unhesitatingly ranged himself with, the forces of change. His view of the course of human events was the simple and optimistic one rooted in the belief in progress, progress that was dependent on freedom. The stage had been reached of an inevitable showdown between the irreconcilable principles of Authority and Liberty. Holding this as self-evident truth, he was never troubled by minor doubts.

But Cavour was a practical man, highly intelligent and clear-headed; contemplative speculation did not provide a satisfactory outlet for the tremendous energy and urge for doing that were his. Having little inclination also for inactive disgruntlement and sterile discontent, he threw himself with gusto into the task of managing the family estates. This he did with striking success, incidentally gaining much valuable experience for the future. Modern as he was, he looked to the more advanced countries of the west, France and England, especially the latter, for models of technical improvements, set an example by revolutionizing agriculture on his own land, later extending his activities to broader economic fields, banking, railroads, and so on. This is worth mentioning as indicative of the man's character and because the influence of his personality was such an important legacy to the Piedmontese, later Italian, state which he molded.

But there is another aspect to Cavour. His unhesitating acceptance of the forces of change has been mentioned. In combination with his interest in economics, this acceptance made of him a typical nineteenth century economic liberal of the English pattern. Recognizing change as desirable as well as inevitable, he believed at the same time in the gradual nature of this change: doctrinaire idealism *à la* Mazzini repelled him as visionary, or worse, ineffective. Revolutions ended in reaction, though he admitted that the blind forces of reaction were more to blame for violent outbursts than the talk and conspiracies of misguided radicals. He welcomed the passage of the Reform Bill in England as an act of statesmanship, but when he first visited that country he was more interested in the development of its industry and the working of factory acts and poor laws than in the grievances which these were intended to mitigate. A sure sense of the practicable was his guide. This does not mean that he did not have firm beliefs: his liberal convictions were never shaken. Once in office, he fought without pause or wavering for two causes, the modernization of Piedmont and the liberation of Italy. Guided by these long-range goals, he was content to work toward their realization, making use of what possibilities circumstances would offer. Thus his behavior was opportunistic, though his policy not unprincipled, but highly flexible and adaptable. Eminently practical, realistic, and sane, he was little troubled by the issue of ends and means. As he put it himself: "There are times for compromises and there are times for decided policies. I believe that there is neither in history nor in statesmanship any absolute maxim. . . . But the wisdom of the statesman lies in discerning when the time has come for one or the other." Of the highest integrity in personal relations, he simply accepted (though regretting it) the fact that the personal code of behavior did not govern the relations of states. Piedmont's participation in the Crimean war proved to be a shrewd investment, yet one may see in it a manifestation of the so-called Machiavellian tradition of Italian politics. That Cavour's goal of a united and liberal Italy was a noble ideal need not be questioned; given the goal, practical man of affairs that he was, he would use whatever means were at hand, perhaps oblivious of the possible effect of these means on the nature of the final result.

Such was the man who was destined to bring about Italian unity. The measure of his achievement lies in the contrast between the means at his disposal, a minor state of some 5,000,000 people, and the result attained, a nation of some 25,000,000, which was soon to achieve the status of great power. Bismarck's Prussia, setting out to accomplish a task of similar nature, was from the start a major European power; no wonder that many consider Cavour the greater statesman. Some phases at least of the manner in which he reached his goal are worth recounting, not for the sake of retelling a well-known story, but, again with an eye on later Italy, because of tendencies and precedents that were thereby established.

The reactionary nature of the Piedmontese regime in the thirties had forced Cavour to give up hope of political activity, and he had become reconciled with good grace to the narrower opportunities of a business career. But the liberal outbreaks of 1848, with their establishment of constitutionalism in Piedmont—Piedmont alone of the Italian states retained its constitution—reopened the possibility of returning to his first preference. Called to the ministry in 1850, albeit in a minor post, he soon became the leader of the cabinet by sheer weight of personal competence and strength. In 1852 he was Prime Minister and from that time, virtually until his death, dominated the scene where he controlled all the moves. Piedmont must continue to advance along the chosen road of progress; preservation of the constitution, outward symbol of this progress, remained his first care. While negotiating the preliminaries of his "unprincipled" aggression against Russia, he yet refused to make his task easier by interfering with the freedom of the press in order to placate Austria. The story of his role in the whole episode of the Crimean war and the subsequent Congress of Paris is worth rereading as a model of the sure and deft handling of a long-range plan. Piedmont had no quarrel with Russia; if ever there was a deliberate foreign war, this was one. Nor did Piedmont secure any advantages, either territorial or pecuniary, from being among the victorious allies. The advantages were all of a moral nature and, from the point of view of the practical politician of limited range, hardly worth the cost. Cavour sat in the Congress along with the great powers—on the understanding that he would only participate actively when the interests of his country were directly involved, which was hardly ever the case. He did manage, only after the completion of the final treaty to be sure, to have the whole Italian situation aired before the Congress, not so much by himself as by Lord Clarendon, the English representative, whose vigorous exposition he, with consummate craft, was content to support in restrained and moderate language. We should call this excellent advertising, and such it was, or perhaps a long-term investment. Even with Russia, he managed to emerge on good terms. Only Austria was irritated and antagonized. But that was precisely what Cavour wanted. And he did not let the seed lie fallow. Despite outspoken English sympathy contrasted with the tortuousness of the policy of the Second Empire, Cavour realized that France was his best hope. Power must be used as it is available.

Meanwhile, in Italy, in the very midst of preparations for the Crimean enterprise, he had definitely put Piedmont at the forefront of the movement of liberation, going so far as to indulge in a contest with the papacy in order to establish the principle of the supremacy of the state in all matters internal. "The wisdom of statesmanship lies in discerning when the time has come for one [compromise] or the other [decided policies]."

Within three years the seeds planted in Paris bore fruit. The Plombières meeting, or conspiracy, with Napoleon III was in part the result of Cavour's patient endeavors, even though the initiative was Louis Napoleon's. The terms of the bargain are in themselves of interest: to all outward appearances, this was little more than a move in the game of dynastic politics. Napoleon would secure concrete territorial advantages for France in the form of Nice and Savoy. The House of Savoy would be handsomely compensated for this cession—and that of Princess Clothilde—by heading a Kingdom of Northern Italy reaching to the Isonzo. There would also be a Kingdom of Central Italy; the Pope, ruling over much reduced estates, would preside over an Italian confederation, where, in the south, Murat might supersede the infamous King Bomba in Naples. French influence would replace Austrian in the peninsula. Such at least was Louis Napoleon's perhaps too clever way of attempting to ride the twin steeds of liberal nationalism and imperial and dynastic advantage, without antagonizing suspicious conservative Catholicism at home. But, from Cavour's point of view, let Napoleon indulge his oversubtle schemes: if once the Austrian hold over the peninsula could be broken, things might happen that neither Napoleon, nor Cavour, could control. Just how clearly Cavour saw the final vision and how set his heart was on it we do not know. The coolness of his approach is well reflected in his correspondence. For example, speaking of Manin's agitation in Venice, Cavour judged it thus in a letter written in April, 1856: "He [Manin] is still somewhat Utopian. He has not abandoned the idea of a war frankly popular; he believes in the efficacy of the press in stormy times; he desires the unity of Italy and other trifles; but, nevertheless, if the practical issue should arise, all this might be made use of." He would take what he could and let go unanswered the critics who charged him with being moved by narrow territorial ambitions for Piedmont. But the road was clear, and, whenever the goal might be reached, that goal was also plain. Skillful combination, the test of high statesmanship, of far-reaching aims with single-minded concentration on the immediate and the possible. Cavour left Plombières in a state of elation and urged the King to accept the bargain.

Carrying out the plot, for such in essence it was, was largely his achievement. He soon discovered—no cause for surprise or indignation to him—that holding wavering Napoleon to the bargain was not simple, once the broader international implications of the scheme had begun to appear. His own task was clear: to keep Napoleon's purpose firm while goading Austria into taking the initiative in hostilities. As to the means of bringing about this last result, he was no more troubled than was Bismarck when he engineered the Gastein Convention or edited the Ems Dispatch. Machiavelli would have approved. Such relative and shifting standards once accepted, however high the ends, the precise meaning and value of the plighted word become values difficult of appraisal. No wonder Cavour was considered by some a shifty intriguer.

Austria obligingly played into Cavour's hands and the war went well for the Franco-Piedmontese forces. Villafranca, the armistice which Napoleon III negotiated directly with the Austrians unbeknown to his ally, nevertheless was a shock for which even the realistic Cavour was not ready. He resigned his Prime Ministership, but his sense of the possible brought him back to office within a few months, at the beginning of 1860. Unpleasant and unexpected as it was, the Villafranca armistice was after all consistent with the standards of intrigue in which Louis Napoleon and Cavour had indulged at Plombières. What took Cavour by surprise was less perhaps the deed itself than the clumsiness of the procedure.

The outcome of the whole affair was somewhat different from what its initiators had planned, but Cavour was prepared to seize the larger opportunity which offered, sooner perhaps than he had thought it would. Austria remained in possession of Venetia, but on the eighteenth of February, 1861, an all-Italian Parliament, assembled in Turin, bestowed upon Victor Emmanuel the title of King of Italy; in addition, it passed a resolution to the effect that Rome should be the capital of the new kingdom. Having failed to deliver his whole part of the bargain, Napoleon acquiesced in the *fait accompli,* which in the end far exceeded the original terms of the arrangement. The political structure of Italy, propped up solely by Austrian power, had irretrievably collapsed. From the paramount power in the peninsula she was now reduced to the mere holder of an unredeemed province. French assistance had been useful, but the behavior of Napoleon combined with his territorial acquisitions caused him to earn little gratitude from the Italians. Nor did he succeed in replacing Austrian influence with his own as he had hoped to do. He, too, had played with power, and it was perhaps fitting that the consequences of having set in motion forces which escaped his control should be visited upon him. There was additional irony in the fact that it should fall to France, Cavour's greatest hope and aid, to assume the role of chief obstacle to final unification. For now that Austria was reduced to Venetia, the absence of Rome in an otherwise complete Italy loomed proportionately larger, and the Pope's hold on Rome was wholly dependent on the presence there of French troops and on the exercise of France's veto. To that extent had France taken Austria's place.

Cavour survived by less than four months the meeting of the first Italian Parliament. But his work was essentially done, and the formal completion of it, which took another decade, may be said to have been the mere dropping of the fruit which he had caused to ripen. The stamp of his personality and of the policy which was his legacy continued to dominate the Italian scene in the sixties: Ricasoli, Rattazzi, Farini, Lamarmora, and others who led the country during this period had been his close and trusty associates. The final resolution of the age-old Habsburg-Hohenzollern feud in 1866 provided the opportunity of securing Venetia. For Italy, this was a relatively minor episode by comparison with the great events of 1860. Italy's share in that war was inglorious and her participation in it comparable, to a certain extent, to that in the Crimean war: unprincipled by standards of ethics which politics does not recognize, yet able and consistent use of power, the sort of thing which has gone to establish what some have called the "jackal tradition" of Italian politics.

Attempts to form an Austro-Franco-Italian combination designed to check the rising power of Bismarck's Prussia failed. Italy's price was Rome, and it was Napoleon rather than Austria—Napoleon frightened at the too great consequences in Italy of his earlier war against Austria and seeking to propitiate conservative Catholic opinion at home—who, this time, proved the chief stumbling block. But Louis Napoleon was no match for either Cavour or Bismarck, the two outstanding statesmen of the period. His final showdown with Prussia—Bismarck's handling of that episode is quite comparable to Cavour's earlier performances—proved his and France's undoing. There were those in Italy who, for practical or sentimental reasons, would have gone to France's assistance; but the Roman question, the bad after-taste of the Villa-franca episode, and wise caution, kept her neutral. Instead, she took advantage of French embarrassment to crown the edifice of unity. Rome was entered by Italian troops on September 20, 1870, henceforth Italy's national holiday, and became the capital of the country.

CONCLUSION

Italy was now one. From the story of her unification what emerges? If one take the deterministic view, the result was inevitable in any event. And, no doubt, Cavour was successful because, unlike Metternich, he was working with, instead of against, the active forces of his time. But the manner in which the deed was accomplished is of capital importance, for it was bound to leave a mark on the future.

Once unification had been achieved, it was possible to recall Mazzini's nebulous idealism and to set it up in high place among the formative influences: this in itself made it perhaps a greater force after unification than before it. For the fact remained that, first, Mazzini's reliance on the people, on Italy alone, and all his attempts rooted in his faith had been dismal failures or worse; secondly, the Italy that was created was not the Italy he had envisioned (and he, consistently, never recognized her). If one chose to forget much, if not most, of what he had stood for, the fact of unification itself could serve to focus attention on a small part of his visionary program; thus he found himself canonized among the patron saints of the movement. Mazzini had come to hate Cavour bitterly, a feeling which was cordially reciprocated. Yet, Cavour's successors, once his task had been done, were willing to forgive Mazzini, even to let him share the glory.

To Mazzini, the literary man, the grandeur and memory of Rome meant much. Since the *Risorgimento* was to a considerable extent the property of middle class intellectuals, the shadow of Rome through the idea they conceived of it was in itself a force that cannot be denied. But in terms of the more solid realities of a modern age, and especially if one thought of the future ahead of the new Italy, the legacy of old Rome should not be overstressed. In point of fact, the second Rome, that of the Christian Popes, had been an obstacle to unification. Old Rome was too far away, overlaid in the memory of the masses by too many other forces and vicissitudes. Far more alive was the communal tradition of the Middle Ages, of which the division of the peninsula into distinct states had been the continued expression.

Cavour, the real architect of unity, did not expatiate on old Rome. Cavour was dealing with power, and it is through the skillful manipulation of power that he obtained results. This is one major aspect of his legacy to Italy. Cavour was Prime Minister of the Kingdom of Sardinia and always acted first and foremost in that capacity. The magnitude of the physical resources at his disposal, those of a state of some 5,000,000 people, a country not overendowed by nature, make his accomplishment all the more remarkable in a sense. But, in another sense, they also made it easier. For the Piedmont around which Italy united was in many respects his own creation. He it was that made it into a modern state, thereby giving it the position of unquestioned leadership among the other backward-looking regimes of Italy tarred with the brush of foreign support. To Piedmont he introduced the modern parliamentary system. The infant steps of Piedmont's first parliament amidst the stress of war were not a very inspiring spectacle: the rapid succession of ministries represented gropings which, if unguided, might have led to the verdict of impracticability. Cavour played a major role in getting the system to function, and the very fact that it was new made it easier for his personality to impose itself upon it. The size of the country and the extent of the franchise made political life in Piedmont an altogether different thing from what it is in a large country with an extensive electorate. The gradual extension of the franchise was a logical consequence of the initial step, but the difference in degree almost changed the nature of the problem by comparison with later times. Cavour evinced no dictatorial leanings, but his power was seldom challenged. An arrangement of the nature and on the scale of Plombières would be a difficult one for the government of a modern parliamentary democracy to contrive.

Thus Cavour played power politics of the kind that had been traditional in the game of dynastic rivalries. Had he been solely concerned with the aggrandizement of Piedmont, he would not have acted other than he did. The weakness of Piedmont, moreover, made it impossible to go about his task after the fashion of a Bismarck in Prussia. All the more credit to Cavour's skill, but the result was to place greater stress on diplomacy and *combinazioni* rather than on brute strength. All of which fitted well enough into the traditional pattern of the petty politics of the Italian states of the Renaissance as depicted by Machiavelli. Nineteenth century England, secure in her overwhelming strength and resources, could afford to blunder and, if need be, lose battles, confident that she could always in the end right the balance. Not so Cavour's Piedmont in 1860. It is not that Italian politics or the Italian man are fundamentally different from others, but that the lack of strength put a premium on wiles. We shall observe later on the permanence of this tradition at work. Cavour's ability and his successes served to create, or rather to revive, a school of Italian statesmen and politicians. The future of that school was to be of capital importance for the future of united Italy.

The other aspect of Cavour's legacy to Italy lies in the fact summed up in the description of him as an English economic liberal of his period. Had he done nothing more than put through the renovation of the Sardinian Kingdom, that would have been sufficient title to fame. His successes in the wider field of international politics have tended to obscure that other aspect of his activity. His belief in constitutionalism was unshakable and his adherence to constitutional practice unwavering. Believer in the party system as constituting the essence of parliamentary democracy, he was yet no narrow party man and he applied to the domestic field the same enlightened opportunism that guided his foreign policy. Thus, for instance, during the early days of his tenure of office, he did not hesitate to face the criticism that attached to the famous *connubio,* his alliance with Rattazzi, leader of the Left-Center, when he saw that it would serve to forward the policies which he really had at heart. That tradition, too, was to survive in the politics of united Italy and, in the hands of less high-minded men, was to yield less inspiring results.

The comparison and contrast between the story of the unification of Italy and the similar and contemporaneous unification of Germany is inevitable and has often been made. The parallel is enhanced by the fact that in the case of Germany also, one man, Bismarck, was overwhelmingly responsible for carrying the task to successful completion. Of the two, Bismarck's influence on his creation was the greater for the purely accidental reason that he survived Cavour in office for nearly thirty years. This gave him the opportunity to guide for twenty years the Germany that he had made, while Cavour's influence was at most that of a powerful tradition.

If we examine the manner in which the two tasks were accomplished, the similarity is close. Both are primarily examples of masterful diplomacy which accepted the use of war as one of its instruments, but an instrument held definitely in a subordinate role. Even Bismarck, for all his blood and iron, once his goal had been achieved in 1871 became a man of peace. The chief difference between the two countries and their unifications lies in two things. First of all the difference in power; for Prussia by itself was rated a major power, hence Bismarck could afford to guide events to the crisis of open conflict confident in the sufficient strength of Prussia alone. This Cavour could not do, for, guide events as he might, he must in the end always depend upon external circumstances over which his control was limited. This accounts for the tradition of the new German state in which force has held such an honored place, whereas there was little strength and less military glory to hold up before the Italian nation.

The other aspect of the difference may be summed up in the contrast between conservative Bismarck and liberal Cavour, oversimplification though this be. Bismarck's success served to kill in its infancy the hesitant German liberalism of the first half of the century and to set the country back on the path which Frederick II had outlined when he spoke of war as Prussia's national industry. Even though Bismarck sincerely strove to maintain peace after 1871, the association with power and the glorification of the conservative military strain continued to color German life after the birth of the Empire.

Cavour, too, fitted well into the old tradition of Italian politics, but in that tradition war had never been suggested as a national industry. Force could be used, but greater respect was granted skill, accommodation or *combinazioni*. And we never find in the new Italy—not at least until the synthetic aberration of Fascism—any great glorification of brute force as a virtue. Thus the legacy of the two movements and of the two men that led the movements in their respective countries was destined to be heavy upon their creations.

But there is another similarity between the two developments. In both cases, one political unit played a preponderant role. United Germany bore increasingly the stamp of the Prussia that had made her one. Likewise, the circumstances of Italian unification gave Piedmont a disproportionate importance in the molding of united Italy. For that reason, that influence cannot be overstressed. The complete bankruptcy of all the discredited Italian regimes after 1860 left a vacuum which was filled by the extension, to the whole kingdom, of the Piedmontese framework of administration and government. It is almost no exaggeration to say that united Italy was a mere extension of Piedmont—with what consequences we shall examine.

Chapter III · ITALY AS A NATIONAL STATE
(1870–1915)

There was no reason for, and no possibility of, making Italy the centre of the universe, as Mazzini's fond ambition had dreamed. But she might have become a beacon for all, a thing of beauty.
Why did it not happen?
Why was Italy so short-lived?

(G. A. Borgese, GOLIATH, THE MARCH OF FASCISM)

ITALY IN 1870

In some ways, Piedmont was the least Italian of the Italian states. Cavour himself had had to "learn" to use Italian as his chief medium of expression, the members of his social class having been more accustomed to the use of French among themselves and of the Piedmontese dialect for the more common transactions of everyday life. So long as unity and independence had not been achieved, the urge for them acted as a cement that could hold together the forces working toward that common end through the length and breadth of the country. This was still so from 1861 to 1870, but, after 1870, with the Venetian and Roman provinces brought into the fold, there remained of the uniting fear of foreign intervention only the possibility, increasingly remote, that the clerical party in France might prove strong enough to attempt a restoration of the papal dominion. By 1874, even the *Orénoque*, a French ship whereon the Pope might seek refuge, symbol of this possibility, departed from Civitavecchia. The immediate goal of union once achieved, the component parts of the union could again focus their attention on the pursuit of their individual idiosyncrasies.

Not that the country was ever in serious danger of returning to the division of separate states, but the fact of regionalism reached too deep for a mere legislative act to erase it. The significance of this regionalism will be even more apparent if we recall that the active force in the drive for unification was the appanage of a very small fraction of the population, the educated middle class for the most part, for whom the intellectual and historical aspects of the goal were important. The masses did not share in the movement, as witness their passivity while the event was taking place. At best, these popular masses, resentful of the oppressive regimes under which they existed, especially in the southern part of the peninsula, felt that they had no stake in the defense of these regimes. But passive acquiescence should not be mistaken for active and understanding support. A peasantry that was capable of attributing epidemics to the deliberate poisoning of its water supply could with equal indifference have witnessed the coming of Victor Emmanuel or a Murat restoration in Naples.

Now that the country was one, these differences were bound to make themselves felt in its political life. The result was a cleavage which, leaving aside relatively minor differences, was essentially between North and South, Rome being, appropriately enough, the meeting point and dividing line of the two. The North, despite its variety, had much in common. Piedmont had long been free, relatively well administered even before Cavour, and, under him, definitely a progressive state; in Lombardo-Venetia, the Austrian administration, if politically and financially oppressive, had been at least efficient. If Venice had suffered from advantages granted Trieste, Milan was an important commercial center. These northern provinces found themselves in contact with the main currents of European life; the proximity of the Duchies, Tuscany, and the northern part of the papal domain caused these regions to gravitate toward their northern neighbors and effect the fusion with comparative case.

Quite different was the condition of the South. Without even going back to the peculiar influences which had shaped its course through the centuries (Greek, Byzantine, Moslem, and Norman), during the nineteenth century the management of the Kingdom of the Two Sicilies had become a stench in the nostrils of civilized Europe, a fact given vigorous and fitting advertisement in Gladstone's indignant protest. The epithet "unspeakable," which his alert sense of moral indignation later applied to the Turk, would have been no less descriptive of the regime of King Bomba. The condition, deeper rooted than the neglect of one ruler, was reflected in the degradation and poverty of the population. The wise and mildly sceptical cynicism often credited to the Italian peasant, which makes him look upon the state as an inevitable evil whose officers must be appeased, produced in this region the extreme reaction of banditry and the famed Neapolitan *Camorra* and Sicilian *Maffia*. The southern third of Italy was truly on the fringe of European civilization.

As previously pointed out, the circumstances of unification in 1861, in particular the leadership of Piedmont, all the more outstanding from the complete collapse of the other regimes, and the still unresolved Roman question which loomed large in the relations of the new country with the outside world, had served to induce the adoption of the expeditious and outwardly simple device of merely extending to the whole country the administrative and legal framework of Piedmont. The device may have seemed attractive and beneficial, since Piedmont was the most modern part of Italy. But the pace of history is difficult to force. The mere blanket freeing of the slaves and the ruthless introduction of Northern ways after the American Civil War are generally not considered to have been the happiest solution of the problem of the American South. Granting the need of reform, in the American as in the Italian South, the attempt to accelerate the pace of historic growth through the application of doctrinaire logic is apt to create problems of its own—when it does not defeat its purpose.

In the case of Italy, the result was a highly centralized administration, somewhat resembling the French model introduced by Napoleon. But, in this respect, Napoleon in France was essentially the continuator of the tradition of Richelieu and Louis XIV. Italy had no such tradition, or rather she had the opposite one of municipal vigor. The result was also the above-mentioned cleavage, a perpetual "problem of the South," and mutual recriminations: the North, contemptuous of the backward South upon which it looked as a burden to be subsidized; the South, resentful and suspicious, leveling the charge of exploitation against the North. With the dimming memory of Bourbon maladministration constrasted with less serious, but more vivid because present, grievances, people could be found in Naples at the beginning of this century who spoke wistfully of these erstwhile Bourbons. Internally, as we shall see, these conditions were to have unfortunate results on the political life and morality of the country. One might be tempted again to make certain comparisons with the evolution of American political life and the influence of the South on this life through its role in the Democratic party. If we look to the European scene for comparisons, we find in our own time problems of a similar nature in the new countries, such as Czechoslovakia and Yugoslavia, creations of the First World War.

But the American scene also presents two fundamental points of difference with the Italian, differences which go a long way toward explaining the subsequent course of Italy's development: by the time of the Civil War, a long democratic tradition had struck deep roots in the American consciousness; in addition, the resources of America are, by comparison with those of Italy, immeasurable.

The poverty of Italy must be stressed, and the backwardness that went with this poverty, partly cause and partly effect of it. Past were the days when the luxury trade with the East, centering in the Mediterranean, had made the Italian cities great centers of wealth, culture, and even power. We have referred before to the decline that began to set in with the sixteenth century. The commercial revolution had benefited many Italians, teachers of Europe in the ways of trade and banking, but not Italy as such. Now, a newer factor was making its force felt; industry was further increasing the discrepancy. Up to a point, the difficulty was political, for the obscurantist regimes of the peninsula, consistently enough in a way, realizing the connection between the new economic forces and the political ferment of the age, had been steadily opposed to the introduction of economic progress. By 1870, despite a few railroads and a certain amount of industry in the North, the country remained overwhelmingly agricultural. Even this agriculture was for the most part very backward in its methods, especially in the former Neapolitan and papal domains. With the best of intentions and management at the upper levels of administration, it could be no easy task to alter these conditions, intimately tied as they were with the whole structure of society. The ignorance of the mass, 90 percent illiterate in the South (as the result of deliberate policy), would have to be overcome to begin with.

This, then, was one of the first tasks of the new Italy: to break through the vicious circle of an antiquated social system that acted as a fetter on any attempt at economic improvement, while the very existence of this system drew strength from the backwardness for which it was responsible. Yet this was necessary if Italy was to have a place among the powers of Europe. Till 1870, the leadership in industrial development was largely confined to the two sides of the English Channel. Thereafter, Germany joined the ranks, forging rapidly to the fore. It would be interesting to speculate how far Cavour would have emulated Bismarck had he, like the latter, survived to mold the first twenty years of the life of his creation.

Economic and social reforms cannot be divorced from the problems of finance. Piedmont, ever since 1848, had assumed heavy obligations in connection with the role that she had chosen for herself. Her finances were well managed, and Cavour had succeeded in making her accept an increasingly heavy burden of taxation. Believer in balanced budgets though he was, his vision was nevertheless broad enough to make him realize that there are times when economy must take second place; through his wars, he had considerably increased the national debt, the service of which absorbed an ever-growing portion of the national income. Unification brought with it a host of financial problems: the various currencies and state debts were merged and unified amidst inescapable demands of an immediate nature on the national treasury. The war of 1866 with its additional and large expenditures brought about in that year the forced circulation of paper. With the acquisition of Rome in 1870 the state assumed the additional charge of compensation and subsidy to the Pope.

Such was in brief the country which appeared finally complete on the map of Europe in 1870. It was faced with two kinds of problems, which may be classified for convenience as internal and external. The internal problem was essentially that of creating, or rather getting to function, the various organs of a unitary state, as distinct from the single political fact of unification. The solution of this problem had been sketched ten years earlier, through what may be called the Piedmontization of Italy. But the making of laws is one thing; their application, enforcement, and workability, quite another. Internally, the chief issue of Italian political life was the impact of unification upon the distinct sections of the country and the problem of adjustment to new conditions.

Externally, the new country had to find its place in the European community of nations. There was little precedent in the life of the

petty Italian states and their politics—not for some centuries at least—
for the role which would fall to a country of 25,000,000. This raised
the great issue of power, at which point the internal state of affairs would
impinge upon the external. Would Italy, Benjamin of European nations,
seek to play on the European stage a role comparable in some ways to
that of Piedmont on the Italian scene, perhaps in the sense of becoming
the beacon of which Professor Borgese speaks? Or would she engage
in the game of power politics to the extent that her resources warranted?

These are the questions we wish to examine. Italy was of course im-
mersed in the European stream and subject to the currents that moved
within that stream. Until 1915, her development seemed parallel to
that of the rest of the continent. Yet, in 1922, she suddenly gave herself over to Fascism. This was neither wholly inevitable, nor wholly
accidental. The forces that came to dominate in Italy were by no means
exclusively Italian. Why should they have been triumphant in Italy,
and not in Britain or in France? And why in 1922? With the benefit of
the perspective of time, we shall examine first the course of her development from her unification to her entrance into the First World War,
then the impact upon her of that war and of the settlements and circumstances that issued from it. As before, the purpose is not to retell
a story that may be found written in many places, but, with selective
treatment, to trace those lines of development which appear in retrospect
most significant.

DEMOCRATIC DICTATORSHIPS

Along with the extension to the whole of Italy of the Piedmontese
system of government went the dominance of the Piedmontese in
politics. This was quite natural in view of the part Piedmont had played
and of the all important role of Cavour. Cavour had died in 1861, but,
if power fell into the hands of lesser men, these were nevertheless, to
a large extent, men who had been associated with him and may be said
to have carried on his tradition. This group was known as the Right in
Italian politics. It contained a goodly share of ability among its members
and carried on with the momentum and high-mindedness characteristic of the *Risorgimento*. Its achievement was to bring the country successfully through the critical period of unification; its policy was, in all

respects, cautious and sound. In 1876, for the first time, the budget showed a surplus, no inconsiderable achievement in the circumstances. The government's foreign policy was also one of caution: parsimonious to the military establishment, its attention was largely centered on the Roman question and the possibility of external complications in connection with this problem.

But the influence of Cavour and the spirit of the *Risorgimento* were becoming gradually attenuated with the passage of time. Also, the Right drew the main body of its support from the northern part of Italy. Ranged against it, as the chief opposition, was the so-called Left. The use of these terms, save in a very broad sense, is apt to be misleading. The issue was not a clear-cut one between conservatism or reaction on the one hand and progress on the other. There was as yet in Italy no significant body of industrial proletariat; but the backwardness of the South with its peculiar problems found vent in opposition to the ruling group. It is also well to remember that the franchise at this time did not extend beyond some 2 percent of the population. The personal factor, then as later, was large in Italian politics.

In March, 1876, the reign of the Right came to an end with the defeat of the Minghetti ministry. Depretis, leader of the Left since 1873, organized an exclusively Left administration. In order to secure its hold on power, elections were held in the following November, with results eminently satisfactory to the group in office. These results were not due to any overwhelming change in the temper of the electorate, but rather to the wholesale pressure which the government had exerted through patronage; in many cases, prefects were displaced in favor of others who could be counted on to produce the desired majorities. In itself, the phenomenon was not new, nor was it peculiar to Italy, either then, before, or since, but the scale on which the government "made" the elections was broader than had hitherto been the custom.

Such a phenomenon might be no more than a passing phase, the early clumsy steps of an infant democarcy, which the passage of time, the enlargement of the electorate, the growth of parties with programs rooted in a real philosophy, and the spread of education, would cure. The Left indeed had no objection to enlarging the electorate, which it did for the first time in 1882—on a very modest scale to be sure, extending the franchise to some 7 percent of the people. But, for the most part, the possible changes just mentioned, most of which did come to pass, were not to cure the situation. A broader franchise could mean a more independent electorate, but it could also mean manipulations, *combinazioni,* personal bargains on a broader scale. This condition in Italy, different from that in other countries in this respect in degree rather than in kind, must be considered against the background of the recent past, the long tradition of misgovernment in a great part of the peninsula. The tradition of distrust of the state, whose chief point of contact with the people had taken the form of financial exactions for the benefit of a corrupt ruling clique, especially in the former Neapolitan and papal domains, needed to be broken. It could not be broken, or at least the breaking of it would be of no avail, by merely substituting for it a different kind of abuse, whereby deputies became in many cases advocates for petty local benefits which they might secure from the government in exchange for their vote. And taxation in Italy remained heavy, not necessarily heavier in absolute terms than in other European countries, but owing to the poverty of Italy, claiming a much greater share of the national income than was the case elsewhere. It was, besides, taxation of the regressive type that bore heaviest on the poor.

It is not that the Left did not have high-minded men in its ranks. Erstwhile Mazzinians and Garibaldians were attracted to it. But the enthusiasm of a Garibaldi or the visionary, if lofty, intransigeance of a Mazzini, useful in their place, are not the qualities desired for the everyday management of a state whose main task was the undramatic one of organizing and keeping up an efficient and progressive administration. Nor was efficiency alone all that was needed, but a bold policy such as Cavour had pursued in Piedmont during the fifties, whose twin mainstays would have been education (in the broad sense) and social reform. The task was harder for Italy than it had been in Piedmont because of the greater size of the country and because of its lack of homogeneity and greater backwardness when taken as a whole. The right combination of practicality and vision that was called for by the circumstances failed to make its appearance among those that emerged as the leaders during the period under consideration. As a result, the political life of the country offers a spectacle both uninspiring and un-inspired.

The leaders of the Left held office, either in person or through tem-porary substitutes, for nearly the entire period from 1876 to the First World War, but, instead of building up a great political party with a program founded on a real philosophy of society and the state, there developed groups attached to the leadership of individuals out of whose manipulations and bargains governments were manufactured. Three individuals in particular came to dominate the scene through the shifting combinations to such an extent that their tenures of office have been described as "reigns" or "dictatorships." Depretis ruled for the first ten years of the period, followed by Crispi for a roughly similar duration. After a troubled interim during the latter part of the nineties, Giolitti came to the fore at the turn of the century to remain the acknowl-edged master of Italian politics until the war broke his hold. His at-tempted comeback after the war was a failure and we shall see how the collapse of his system gave way to a far more unfortunate experiment.

Depretis, if competent, was neither a strong personality nor a real leader, and the early enthusiasm for a program of reforms that attended the coming of the Left to power was soon dissolved in the niggardliness of their enactment: the degree of the extension of the franchise may be cited as an illustration of the spirit that came to prevail. The role of Italy at the Congress of Berlin, the policy of "clean hands"—clean, but empty, as was soon remarked—is another aspect of this uninspired timidity. The French occupation of Tunis in 1881, aftermath of Berlin, shook the government. There had meanwhile been various Cabinet reshufflings, of minor significance in retrospect. In 1881, Depretis made his "great" contribution to Italian political life, if such a term may be used to describe the administration of a soporific.

Faced with the disintegration of his following, Depretis resorted to what came to be known as *trasformismo,* a term which could pass for the description of a policy in default of one: with the assistance of Minghetti, leader of the old Right, he organized a government which brought in elements of the Left as well as of the Right. Under the stress of great emergencies or novel issues, political parties will split and their component tendencies regroup themselves according to a different pattern. But the advent of *trasformismo* was very different from Cavour's *connubio* of 1849. For Cavour, holding to certain goals and ideas, was willing to accept support from whatever forces would assist him in their pursuit. But no such issues were present in 1881 when it was merely a matter of patching together an administration that would command sufficient support from the more or less personal following of the chief architects of the combination. Having made this contribution, well designed to bolster the belief that, in government and politics, *plus ça change plus c'est la même chose,* Depretis carried on to the end of his reign and his life in 1887.

Some changes there had been, small doses of reform, timid essays in social legislation—and, after a period of budgetary equilibrium, growing deficits from 1882 on—but such great problems as the condition of the South remained essentially untouched. Depretis' succession fell to the far more colorful personality of his Minister of the Interior, Crispi. Francesco Crispi came from Sicily, where, during the days of the struggle for independence, he had become one of the leaders of the opposition to the corrupt Bourbon regime. Mazzini and Garibaldi had had more appeal for him than Cavour, but, though a republican originally, like Garibaldi, he had finally accepted the united Italy of the House of Savoy. Endowed with considerable energy, he was attracted by grandiose schemes; his personality as well as his accomplishments have been the object of widely divergent estimates and remain a source of controversy. But Crispi, while strong, was essentially an unstable man, forever smelling conspiracies and plots around him, incapable of the dispassionate and sound appraisal of men and circumstances indispensable to the statesman. His more conspicuous activity was in the field of foreign relations where it had highly unsatisfactory consequences.

In the domestic field, his first administration (1887-91) witnessed a number of reforms dealing with matters of local government, education, and social legislation, a response to the growth of industry and its attendant problems. During his second tenure of office, from 1893 to 1896, there developed serious unrest, particularly in the South whence he came, owing to the miserable conditions of the peasantry which his economic warfare with France was hardly calculated to alleviate. De-

spite his affiliation with the Left, and the presumably liberal tendencies
to which his earlier activity bore witness, he made himself responsible
for the most brutal repression in Sicily. The elections of the following
year, 1894, marked a low point in political morality. Parliament meantime had been treated to the unedifying spectacle of a quarrel conducted according to unusually low standards between two of its leaders
and former cabinet colleagues, Crispi and Giolitti, in connection with
improper dealings between high government officials and the *Banca
Romana.* The disclosures, or rather the investigation and trial (for
candid public disclosures would have been too unsavory) caused neither
man any lasting political injury.

Economically, Crispi had to deal with a difficult situation, for his
accession to the premiership coincided with the economic crisis of
1887. His own activities, however, served to prolong the crisis, for the
tariff war in which he indulged with France, beginning in 1888, was
the cause of considerable dislocation to the Italian economy, especially
in this same South. The fact that industry, almost exclusively centered
in the North, was on the whole in favor of protectionism, did not help
heal the cleavage between the two sections of the country. The tariff
war with France, which lasted for ten years, was but one aspect of
Franco-Italian relations. It is Crispi's experiment in the colonial field
which finally brought about his downfall in 1896, as an aftermath of
Adowa.

The later nineties were for Italy a difficult period during which it
seemed doubtful at times that the orderly process of parliamentary
government could continue to function. The harsh repression of the
troubles of 1893 had done nothing to remedy their cause. From the
South, where the unrest reminds one of bygone *jacqueries,* it spread to
the North, where its source lay in part in the problem of the new industrial proletariat. There were serious riots in Milan in 1898, where,
to use Salvatorelli's gem of ironic understatement, the military "proceeded with redundant energy." The seeming inability of the government to cope with the unrest in the country led to a short-lived attempt
to rule by stronger methods. The government organized by General
Pelloux was the expression of this effort. Responsible for the brutal
suppression of the Milan riots, yet thoroughly frightened at the same

time, this government introduced in Parliament measures designed to curb the freedom of assembly and the press. But this reactionary effort merely served to defeat its own purpose. Parliament, to its credit, refused to be dragooned into acquiescence, but its role was essentially negative, for the failure to put through the proposed legislation was only procured through the resort to obstructionist tactics. We shall see this negativeness reappear in 1922, and again in 1924, when it was no longer to be sufficient. More promising was the action of the Rome Court of Cassation which declared the decree-laws (the government's attempt to enact its measures without parliamentary consent) unconstitutional. This, however, proved to be an isolated act rather than an illustration of a tradition of independence of the judiciary.

By the end of the century, the economic and the foreign situation—the tariff war with France came to an end and there was a political rapprochement with that country at the same time—had both eased and, with the formation of a Giolitti-Zanardelli ministry in 1901, the political uncertainty of the preceding years gave way to a return to "normalcy." From that time on, or from 1903 to be exact, Giolitti played a role comparable to those of Depretis and Crispi as the third "democratic dictator" of Italy.

Giolitti made a thorough contrast with Crispi, although he, too, has been the object of widely divergent estimates. Not from him fire and bombast; he was all calm, coolness, and reasonableness, hiding behind this mask a disillusioned, or even cynical, view of the motives of men, of the working of politics in general, and of Italian politics in particular. Highly intelligent withal, he had a clear, if detached, appreciation of the dominant forces of the twentieth century, in which respect he may be said to have resembled Cavour. Unlike Cavour, however, Giolitti had no particular values or principles to which he firmly held as guides. His administration has been excoriated by a critic under the title *Il ministro della mala vita* (The minister of the Underworld). The extension of political democracy for instance was to him not so much good or bad, as an inevitable trend which it would be merely unintelligent to oppose. By the same standards of practicality, Giolitti could believe, in 1921, that a dose of Fascist tactics might be useful in restoring the balance. Hence the quality of meanness which attaches to the politics which he dominated. Extending the franchise toward the inevitable end of universal suffrage as he did, did not conjure up visions of the millennium; it simply meant that one had to adapt oneself to the changed circumstances in order to "make" the elections as usual. At this game he became a past master; of undisputed probity himself, he was content to hold at his command the strings of power and was highly appreciative of the reputation of superlative foxiness that came to attach to his name.

Depretis' *trasformismo* could hardly be called a permanent system of government, and Giolitti who, in 1900, had been instrumental in the overthrow of the Pelloux ministry with its attempt at unconstitutional action, sought at first to organize a real party out of the constitutional Left and of those elements of the extreme Left who might be attracted by his liberal policy. In this effort, he failed to break the traditional influence of personalities in Italian politics; his own handling of patronage militated against success, and he ended up by reinforcing the tradition, holding power as he did largely by virtue of his own personal following.

Giolitti did not hold power continuously from 1903 to 1915, but whether in office or out, he was the acknowledged master of the situation. His method was to withdraw on occasion, leaving some opponent (Sonnino, for instance) to display his inability to organize a viable combination, or some lieutenant of his to carry on until he was ready to resume power in the open. Unlike Crispi's, Giolitti's tenure of power was facilitated by the general trend of economic progress which coincided with his time. The rising force of the popular mass he handled in two ways. Thus, in 1904, there was a general strike which caused considerable alarm, especially among the propertied classes. Giolitti's reaction was to let matters take their course, and the army, by contrast with its behavior in 1898, displayed the utmost forbearance. Having let the workers use, and even abuse, their apparent immunity, Giolitti called an election to capitalize on the revulsion of feeling throughout the country. But he had no intention of crushing the working class movement. In 1911, he proposed a large extension of the franchise, creating some 5,000,000 new voters. A good many of these were bound to give their support to the Socialist party; but this party he bound to himself, at least to a degree, through treasury assistance to socialist cooperatives. Had not new forces been at work with greater intensity in 1920, his technique of passivity during the episode of the occupation of the factories in that year might well have served to prove the soundness of his methods.

The picture of Italian political life which has just been sketched is a dark one. It would be incomplete without further comment. It will in fact be objected to as unfair, and as against it will be presented the record of Italy's progress during the half century following unification. The shortcomings which have been emphasized will be either dismissed, or at least played down, as the normal accompaniment of learning the use of a parliamentary democratic system. For an exposition of this point of view, we can do no better perhaps than refer the reader to the interpretation given by Croce in his *History of Italy from 1871 to 1915*. And indeed it is conceivable that, had circumstances been different, Italy would have continued along the path of improved democratic technique toward the model of a British parliamentarism. Two questions remain to be answered. How different were the circumstances? How, or at least to what extent, do these different circumstances account for Italy's peculiar course?

The half century which preceded the outbreak of the First World War, allowing for the fluctuations of the economic cycle, was on the whole a period of peace and steady economic progress. Italy, like other nations, participated in the general material improvement. The mainstay of this improvement was everywhere the development of industry, although agriculture also shared in it. Italy developed an important textile industry, chiefly silk and cotton, to the extent that, in the former field, Milan came to displace its rival Lyon as the first center of the continent. Likewise, the port of Genoa gradually overtook Marseilles as number one port of the Mediterranean. A net of railways was built to cover the peninsula and connect with the great trunk lines of Europe, a remarkable engineering achievement considering the difficult nature of much of the terrain. Trade grew, domestic as well as foreign, wages followed the general tendency to rise and the wealth of the country increased.

But this picture of material progress must be considered in the general framework of change elsewhere. Viewed in this perspective, it will appear that Italy lagged behind the rest of the western world, when the differential did not even increase. The discrepancy is particularly sharp if we make comparisons with the countries whose rate of development was fastest during this period, the United States and Germany. This was in some respects inevitable, for Italy is poorly endowed by nature with the basic materials of industry. Virtually deprived of coal, iron, and other minerals, she did, behind a high protective tariff, contrive to build up a steel industry of some size. The Sicilian sulphur industry—one of the few raw materials found in her soil—became a depressed industry owing to American competition. A comparative measure of Italy's standing among industrial nations may be found in the estimate of her per capita income in the nineties at $40, when the corresponding figure was $155 for Britain and $130 for France. In 1905, her exports at $120,000,000 were less than those of Belgium.

This economic backwardness, due in part to the poverty of the country, could only be remedied through becoming a manufacturing nation. This Italy accomplished to a certain extent, as witness the establishment of the flourishing textile industry. The low standard of living and consequent low wages of her workers were an asset in world competition, offset however in many cases by the fact that she was a latecomer in the industrial field. To some extent also, industrial development was retarded by the timidity of capital in finding its way into the newer enterprises, a fact which was itself the result of a predominantly agrarian economy of a backward type in a large part of the country. Here again, it was a case of breaking through a vicious circle. The state could have been of greater assistance than it actually was in breaking through the circle had its policy been less timid. Agrarian reform, the greatest and most urgent single need of the country was much discussed, but not enacted, one reason being the *modus vivendi* which perpetuated the status of the large agrarian interests through political compromise: it was easier not to disturb a state of affairs which fitted comfortably into the system of "made" elections.

In its general economic outlook, the Italian state continued to adhere to the Cavourian inheritance of devotion to free enterprise. Interesting on this score is the contrast with the role of the German state in the development of industry in Germany after the achievement of unification. Italian finances were sound according to the orthodox standards generally accepted during the period under consideration; indeed Italian credit improved and the premium on gold which reflected the weakness of this credit was gradually reduced and finally eliminated. A substantial part of the state debt held abroad had been redeemed by the nineties and the Treasury was able successfully to effect a profitable reconversion. All this was taken as a sign of economic maturity, but taxation was neither light nor well distributed. While the state revenue was considerably lower than in Britain, France, or Germany, it absorbed a much greater share of the national income than in those countries, and, with the passage of time, an increasingly larger portion of this national income. Now, as we know, especially from the experience of various countries since the First World War, a high rate of taxation need not be necessarily injurious to the economic health of the nation. But recent taxation has tended to bear increasingly on income, whereas in Italy at this time the burden of it was very unequally distributed, bearing most heavily on those least able to pay.

It is not surprising, then, that despite over-all economic improvement, one found conditions in Italy at the beginning of the present century such as are not usually associated with life in so-called civilized countries. Again, in sections of the South especially, the peasants lived in a state of utmost destitution, housed in unspeakable hovels and subsisting on a wholly inadequate diet. In some places even, conditions had actually deteriorated with the passage of time until, with a rapidly increasing population to make matters worse, the only alternative to starvation seemed to be emigration—which in fact was the case. Conditions of life in a large metropolitan center like Naples were little more inspiring. It is such a state of affairs which produced the events of 1894 in Sicily.

Education would have been a necessary, though perhaps not sufficient, prerequisite to the successful working of political democracy. A literate people in a modern state may not be capable of operating successfully the machinery of democracy; an illiterate one certainly cannot. And education in Italy at this time was a sadly neglected waif. Italy, home of the humanistic Renaissance and one-time leader of Europe in the arts, the sciences, and generally in the ways and amenities that go to make living civilized, had long since lost her primacy. The tradition was not dead, but it continued to exert its influence at the upper levels only. Important outstanding individuals there were, and the quality of the universities was far better than that of the lower grades of instruction. To be sure, there was a colossal distance to travel after 1860. If we make comparisons with conditions in the Kingdom of Naples and the papal domain where illiteracy was the rule, considerable progress *was* made. But one would get an incorrect picture of the true state of affairs by merely looking at the legislation on the statute books. To legislate universal compulsory elementary education is one thing; the extent of enforcement and the quality of the product are something else again. While much headway was made in reducing illiteracy, it was still high at the beginning of the century, and far higher in the South than in the North. To a considerable extent, the poor quality of instruction was due to the insufficient financial assistance it received: miserable as their pittance was, schoolteachers often had great difficulty in collecting arrears from the municipalities. Mussolini came from their ranks, where, however, his ambition, ability, and restlessness did not leave him long.

This general backwardness had its reflection in the political life of the country, first in the restricted size of the electorate, secondly in the degraded nature of Italian politics which, instead of flowing into great political parties representing various aspects of social philosophy and political thought, degenerated into a highly personalized system of groups centering around dominant individuals. In this desert of political thought, there was an exception, the Socialist party, which, as elsewhere in Europe, made its entrance upon the scene in Italy following the appearance of an industrial proletariat. But the unfortunate tradition of personalities in politics affected, to a certain degree at least, the Socialist as it did the other so-called parties. Despite the fact that it produced a number of able and high-minded leaders, the Socialist party too split into irreconcilable factions, to its greatest damage and ultimate undoing. Here also, the strong personality of Mussolini was destined to play an important role. But the consideration of Italian socialism may best be left to the next chapter, for the reason also that the Socialists, whose activity began toward the end of the last century, still played a relatively minor role, as a political party at least, during the first decade of the present one.

The shortcomings of Italian political life—and the emphasis has been purposely on shortcomings—should of course be viewed in perspective and in comparative terms. The *Banca Romana* scandal in the nineties was a sordid enough affair; yet it would be misleading to isolate it. One could tell many a tale of the corruption of eighteenth century English political life; the nature of American political machines is a familiar story; France had its Panama scandal, its Dreyfus affair, and a peculiarly venal press. Comparisons and contrasts among such isolated happenings lead nowhere. But it is enlightening to contrast, for example, the French development with the Italian considered in their broader aspects.

To one writing in 1949, after having witnessed the collapse of the Third Republic, the temptation to make comparisons is particularly strong. But, confining ourselves to the period before the First World War, between the course of France and that of Italy two chief points of contrast should be stressed. First, as against the poverty of Italy, at once cause and effect of her backwardness, France was a rich country, indeed among the richest. Applied to this rich native endowment, the Revolution had set free the new and progressive social force of the bourgeoisie. France after 1870 had, besides wealth, a large and politically highly conscious middle class, in which element Italy was deficient. France, also, had the most extensive franchise of any European country. The course of internal French politics from the Great Revolution until 1870 had been anything but smooth. After 1870, following uncertain beginnings, the Third Republic became firmly established. But the struggle, going back to the Great Revolution, between the forces of reaction and those of progress went on. For all the influence of personalities, considerable at times, and despite much abuse and corruption, there was in French politics a genuine struggle between opposite ideas and philosophies which found expression in the French political parties. The meaning of Right and Left in France was quite different from that of these same terms in the context of Italian *trasformismo*. Gambetta, Jaurès, Clemenceau were strong enough personalities, but none of them filled a role comparable to that of Crispi or Giolitti on the Italian stage.

This difference may have been a mere lag in development; it is quite conceivable that, given time, Italy too would have developed genuine

political parties and a properly functioning parliamentary system. Looking over the record of what progress she made, especially in view of
her resources and previous history, a good case may be made for the
claim that she, albeit with a lag, was traveling along the road which
seemed to be the same for the whole western world at least. The atmosphere of optimistic materialism which pervaded this western world
affected her no less than other nations. Whether her evolution would
have been the same had not extraneous circumstances intervened, must
remain a matter of conjecture, one of the ifs of history. The fact remains
that she was diverted from this line of development into a different
and novel course. The immediate cause of the divergence was the aftermath of a foreign situation, the impact of the First World War. The
study of this impact will be the object of the next chapter. But, in view
of the fact that the catalytic factor was war, we must briefly cast a
glance at the record of Italy on the international scene during the period
which we have been discussing.

ITALY AMONG THE POWERS

The formation of a united Italy was essentially Cavour's accomplishment. In the course of attaining this end, the international situation had
always been paramount in his eyes. From 1860 on, a wholly novel state
of affairs obtained for, instead of the problem of little Piedmont, a
fourth-rate European state, skillfully exploiting the rivalries of the
larger powers to procure a result primarily confined to the Italian scene,
the question that confronted the new state was that of finding its place
in the European community. No doubt Cavour's skill would have
been equal to the task of guiding with success the destinies of his creation on the larger stage. But Cavour having died in 1861, the task fell
to other hands. Cavour's policy had been characterized by an adroit
combination of caution and daring, either of which he used as occasion
demanded with an accurate sense of timeliness. Few men so well mas-
tered the international politics of his time, but of necessity his role was
limited to a small section of the European checkerboard.

The task of his immediate successors was in some ways simple, for,
so long as Rome remained outside of the Italian state, the Roman
question was bound to be the dominant issue of Italian foreign policy.

The acquisition of Venetia in 1866 was an interlude, important yet secondary. The Franco-Prussian war settled the fate of Rome. With the perspective of three quarters of a century, we can see what the formation of the German state under Bismarck's guidance and with his methods has meant to Italy, to Europe, and to the world. But it would be otiose to expect 1870 to judge with the knowledge of 1949. In 1870, it might seem at most that Prussia was somewhat disturbing the existing European balance of power; even Britain, most sensitive and jealous guardian of this balance, felt more pleased than alarmed at the German victory over France. Looking at the conflict from the Italian point of view at the time, one cannot but agree that those acted soundly who restrained Victor Emmanuel's impulse to go to France's assistance and advised instead taking advantage of her disaster to acquire Rome. Italian assistance, for that matter, would merely have served to join Italy in defeat with France.

From this time, the Roman question took on the more limited aspect of the issue of the position of the Pope in the new Italian state; the fate of Rome itself was never in question. But, owing to the peculiar nature of the papacy, the Roman question could not be divorced from foreign implications. Two things are clear. One, partly because of the sorry quality of papal rule, or rather misrule, and partly because the Pope's subjects were after all Italians, there was never any chance that restoration might be attempted from within Italy. The other, consequence of the first, any restoration could only be the effect of outside intervention. As things appeared in 1870, this danger did not seem wholly nonexistent. It weighed heavily upon the calculations of the Italian foreign office which followed with keen interest the vicissitudes of the struggle in France between partisans and opponents of the Republic. But France was after all busy with reconstruction; it was some years before she felt able to resume an active foreign policy, and by that time the triumph of the Republican forces had removed any likelihood that French policy would turn its eyes toward the Rome of the Popes.

France having declared through Gambetta that "clericalism, there is the enemy," the new Austria-Hungary was left as the only important state on whose support the papacy could rest whatever hopes it might entertain of outside assistance. But if Austria-Hungary, as the leading

Catholic country, was an important factor in the calculations of papal policy, she showed no inclination to interfere in the matter. Certainly nothing would be done by Germany, now predominantly Protestant, where, moreover, Bismarck was engaged in the *Kulturkampf* episode. Britain had seen Italian unification with an approving eye. This unity was therefore secure and it was not long before the Roman question settled down to the compromise of a not unsatisfactory *modus vivendi,* despite the official stand maintained by the Vatican. The result was a unique and curious anomaly, but for the most part relations between Italian and papal Rome were friendly rather than the opposite. Italy was therefore free, soon after 1870, to seek her place as a new arrival in the European community of nations.

This period of the seventies marks a pause in the international activity of Europe. Germany, Austria-Hungary, France, and Italy herself, were all busy in their several ways with problems of internal reorganization. Britain was content to thrive in peace, managing the rapidly growing wealth which her industry and trade brought. Bismarck, central actor on the European stage, wished to live on good terms with all the powers, save unreconciled France. From France, reconciliation was not to be expected, but so long as she were maintained in isolation, she offered no serious threat. Bismarck's policy was successful—while he lasted.

What role would Italy seek to play in these surroundings? Germany, new like Italy, had aggregated around Prussia, a major power in her own right; German policy might therefore be expected to be a continuation and extension of Prussian precedent. But Piedmont had held no position comparable to Prussia's. Italy therefore started on her new career with an unusually clear slate. Would she seek to maintain a position commensurate with her relative degree of power, or would she, indulging in dreams of Roman grandeur, attempt to supplement and overcome the limitations of her intrinsic strength by the use of diplomacy, perhaps essaying on the European or world scene a role comparable to that of Cavour's Piedmont on the Italian? In the course of time she tried both, and her story may be summed up in brief in the statement that she was successful when adhering to the former course, while her dabbling in the latter brought her to grief.

It is well perhaps to look at the position of Italy in Europe as she was about to start on her career as a nation. The foreign policy of nations is apt to show a remarkable degree of continuity, ignoring the vagaries of internal changes of administrations and often, even, major revolutions. This is inevitable, so long as we have a world of nations, for this policy is based on deep-rooted and slow-changing fundamentals. The first fact to be noticed in the case of Italy is that of geography. She is wholly a Mediterranean country, and the circle of the Alps which separates her from the rest of Europe serves to define her frontiers with unusual clarity and gives her an almost insular character. The Mediterranean and its surrounding lands are therefore the logical sphere of Italy's prime interest. This meant that, among the major powers of Europe, Italian relations would give priority in their attention to Great Britain, France, and Austria-Hungary. Germany was to be little interested in the Mediterranean for some time, and Russia was still knocking at the gates.

As stated before, Britain had not been averse to the appearance of united Italy on the map of Europe; the prospect of an eventual rival to France in the Mediterranean was not displeasing to her. Italy's relations with Britain continued to be amicable and, on the Italian side, came to be based on the simple and sound axiom that, in view of Britain's preponderance of naval power and of the vulnerability of her long, exposed coastline, Italy must, under no circumstances, become involved in a conflict on the side opposite the British.

In the western Mediterranean, France in possession of Algeria was dominant. But Tunisia, next to Algeria and just across the straits from Sicily, had been a sphere of Italian economic activity even before unification. United Italy looked upon Tunisia as a natural prolongation of the peninsula which, in time, might fall under her rule. Tunisia was destined to play an important role in Franco-Italian relations. To France also, Italy had recently yielded Nice and Savoy. But any irredentism directed toward these territories—and Corsica—was to be a much later, and on the whole synthetic, discovery. Even Tunisia did not become an issue until after it became a French protectorate in 1881.

Relations with Austria-Hungary were, in many ways, the most delicate. To begin with, unification had been one long struggle against Austria. The tradition of enmity toward Austria was kept alive by the fact that there were still Italians under Austrian rule, to say nothing of the outcome of the war of 1866 which, if it had given Italy Venetia, had also left her with a strategically—and purposely—very unfavorable frontier, well on her side of both the natural and ethnic boundaries. Before the First World War, the cry of Italian irredentism was "Trento e Trieste." Also, Austria was established on the eastern side of the Adriatic across from Italy. Within the Mediterranean, the Adriatic was for Italy a smaller edition of the larger possibilities. Across the Adriatic were the Balkans under Turkish rule. In the steady disintegration of the Ottoman Empire, kept alive by the rivalries of larger powers rather than by its own intrinsic strength, what role would Italy seek to play? Just as Austrian interests in this region came into contact with Russian toward the east, they touched upon a possible Italian sphere in the west.

Such was the general picture of Europe as it appeared when viewed from Rome. The international calm that succeeded 1870, due to the focusing on internal reorganizations, was broken by the Russo-Turkish war of 1876. The military victory of Russia, first sanctioned at San Stefano, turned the issue into an Anglo-Russian one. The Congress of Berlin was the first of the Concert of the new Europe that had emerged from the events of 1870. The principals in this case were Britain and Russia, closely followed by Austria-Hungary. Bismarck, more embarrassed than pleased by a quarrel among powers with all of whom he wanted to be on good terms, proclaimed Germany's role as that of the "honest broker." France, though traditionally interested in the Near Eastern question, was still hesitant and uncertain; she played no significant part in the proceedings. Italy was making her first appearance in the concert, no longer as Cavour had done at Paris in 1856, on sufferance and merely because of Cavour's skillful management of circumstances, but in her own right as a great power. Yet her role was in many respects less significant, certainly more barren of results, than had been Cavour's in 1856. That she should have kept aloof from the chief Anglo-Russian issue is understandable. But such by-products of the main issue as the Austro-Hungarian occupation of Bosnia-Herzegovina and the British occupation of Cyprus might have evoked a reaction from her. However, she put in no claims for compensations on the classical plea of preserving the balance of power. She was content to pursue the policy of clean but empty hands. Too unsure of herself and too wrapped up in her domestic issues, she was not yet even practicing a policy in keeping with the power that she had.

Of greater significance for Italy than the Congress itself, was another by-product of it. From both Germany and Britain, France received encouragement to establish herself in Tunis. Bismarck's motives in making this suggestion were not wholly disinterested: it might serve to ease his task of watching a revengeful France by diverting her energies and attention to other compensatory fields of expansion while holding the additional possibility of embroiling her with Italy. To make doubly sure of the latter result, it was also hinted to Italy that she might go to Tunis. Neither France nor Italy reacted at the time, but before long, France, though not forgetting Alsace-Lorraine, did embark on a large program of empire building. The first step along this path was the establishment of a protectorate over Tunisia. Of the long and bitter controversy which has raged in Italy over the rights and wrongs of this episode and the manner of its performance, we need only retain the intense and well-nigh unanimous feeling of frustration which it produced. Most significant perhaps was the consciousness of isolation which the incident brought home—none of the expected protests were voiced by either Germany or Britain—and the consequent search for ways to end this isolation.

By the time of the Tunisian affair, Germany's power and Bismarck's diplomacy made that country the undoubted center of international continental, if not European, politics. Could Italy attach herself to the dominant constellation? Germany was not overly interested, for what did Italy have to offer? The possibility of French aggression presented some common ground between Germany and Italy, but a great obstacle had to be overcome, for one of the cardinal principles of German diplomacy was the alliance with Vienna. When faced with the unwelcome, but finally inevitable choice between St. Petersburg and Vienna, it was the latter that Bismarck chose. For Italy, as was said at the time, the key to Berlin was in Vienna. Yet from the point of view of the group in power in Italy—nominally the Left, though *trasformismo* had already been inaugurated—there were compensating advantages to be found in a link with Vienna. This group professed to be concerned over republican agitation in the country; republicans would naturally look to France for support, while Vienna had the virtue of being strongly conservative and respectable. An alliance with Austria would also eliminate the possibility that the Pope might find any support in that quarter, not a dangerous possibility, but one which still carried some weight with Italian statesmen.

In the midst of these considerations came the French occupation of Tunis in May, 1881. In the autumn of that year, we find King Humbert paying a state visit to Vienna where, amusingly enough, the heir of the House of Savoy was made a colonel in the Austrian army, and, in May, 1882, the Triple Alliance of Germany, Austria-Hungary, and Italy was born. The treaty of alliance, whose terms of course like those of all such treaties in those days were secret, had for its core the pledge of neutral support in case of French aggression. Of the Balkans and the Mediterranean no mention was made. How unsure of herself Italy still felt at this time, and how limited her foreign horizon, appears from her refusal to act in conjunction with England in Egypt in this same year 1882.

However, with the passage of time, a greater positiveness began to assert itself. When the original treaty had run its five-year course, Italy was able to renew the alliance on terms more favorable to herself. By playing on the European situation of the moment, Italy obtained an extension of the promise of support by Germany to cover the possibility of a conflict with France over Mediterranean issues, meaning Tripoli and Morocco, the last two non-preempted sectors of North Africa. At the same time, she obtained from Austria recognition of a voice in Balkan affairs: while professing a desire to preserve the *status quo* in the Balkans, the Adriatic, and the Aegean, the new treaty of 1887 recognized that Italy would be entitled to adequate compensations for any Austrian advantage, even a temporary occupation in these areas. This arrangement was embodied in a separate treaty between Italy and Austria-Hungary alone, but found its way subsequently into the later tripartite renewals of the alliance and, as Article VII of the treaty of 1912, was destined to play a vital role in 1914.

During the rest of that same year 1887, from May to December, exchanges of notes involving Great Britain, Austria-Hungary, Italy, and

Spain asserted likewise the desire to maintain the Mediterranean *status quo*. Italy also obtained from her allies recognition that her commitments to them would in no way involve her in a conflict against Britain.

It is not our purpose to give a detailed history of the Triple Alliance or even of Italy's role within that combination. The treaties of 1882 and 1887 are of interest as indications of an Italian policy gradually taking shape and asserting itself and of Italy's desire to play a role, albeit still a modest one, on the European scene. Adherence to the Triple Alliance became an established principle of Italian foreign policy; we shall see presently the complicating factors that entered the situation. For the moment, it will suffice to say that the Triple Alliance, through its renewals in 1891, in 1902, and again in 1912, was still in existence at the time of the outbreak of war in 1914.

The renewal of 1887 was one of the last acts of Depretis. The stormy Crispi who succeeded him was given to dreams of grandeur. To the Austro-German connection he remained faithful. His intense dislike, or at least profound suspicion, of France—his overwrought imagination could accept at face value the report of an intended French attack on Spezia—was cordially reciprocated, and relations between the two countries were highly unsatisfactory during his tenure of office. But Crispi's main foreign activity was in the colonial domain. Out of Italy's modest and half-hearted essays at colonial expansion on the shores of the Red Sea, Crispi conjured the vision of a great East African Empire. The attempt ended in the Adowa disaster and Crispi's downfall.[1]

But Crispi and his dreams, which he attempted to transmute into reality with inadequate preparations, represent an interlude, a departure from the caution and moderation which were characteristic of the aims of Italian policy before and after him. This policy, after his departure, liquidated the East African episode, and returned to a clearer view of the proper balance between the ends that could be achieved and the means available for the pursuit of these same ends. Crispi's successors, however, were confronted with a different Europe. The cardinal developments of the nineties were the two related facts of

[1] In view of the importance of colonial policy in the more recent development of Italy, her whole colonial record will be treated as a unit in a separate and subsequent chapter.

Bismarck's departure from the helm of German affairs and the emergence of France from her isolation with the conclusion of the Russian alliance. Italian policy was not slow to perceive, and to take advantage of, the possibilities contained in the new situation.

The beginnings of a rapprochement with France took the form of a liquidation, with the commercial treaty of 1898, of the previously mentioned tariff war. This was soon followed by a Mediterranean *quid pro quo,* similar in character to the Anglo-French agreement (precursor of the Entente Cordiale), whose terms involved Egypt and Morocco. The Franco-Italian arrangement recognized France a free hand in Morocco —as far as Italian interests were concerned—in exchange for a corresponding French undertaking with respect to Tripoli. This was in 1900. Two years later, the Mediterranean agreement was supplemented by an exchange of notes between Prinetti, Italian Foreign Minister at the time, and the French Ambassador, Barrère. It is worth dwelling for a moment on the content of this note for it is one of the most enlightening documents on the nature of Italian foreign policy.

The Prinetti-Barrère exchanges contained a promise of neutrality on the part of either country in the event that the other should find itself at war as the result of aggression, direct or indirect. But they went further by guaranteeing this neutrality even in the event that either country should find itself in the position of having *"to take the initiative in a declaration of war,* as the result of a direct provocation, *to defend its honor and security."* This famous declaration, secret of course at the time, has been the object of endless discussion, especially on the part of Italian statesmen, publicists, and historians, who have endeavored to explain how it was not inconsistent with Italy's commitments under the Triple Alliance. It is well to bear in mind that the fourth treaty of this alliance was signed on June 28, 1902, and that the Barrère-Prinetti exchanges bear the date of June 30. The near identity of dates may have been accidental, but it creates a strong presumption in favor of the belief that the two sets of engagements were part of one policy. That their juxtaposition should provide scope for the exercise of the legalistic mind was inevitable; this may indeed be said to have been its very purpose. We need not be concerned here with the issue of whether, or how far, the two commitments were morally and legally consistent.

As an indication of Italian policy, their significance is clear: they meant quite simply, as Poincaré put it later, that, in the event of conflict, one could not predict Italy's behavior for she was reserving her freedom of action. The state of affairs created in 1902 bore its logical fruit in 1914. Yet it should also be said, at least parenthetically, that the moral aspect of the matter was not wholly insignificant, even from the pragmatic standpoint of expediency, for it served to bolster the belief in the unreliable shiftiness of Italian policy, or, if one prefer the more colorful expression previously mentioned, in the "jackal tradition" of Italian politics.

But this "jackal" behavior, or fence-sitting attitude, represented a sound appraisal of Italy's position in the world community. It was in essence an acknowledgment of the fact that Italy, smallest of the great powers, could not play the role of initiator in world politics. With the change in Europe which crystallized at the turn of the century, from German dominance to a system of balance between rival alliances, Italy stood to gain most by attaching herself to the winning side in any conflict the initiative of which was likely to rest with stronger powers. At the same time, while relatively weak, her power was not wholly negligible, and, in a state of delicate power balance, might be sufficient to tip the scales, and hence command an attractive price. For this reason, the agreement of 1902 with France is extremely important, representing as it does this fundamental aspect of Italian policy. For those concerned with moralistic judgment and parallels between the behavior of individuals and of nations, it may be pointed out that the secure possession of wealth makes easier the practice of disinterested generosity than the penny-pinching necessity of the man struggling for existence. But this, in turn, does not alter the fact that generosity is more attractive and desirable than penny-pinching.

The position that Italy had evolved for herself around 1900 was in the true tradition of her politics. It was not accompanied by any disproportionate dreams of grandeur, imperial or otherwise, but was based on a correct appraisal of the shifts which had taken place on the European diplomatic checkerboard during the decade following Bismarck's relinquishment of office. Those responsible for the conduct of her policy were sober men, of a higher caliber as a rule than the average of her political leaders, a description which, for that matter, is also fitting of

European diplomats in general during this period. Conservative as a group, for diplomacy was still to a large extent the appanage of the old aristocracy, narrow in some respects, yet on the whole high-minded and, despite later fashionable aspersions, devoted as a class to the preservation of peace.

At the same time, the successful exploitation by Italy of the power relationships of Europe, if it served to enhance her bargaining price, hardly went to heighten her moral standing. We shall see the effects of the widespread feeling that Italy could not be depended upon when the fundamentals of the situation which she had skillfully exploited came to be changed after the First World War. The position of cautious balance continued to be hers until 1915. How it operated at that time will be examined in the next chapter. The same will be done with the Tripolitan War, for the acquisition of Libya, if it was one of the fruits of the policy which has just been outlined, was also the result of other forces which were beginning to make their influence felt in Italy. These and their consequences during the second decade of the present century can be most conveniently discussed as a unit.

Chapter IV · THE TRANSITION OF WAR

La nostra guerra (Our War)

NEW FORCES AT WORK

It is now necessary to go back a little in time, to the beginning of the present century, in order to follow the development of forces which might appear of little moment to the contemporary observer but which were destined, in time, to supplant those tendencies that seemed dominant in the life of the country. Small groups or parties and the ideas to which they are dedicated are apt to be the leaven of the larger and more inert mass; under the impact of great events giving birth to novel circumstances, these groups and ideas may be thrust into a commanding place or find themselves in a position to seize leadership and divert the course of a country's life into new channels. The First World War created precisely such a set of circumstances in Italy. How this happened, and the unforeseen result of its happening, are the objects of the present chapter.

To the Giolittian type of mind, shrewd and prosaic, Italy after 1900 was making steady progress, economically as well as politically. The economic progress was undeniable, and its pace seemed to be gathering momentum. It is often said, in fact, that Italy's industrial progress was greater than that of other European countries. This is true, in certain important lines at least, yet does not invalidate the picture given earlier of her economic backwardness. If we read, say, of a fivefold increase in her output of steel as against a mere twofold increase during the same period in England, such percentages give a misleading impression unless remembered in conjunction with the fact that England had the world's largest steel output to begin with while Italy's steel industry was still virtually nonexistent.

But, bearing this qualification in mind, there is no denying that by the first decade of the century Italy had developed a substantial amount of industry—and an industrial proletariat. The most pregnant consequence of the appearance of a large body of industrial workers in the European economy has been the emergence into the political life of the Continent of the Socialist parties dedicated to the ideology of Karl Marx. As logic would expect, there was in the various countries of Europe a fairly close correlation between the strength of the Socialist parties and the degree of industrial maturity of these same countries, for Marxism was definitely an urban product, taking little interest in— in fact rather suspicious of—the agricultural laborer.

The Marxist ideology penetrated Italy like the rest of Europe, but, in keeping with the size of her industry, made relatively little progress during the latter part of the nineteenth century. Moreover, owing to the peculiar conditions of the Italian scene—the slow-dying legacy of the tradition of misgovernment and the tendency to resort to direct, uncoordinated action—the influence of Socialism as a political party was weakened by the comparatively strong appeal of the version associated with the name of Bakunin. But anarchism, if it continued to retain a certain disruptive hold, was, by its very nature, precluded from becoming a significant movement in politics. Also, Socialism in this period derived much of what strength it had from its appeal to the intelligentsia.

However, with the passage of time and with somewhat of a lag, Socialism followed the same course of development in Italy as in the other countries where it came to be an important influence. The general strike of 1904 and its aftermath have already been mentioned. Thereafter the issue came to be mainly between the two wings of the party, both adhering to the same philosophy of society, but differing on methods: the revolutionary Socialists believing, as their name implies, in the inevitability of violent revolution, with the corollary that the attempt to install Socialism by constitutional means was futile, if not dangerous; and the so-called reformists, believers in the possibility of evolutionary transformation of the state. Syndicalism was also strong in Italy, as in France, but the reformist tendency seemed to be dominant during the first decade of the century. The leaders of this tendency, men like Turati and Bissolati, might well have accepted Giolitti's offer of Cabinet posts had it not been for the fear of losing their hold on their followers through what might have been termed in those days a betrayal. The organization of the General Confederation of Labor in 1906 strengthened the reformist tendency.

The struggle between the two wings of the Socialist movement continued bitter nevertheless. No doubt there was an element of weakness in the reformist position, for, in view of the small size of the party in Parliament, the likelihood that the socialist state would come into being through the achievement of a parliamentary majority was so remote as to be little more than theoretical. Hence the demoralizing temptation to settle into the accepted position of a permanent opposition, without prospects of ever having to shoulder the responsibilities of power, content to work for small installments of social reform while paying safe lip service to the tenets of the authentic gospel. That tendency and that danger were not peculiar to Italian Socialism. Some of the reformist leaders, moreover, became tainted with the capital sin of nationalistic, or at least national, leanings, with the result that at the party congress of 1912 the reformist leadership was defeated and ousted, largely through the attacks of one of the more fiery leaders of the revolutionary tendency, none other than Mussolini himself.

But the important thing is that, whatever their shortcomings and internecine quarrels, the Socialists introduced a new element in Italian political life. It was new because it represented those elements which had in the past been condemned to dumb acquiescence in the leadership of their "betters," indulging at most in occasional, but generally aimless, revolt when conditions became unusually unbearable. It was, and is, the inevitable trend of the times that the impact of economic change should result in the growing political consciousness of the masses, and that this consciousness grafted onto the democratic ideology of the English and French revolutions should transfer to these masses the weight which the bourgeoisie had carried in the body politic during the nineteenth century. What use the masses will make of this power is another question, to which the subsequent course of Italy herself has supplied a possible, if not very fortunate, answer. To be sure, in the early days especially, and in Italy as elsewhere, Marxist leadership was in the hands of middle class intellectuals, largely attracted to it through humanitarian motivation; but they alone could not carry much weight until the backing of the real proletariat had been secured. There was nothing peculiarly Italian about all this. But what was peculiarly Italian in the appearance of Socialism in Italy was the fact that in the rather drab context of Italian politics previously described, here was a political party devoted to a real idea; whatever one think of the merits of Marxism, it is undeniably a serious philosophy, one of the major developments of nineteenth century thought. There were those, in Italy and outside, who considered that Socialism, because of this very quality, was the most hopeful development in Italian political life since the initial driving force of the *Risorgimento* had spent itself. But the possibility also existed, and was contemplated by some, that Italian Socialism, especially its more moderate reformist aspect, might become absorbed in the tradition of *trasformismo* or of Giolitti's newer version, sometimes called *neo-trasformismo*.

As a party in Parliament, before the war, it must always be remembered that the Socialists were a small group. Effective control of the state was securely in the hands of what might be called indifferent liberals. The old conservative tendency, fearful of even any small extension of democratic practice, was definitely becoming a thing of the past. Even Sonnino admitted to Giolitti that he had come to the conclusion that Italy could no longer be governed by other than parliamentary means. For the most part, however, these indifferent liberals thought of socialism in terms of the Red menace. Not so Giolitti, who felt that the Socialists could be tamed into participation in the normal political life of the country, in order to do which he offered them representation in the Cabinet. Thus Socialism, before 1914, was an uncertain force, a great potential factor for the future, but a force whose ultimate course was unknown. The split of 1912 is an indication of its unreconciled gropings. Mussolini, who won the day and the editorship of the party newspaper, *Avanti*, was the sort of Socialist best calculated to instill fear of the Red bogey. Forceful and unrestrained in expression, yet consistent Marxist that he was in those days, he could condemn the Tripolitan war as a typical capitalist, imperialist adventure to be paid for by the blood of the workers, and logically advocate direct action to interfere with the movement of troops.

But Socialism was not the only leaven stirring at this time. For the poor, ground in misery—and the standard of living of the Italian masses was very low—the alleviation of this most pressing burden may understandably suffice to fill the horizon of desire. For those to whom economic necessity is less pressing, the alleviation of social injustice may exert an appeal, but the question is soon bound to arise, what then? Socialism, as mentioned before, had exerted a considerable appeal among intellectuals whose response to economic advantage is relatively emasculated (they themselves largely belonging to the bourgeoisie, for that matter) and among the young whose idealism and normal rebelliousness is not yet tamed into acceptance of the world that is.

Socialism, growing out of economic change, was an indirect product of scientific development. But science, delving into the nature of matter and life, had done much more than produce gadgets, revolutionize material conditions of life, and give birth to Socialism as a response to the problems which it had bestowed upon society. Its remarkable successes had caused it to become for many a substitute for religion. To be sure, there were many questions, of a fundamental character to man, for which science had no answer. But so much had been done in so little time that the only reasonable position to take was that of a well-bred agnosticism, content with knowledge so far acquired, in the confidence that all secrets would eventually yield their key. Meanwhile, it was obvious that the boundaries of understanding were steadily advancing and that man was conquering nature.

Thus came to pass a strange reversal. Mankind, from time immemorial, had cherished the dream of a Golden Age; but classical Greece no less than Christendom, believing in man's original fall from grace, had placed this millennium in some dimly remote past. Now, under the impact of scientific accomplishment, the nineteenth century projected this millennium into some indefinite, but not too distant, future. Belief in unlimited progress came to be the accepted ideology of all that was up to date, new, in the current of contemporary thought. The steady stream of invention and material improvement made the latter part of the nineteenth century what may be described as an age of optimistic materialism. Yet, as a belief, this was a static condition, best exemplified perhaps by the state of development of physical science around the turn of the century. Physicists at that time seemed to have evolved a complete explanation of the constitution of matter and its behavior—even if they had found it necessary, in order to achieve this end, to endow the evanescent ether with seemingly inconsistent attributes. The satisfaction of full understanding did not long prevail in physical science and was soon shattered by the opening up of new vistas.

Likewise in the domain of thought in general, even while the idea of progress seeped to the popular level and became the official theme of a Fourth of July type of oratory, doubts and questionings were beginning to disturb the more serious thinkers. But there is normally a quarter-century lag between the birth of new ideas and their seepage into the popular consciousness, or at least into the consciousness of that elusive being, the educated layman. The stirrings which had been taking place behind the seemingly unshakable façade of a Victorian solidity were beginning to agitate broad layers of society at the turn of the century. The climate of thought just described was common to the western European nations as a whole and penetrated Italy like other lands, though, here also, Italy was perhaps more a recipient than an originator.

This restlessness of thought manifested itself in a renewed interest in polemics in which the young especially, the literate youth at least, participated with gusto. Many, attracted at one time to Socialism, were, in the succeeding disillusionment of another generation, groping for other idols, preferably of a less material nature. The old faith of the Roman Church did not reclaim them. The Church of Rome was indeed not immune from the prevailing unrest of the intellectual atmosphere. But, perhaps not incorrectly from its own point of view, sensing the danger of attempts which might lead to the same result as the Protestant Revolt of four centuries earlier, Rome deemed it wise to fall back on a strict reassertion of the authoritarian principle. It lost a few adherents, unable to deny the logic of their thought, but the modernist movement within the Church was successfully quashed. A renewed and revitalized Catholicism did not emerge during the first decade of the century.

Of the various, and not unrelated, movements which made their appearance in Italy during this same first decade of the century, in politics, in literature, in the arts, the most interesting and significant from our point of view is the revival of nationalism. Nationalism in Italy was no novelty. The very formation of the country had been one of the outstanding manifestations of that force in the European world. But the nationalism of the *Risorgimento* was liberal and willing to apply its own criteria to other nationalisms toward which it nourished no antagonisms. Much had happened to change the atmosphere since the middle of the century. Such things as the manner in which Venice and Rome were acquired—the first ceded by Austria to Napoleon who passed it on to Italy, the second ingloriously entered while the same Napoleon was meeting disaster—had left a slightly unpleasant aftertaste and a certain feeling of inferiority. Despite her recognition as a great power and her membership in the Triple Alliance, Italy as a power was not held in very high regard. What is more, Italians gave the impression of acquiescing in large measure in the foreign judgment. The Crispian adventure hardly enhanced the prestige of the country either abroad or in its own eyes. But with the dawn of the new century some Italians, young ones especially, began to voice their objection to being forever relegated to the role of "a nation of mandolin players." The new nationalism was therefore bellicose and aggressive.

This revival of nationalism was in large measure a literary phenomenon, as is often the case with nationalism. Its most articulate and conspicuous spokesman was Gabriele d'Annunzio. The Prince of the Snowy Mountain, as he was later to be formally dubbed, was a picturesque personality. As an individual, his character may best be described as unsavory; as a dabbler in politics, theatrical is most fitting; as a master of words, his place must be high. Master of words is used advisedly, for his mastery of their use was supreme. This very skill served to conceal the dearth of ideas; by no stretch of the imagination may D'Annunzio be called a thinker. This made him all the more suitable as the representative of the new nationalism which harbored a confusion of vague and undigested yearnings. This aspect of modern nationalism may be found elsewhere. In France, for example, the names of Barrès and Maurras come to mind. The case of Maurras is of particular interest. For Maurras, while a superior mind, has lived long enough to bring out in full the vice of contradictory weaknesses which make up the aberrations of modern nationalists. Violent xenophobe like all his ilk, he has yet been able to give his support to the subservience of Vichy France. It is not often that circumstances offer such an opportunity to bring out in full light intellectual dishonesty, which is why the case of Maurras has been cited.

Yet, even in its perverted form, such nationalism contains a share of idealistic appeal, if for no other reason than because it evokes a response, among some at least, from the individual's yearning to surrender himself to some value other, hence presumably higher, than his immediate narrow self. This explains the appeal of nationalism to some who felt that the atmosphere of optimistic materialism had left an unfilled vacuum in their souls. Colorful literary imagery was best calculated to convey the appeal. When D'Annunzio discovered nationalism, he was approaching the middle of life rather than entering it with the freshness of youth, and his literary reputation was already established. A decadent sensualist in search of new sensations, the perceptiveness of his poetic antennae may have caused him to sense the possibility of new fertile fields, although this must be said of him that he remained faithful to the end to this new love of his middle age. We shall dwell a little later on the extraordinary role which fell to him after the war. Around this time, in 1908, there appeared a play of his, *La nave* (The Ship), which may serve as an excellent illustration of the nature of this phase of his work and of the ingredients that went into the Italian nationalistic brew. The play, later made into an opera for which it provides a most colorful *mise en scène,* is essentially a poetic exaltation of the glory that was Venice, couched in the usual D'Annunzian mixture of violence, cruelty, and vague aspiration, all wrapped up in brilliant imagery, whose theme is expressed in the recurring phrase: *arma la prora e salpa verso il mondo* (arm the prow and sail forth toward the world). It was in short a recalling to Italy of former high deeds, a sounder appeal than that to the too remote glory of Rome, and a call to perform some great, if unspecified (sail forth toward the world), deeds through the assertion of power (arm the prow). This is an isolated example; others could be given, just as other names than D'Annunzio's could be cited, but it has been chosen as a good illustration of a tendency and a state of mind.

Italian nationalism was somewhat handicapped by the difficulty of choosing the direction of its possible attack. French nationalism had a ready-made issue in Alsace-Lorraine. To be sure, Italians could produce a counterpart with the cry "Trento e Trieste." The complication in this case came from the fact that early twentieth century nationalism drew its recruits in the main from the conservative layers of society, and in the case of Italy the conservatives tended to be the stanchest adherents of the Triple Alliance, partly from fear of facing a possible conflict with Austria, partly because Austria stood for conservatism whereas anti-clerical, republican France, was too tainted with radicalism.

In actual fact, relations with Austria continued to deteriorate after the turn of the century. Governmental policy turned to the fence-sitting attitude which has been described in the preceding chapter, but, quite independently of this, there was a genuine recrudescence of the anti-Austrian irredentist agitation. While the government did not encourage the agitation, neither did it try to suppress it, and there developed between the two countries a continual friction, kept alive by a series of minor incidents over which Germany sought to pour the oil of her mediating influence. Unfortunately for the central European combination, Bülow's *tour de valse*—the urbane manner in which he sought to minimize German concern over Italy's flirting with France—seemed to be followed by "sitting out" the next dance, and Vienna's policy assumed increasingly a disgruntled snarliness that vented itself in pin-pricks.

Nationalism, if it could thrive on the irredentist grievance, also became colored with an imperialist tinge, Italy in this respect following the same pattern as the rest of the major powers. The various international crises of this period arose out of the clash of imperial interests for the most part. There were common elements between the poet D'Annunzio, holding up to his contemporaries the model of imperial Venice, and the poet Kipling extolling the mission of imperial Britain—despite differences in other aspects of their work: Victorian Kipling, for example, would hardly be associated with decadent sensuousness. Italy's imperial ambitions turned east and south. To the east, the issue was control of the Adriatic and influence in the Balkans, which again meant a collision with Austria. This took the specific form of rivalry for the control of Albania, compromised by agreement to uphold the independence of the small country should Turkish rule be removed. In the increasingly delicate and tense power balance of Europe, the very friction nourished by this rivalry and by the irredentist agitation at home was used by Italy to enhance the price of her continued adherence to the Triple Alliance.

To keep things in their proper perspective, it must be emphasized that this nationalistic, imperialistic movement did not penetrate very deeply into the masses. A nationalistic party as such made its appearance on the political scene, but its parliamentary strength was wholly insignificant. But, then, the Socialists were also not numerous in Parliament at this time. These two movements have been discussed at some length because, while small in terms of votes in Parliament, they represented new, live, and active forces. Of the two movements, Socialism seemed the more solid, drawing its strength from the fundamental forces that carried the modern world along. Assuming that Europe and Italy would continue to move along the paths they had been treading for some decades, there was every reason to predict that, with increasing industrialization, a growing urban proletariat, and a steady enlargement of the franchise, the Socialist party could look forward to steady and continued growth. The future of nationalism would have seemed perhaps less predictable. Its negligible voting strength was not an altogether accurate measure of its significance. For, if its recruits were few, these were drawn from the educated classes; they were literate, and even more highly vocal than literate, and counted among them a fair share of ability. While D'Annunzio was their poet and successful advertiser, men like Corradini, Federzoni, or Prezzolini represented something more substantial. To be sure, the movement also had its lunatic fringe, the sort of individual that was attracted, in the field of the arts, by Marinetti's futurism. Highly emotional, hence unstable, the future influence of the nationalistic agitation was, in the early 1900's, in the nature of a question mark.

Nationalism and Socialism stood at the opposite poles of political life, extreme Right and extreme Left. Yet, curiously enough, or perhaps not so curiously after all, there were common elements between rabid Nationalists and the more extreme type of Socialists who found their home in the revolutionary wing of the group. Those who took to heart the teachings of Sorel's *Reflections on Violence,* a book first published in 1906 which had perhaps more influence in Italy than in its native land, and those who reveled in D'Annunzio's approving picture of bloody, if aristocratic, brutality may have execrated each other. Both, however, joined in the exaltation of violence and strength as qualities desirable in themselves, hence had a meeting ground of common motivation and outlook. To have spoken of any possible union of the two would have seemed wholly ludicrous around 1910. It would be anticipating our story to show how the unholy union was eventually consummated, and not in Italy alone. At this point, we wish to do no more than point to the existence of certain situations, states of mind, and moods.

LIBYA AND ITS INTERNATIONAL REPERCUSSIONS

Over this scene, unruffled, Giolitti was presiding. Sensitive to the currents of opinion, but evaluating them from the height of his sane practicality, he thought the time had come for a small installment of adventure. The nationalistic ferment could be at once assuaged and exploited, turned the while into carefully directed channels. War, in addition, tends to be a unifying factor for the nation and may be useful in diverting attention from nearer sources of division. The ground had been carefully prepared through long negotiations, as the result of which Italy had obtained *carte blanche* from her allies and friends, on both sides of the fence she was straddling, for whatever she might wish to do in Tripoli. In this respect, the matter was handled in the tradition of Cavour rather than in that of Crispi, though relatively little was at stake this time in terms of real value. The provinces of Tripoli and Cyrenaica, centers of a certain amount of wealth and culture in the days of ancient Rome, were now little more than desert, supporting a sparse population of some 1,000,000 souls, totally devoid of any resources. Assets of strategy and prestige, glory at not too great expense, were the advantages to be found in the desert.

In 1911, accordingly, war was declared on Turkey under whose suzerainty, largely nominal, the two provinces still were. Good reasons for attacking Turkey there were none, but pretexts were easy to find— or manufacture. Turkey, degraded and maladministered, and for some time suspicious of Italian designs, had indeed been not overfriendly to the extension of Italian enterprise in the provinces. But this aspect of the matter is, from our point of view, irrelevant. The Tripolitan War was just one more of the many colonial wars which had become a commonplace in the activity of European nations, especially since the revival of imperial expansion which began in the 1880's. In this context,

Italy's claim to Tripoli was no better, nor any worse, than Britain's to the Sudan, France's to Morocco, or Germany's to the Cameroons.

The course of military operations need not detain us either. Never conducted on a large scale, they involved a somewhat greater effort than had been originally envisaged, but the outcome could hardly be doubtful. By 1912, yielding to the combined pressure of diplomacy and brute force, Turkey ceded her last African possessions and allowed Italy to occupy "temporarily" the Dodecanese Islands, pending fulfillment of the terms of peace. The Italian domestic reaction to this war was interesting. The popular enthusiasm for it was small, though there were but few who, like Mussolini, outspokenly condemned and openly opposed the undertaking; the majority, while passive, were at the same time inclined to find satisfaction in the results. In Italy, as elsewhere, the active driving force of imperialistic expansion has been guided by small groups of individuals, with the mass of popular opinion following in indifferent acquiescence. But this same opinion has been keenly sensitive to foreign opposition arising from the clash of imperial interests. In this fashion, imperialism has acted as a stimulant of national consciousness. We shall observe the same phenomenon, in sharper manifestation, at the time of the Ethiopian episode in 1935. Whether Italy was earnestly embarking upon an imperialistic career or merely playing at imitating the game in which the other great powers were by this time deeply committed, the Tripolitan episode was too small to tell.

But small as it was, its repercussions went deeper than those of far more important happenings which had taken place only a decade or two earlier. This was due to the fact that, by 1911, there was but very little territory which had not been preempted by one or other of the imperial powers; as a consequence, their expansion had brought them into direct contact, and clash. Franco-British and Anglo-Russian imperial differences had been composed through amicable compromise. But German ambitions, and Austrian, collided with the interests of all three members of the Triple Entente, chiefly at the two ends of the Mediterranean. By 1911, Europe was an armed camp in a state of precarious equilibrium. That is why the Tripolitan War had wide repercussions and the European chancelleries, indifferent to the Italian acquisition for its own sake, displayed concern over the fact of hostilities.

The Italian expedition to Tripoli, part and result of the Franco-Italian *quid pro quo* in Morocco, came close on the heels of the Agadir crisis, generated in this same Morocco, focus of Franco-German colonial rivalry. In the end, Italy was able to exploit these fears of the powers who, reluctantly, acquiesced in the Italian solution for hastening the termination of hostilities. This solution consisted in having them exert joint pressure on the Porte to induce acceptance of Italy's terms. The delicacy and complexity of the European balance may perhaps best be judged by the behavior of Austria-Hungary during this war. Unfriendly ally of Italy as she was at the time, she raised the issue of Balkan equilibrium and compensations in order to check Italian action in the Aegean. Italy was thus circumscribed in her conduct of operations and she, in turn, when confronted with Turkish tergiversations, resorted to the threat of naval action at the Straits in order to frighten the powers into supporting her claims. Perhaps skillful, but certainly dangerous—some would say irresponsible—playing with fire.

The gamble was successful, from the Italian point of view, but the fire was not put out. For Turkey's yielding was due only in part to the pressure exerted upon her by the powers; it was also due to the fact that she felt she must prepare to cope with trouble nearer her own center, in the Balkans. And one of the reasons the Balkans were astir and judged the time opportune for action was this same fact that Turkey was involved in war with Italy. Between the Tripolitan War of 1911–12 and the attack of the Balkan League in 1912, there is a direct, if not exclusive, connection. The Balkan Wars of 1912 and 1913 resulted in the virtual expulsion of Turkey from Europe. Balkan nationalisms showed themselves no less intransigeant than those of older vintage. One outcome of their bitter antagonisms and of the relations between Austria-Hungary and Italy, suspicious rivals rather than allies in this area, was the birth, or perhaps one should say the abortion, of the independent state of Albania which issued from the Congress of London in 1913.

TO BE OR NOT TO BE

The Balkan turmoil did not subside until the autumn of 1913. By that time, the members of the Russian-sponsored Balkan League had fallen out among themselves. The great powers were anxious to prevent a spreading of the conflict to themselves, but no less anxious to prevent any one of them from securing exclusive advantages. The antagonism was especially sharp between Russia and Austria-Hungary. The former, still smarting under the effects of the diplomatic setback represented by the Austrian annexation of Bosnia-Herzegovina in 1908, was further disgruntled by the success of Austrian diplomacy in Sofia. Austria, on her side, genuinely and rightly concerned over the growing restlessness of her Slavic population, was irritated by Serbian aggrandizement which she contrived to curb to the extent of preventing Serbian access to the sea. This, in turn, focused against her the frustration of Serbian nationalism which ever more turned to dependence on St. Petersburg. Bulgaria, equally frustrated and resentful, became likewise more than ever Vienna's client. Austro-Russian rivalry thus added fuel to the rivalry of their Balkan pawns. The connection between the events of 1912–13 in the Balkans, the situation just described, and Sarajevo is not far to seek. And the time interval between them is short: from September, 1913, to June, 1914. This, to be sure, is only part, albeit an important part, of the story, and it would be even more incorrect to charge Italian action with undue influence on the course of events. But it is no exaggeration to say that the Tripolitan War was a match lit in the midst of an explosive situation, or that a continuous thread of development runs from that war, through the Balkan Wars, to the Sarajevo murder.

Despite the growing tension of preceding years, the mounting burden of warlike preparations, and the accelerating pace of successive crises, the Sarajevo murder caught the world of 1914 unprepared. That world accepted the idea that a conflict among the major powers was a thing of the past, cheering itself with the thought that the very destructiveness of improved scientific warfare precluded the possibility of its occurrence among nations that boasted of the degree of their civilization—and of the quality of their weapons. Looking back to these thoughts in 1949, they may seem not devoid of irony. Yet, despite much unforeseen improvement in the arts of destruction since 1914, one can hardly deny that the world of 1914 was rather more civilized than the one we have been trying to cope with in recent years. Ever larger military appropriations, in which even the Socialists at times concurred, were thought of as defensive. If we leave aside the otherwise perfectly legitimate and relevant discussion of responsibility, either immediate or long range, for the catastrophe which engulfed Europe in 1914, it is true to say that this Europe blundered into a war which it did not want. Even Austria-Hungary, whose Foreign Minister Berchtold acted with greatest rashness and least sense of responsibility, was moved at least as much by the defensive desire to prevent the disintegration of the Dual Monarchy under the disruptive impact of its disparate nationalisms (one of whose chief foci of agitation lay in Serbia), as by the aggressive search for territorial acquisitions.

Berchtold's handling of the situation was the most important single and immediate cause of Italy's behavior in the hectic month of July, 1914. This behavior must be examined at two levels: at the level of momentary action in the context of immediate events, and at that, ultimately more significant, of long-range policy.

The diplomatic negotiations which unfolded at an accelerating tempo during July, 1914, found Italy in the situation which has been described before. She had, on the one hand, definite commitments formally expressed in the treaty of 1912, latest version of the Triple Alliance; on the other, there were the Prinetti-Barrère exchanges of 1902, to which should perhaps be added the Tittoni-Izvolsky agreement made in 1909 at Racconigi.[1] The commitments to the Entente were loose and ambiguous, those contained in the Treaty of the Triple Alliance, on the contrary, quite precise and clear. These came under two heads: the *casus foederis* and compensations; in other words, the circumstances under which Italy was to join her allies in war on one side, and, on the other, the *quid pro quo* she might be entitled to expect in compensation for any advantage Austria-Hungary might obtain in the Balkans. So long

---

[1] The Prinetti-Barrère exchanges of 1902, culmination of the Franco-Italian rapprochement, have been described in the preceding chapter (pp. 74–75). The Austrian annexation of Bosnia-Herzegovina had antagonized Italian as well as Russian feeling. The Russian and Italian Foreign Ministers, meeting at Racconigi, concluded an agreement one of whose purposes was the checking of further Austrian encroachments in the Balkans where the *status quo* should be preserved; in addition, the two countries promised each other support for their respective ambitions, Russia's at the Straits and Italy's in Tripoli.

as the dispute concerned Austria and Serbia alone, there could be no question of the former coming into play. But Article VII of the treaty of alliance was designed to meet precisely such a situation as had arisen and provided specifically for consultation prior to action. For reasons of his own, some plausible and others not, which need not detain us here, but, in the last analysis because of the strain and mutual distrust which had been accumulating between Austria and Italy, Berchtold made it a point to keep Italy in the dark about his activities with the intention of confronting her with a *fait accompli;* meanwhile, he consulted only with his German ally. When, therefore, Italy learned the content of the Austrian ultimatum to Serbia of July 23 (she did not even receive the twenty-four hour advance notice of it originally intended), she was wholly justified in considering Austria's action a breach of the spirit as well as of the letter of the alliance. When the area of conflict began to spread (involving Russia first, then through the play of the alliances, Germany and France), and Austria then sought to invoke the *casus foederis,* she could hardly expect a friendly hearing in Rome.

Nevertheless, the involvement of the major powers completely altered the nature of the impending clash. At this point Italy was confronted with a major decision, far transcending petty Balkan bickerings or Berchtold's fine spun casuistry about temporary versus momentary occupations of territory. The outcome was that Italy declined to join her allies, on the plea that the war was the result of their own aggression, while the Triple Alliance was a defensive instrument. This decision implied a judgment on her part, a judgment for which a good case could indeed be made, and there is no denying that, from the standpoint of strict legality, Italy's behavior was formally correct. But that was really, if not beside the point, at least of secondary importance, just as it would be irrelevant at this juncture to review the issue of war guilt. The really decisive factor was the consideration of self-interest. The fact that Italy was militarily and financially unprepared for war, not having yet made good the drain on her resources of the Tripolitan War, and that the state of public opinion was antagonistic to Austria, had to be taken into account; but had the government felt convinced that the country's interest would have best been served by adhering to the alliance, its decision on the applicability of the *casus foederis* could easily have been

different. It is true that public opinion, in Italy just as in Britain, became quite aroused over the German violation of Belgian neutrality,
but that event took place *after* the government's decision had already
been reached. At the same time, it would have been difficult to justify
at the moment so violent a reversal of policy as turning on her allies; the
only course was thus neutrality. By August, 1914, Italy was the only
important power in Europe not involved in the conflict: she was still
sitting on the fence.

The government at this time was presided over by Salandra, Giolitti
enjoying one of his periodic self-imposed retirements. He was still the
dominant figure on, or at least behind, the political scene, and approved
the policy of neutrality. But, with the passage of time, even in neutral
Italy, the war situation came to override other considerations. The general expectation throughout Europe, once the unthinkable had happened, was that the war would be of short duration, for technical, if
for no other, reasons—another myth the irony of which we may now
appreciate to the full. The course of military operations during the first
month of hostilities seemed to support both this belief and that, for those
who held it, in the overwhelming superiority of German arms. But the
German strategy which succeeded in 1940 failed in 1914. After the
Marne, and the race to the sea, the struggle in the west soon settled down
to the stalemate of trench warfare.

The successful French stand was on the whole welcomed in Italy.
Leaving sympathies aside, a crushing German victory would have
faced Italy with some difficult, perhaps unpleasant, problems. But the
stalemate also altered the diplomatic picture. The Allies, Britain especially, were less well prepared for war than the Central Powers; if they
could withstand the initial shock, time, enabling them to mobilize their
greater resources, might work in their favor. If the war was to be prolonged, Italy was confronted with two issues: one, could she maintain
her neutrality, even if she wanted to? the other, how could she best
profit from the situation? It is at this time, in October, that Salandra,
taking charge temporarily of the Foreign Office, owing to the death
of its incumbent, the Marquis di San Giuliano, coined the since famous
phrase *sacro egoismo*. It was meant innocently, and soundly, enough as
an expression of the government's devotion to the national interest.

As such, there was little novel in the sentiment, save perhaps in the terse neatness of its expression, quite comparable to what might be termed a "purely American" or a "primarily British" policy. But the ambiguous position of Italy and her subsequent actions explain how the innocuous phrase came to be seized upon as the classical expression of the unprincipled cynicism of Italian policy, thus endowing the phrase with overtones that it did not originally possess.

Meanwhile the emotions of the belligerents and the heated debate which they carried on, both for home consumption and with an eye to enlisting neutral sympathy, evoked in Italy an increasingly loud response. In this debate, Germany had placed herself at a disadvantage; even if one discount early tales of atrocities, invented and true, there was the incontrovertible fact that Germany, not Britain or France, had violated Belgian neutrality—in a particularly clumsy and brutal manner to boot. In the atmosphere of 1914, this event, which as the result of postwar disillusionment has been since then too easily forgotten and written off in America, deeply stirred the conscience of the world. Such a manifestation of Teutonic arrogance, combined with the mounting dislike of Austria, served to create in Italy an increasingly strong body of pro-Allied opinion, part of which at least went the length of advocating active participation in the conflict. At any rate, intervention on the side of Italy's Central European allies, once the original neutrality had been declared, became out of the question. As to the government, the thought of British naval strength furnished a clinching argument, if one had been needed, toward the same conclusion. Thus Italy became the scene of a debate, conducted with increasing vivacity, between the advocates of intervention on the Allied side and those in favor of continued neutrality.

On that issue the country was divided. Conservative opinion was on the side of continued neutrality. Giolitti, from his Piedmontese retreat, kept his counsel, watching events develop, probably expecting to return to the helm at the auspicious moment; he himself was a convinced neutralist. Moved by entirely different considerations, the bulk of the Socialists were also opposed to intervention, adhering to the orthodox Marxist interpretation of the war as a clash of rival imperialisms—an explanation which was true, but only partly true, prime example of the limitations of an exclusively economic, materialistic view, and, for that reason, in the long run, one of the sources of weakness of the movement.

The interventionists were an equally oddly assorted lot. What there was in Italy of the Mazzinian tradition, vague and uncrystallized but not dead, was strongly drawn to republican, anticlerical, Masonic France and to liberal England. Enthusiastic nationalists were attracted by the prospect of combat, of action for the sake of action. D'Annunzio, returning from France, whither personal embroilments had caused him to seek shelter for a time, put his eloquence at the service of the pro-Allied agitation. An unexpected recruit joined the ranks. Mussolini, so outspokenly opposed to Italy's own imperialistic Tripolitan adventure, after some intense soul searching, came to the conclusion that Italy would stand diminished if she continued to adhere to a mean and uninspired neutrality; with events of such magnitude as were taking place, the country must join in the stream of action. This conclusion reached, he wasted no time in putting the implications of it into effect. In October, he resigned the editorship of the *Avanti;* to the accompaniment of great bitterness and turmoil he was expelled from the party in November, having meantime started in Milan his own newspaper, the *Popolo d'Italia,* where, with his wonted gusto, he carried on an active campaign of interventionist propaganda. D'Annunzio and Mussolini were strange bedfellows to contemplate. There is no lack of irony in the charge brought against both that French money was the agency that accounted for the position that they took. Quite possibly, French money was used, but this as the sole and complete explanation of the change would be highly misleading. Mussolini did not shed his revolutionary ardor, and the *Popolo d'Italia* blazoned Blanqui's motto, "Who has steel has bread," and Napoleon's apt remark, "The revolution is an idea which has found bayonets."

The government meanwhile was holding to a steady course between the growing clamors of divided opinion. In November, Sonnino accepted the foreign portfolio which he was destined to hold for four years. He was the only Foreign Minister among the Allied powers who held office uninterruptedly throughout his country's participation in hostilities and beyond that through the peacemaking at Paris. That fact alone would have sufficed to make his influence considerable. Sonnino was a rather lonely character on the Italian political scene. He was the unusual combination of a Jewish father, a Scottish mother, and Levantine antecedents. For all the affinity Calvinism may have with the Old Testament, a Hebrew Presbyterian was a rare object in Italy. But in the liberal Italy of that time, it was not his origin as much as his personal character that made him stand apart. The motto he adopted, *quod aliis licet, non tibi,* was suited to the man, though the display of it perhaps reflected on the quality of his taste. Rigid, stubborn, and taciturn, Sonnino's rise was due to his ability, so far displayed mainly in connection with financial matters, but he thoroughly lacked the art of managing and humoring men, and his two tenures of the Prime Ministership had collapsed within a few months. Thoroughgoing conservative, known and respected for his integrity, Sonnino had been initially one of the few advocates of going into the war on the side of the Central European allies. He now accepted neutrality and was the person best calculated to direct the country's policy according to Salandra's slogan of *sacro egoismo.*

There was one simple question before Sonnino: how could Italy derive most advantage from the war? Or, to put it differently, and more crudely: what price could she get for continued neutrality? and, as an alternative: what price could she get for intervention? The second must, of course, be higher than the first, for it would involve the costs and risks of active participation in the war. From his accession to office, Sonnino carried on negotiations with both groups of belligerents until the query was answered with the signature of the Treaty of London in April, 1915. The negotiations with Austria never came within sight of success. The Italian demands were moderate, amounting to little more than the cession of *Italia irredenta*. But, despite German pressure in Vienna and Bülow's trip to Rome in an effort to bring about a compromise, it proved impossible to agree either on the physical extent or the time of the cession. Austria's understandable feeling of being blackmailed was a reaction more human than statesmanlike.

The feeling of the Allies was not very different from that of Austria. From their point of view, the cost of Italy's assistance was boosted to an inflated value because she was in a position to take advantage of their predicament and set her own price. However, in the military equilibrium that had been reached, it was thought that Italy's power might be sufficient to break the stalemate. Moreover, it was obviously easier for the Allies than for Austria to make a promise of Austrian territory. After some haggling, the bargain was therefore concluded, and, save for a compromise in Dalmatia, fruit of Russian objections, it was made on Italy's own terms.

This Treaty of London must be examined in some detail, for its importance to Italy was destined to be great. Its incompletely fulfilled terms may be said to have kept it alive until June, 1940, at least, and the vicissitudes of its fate gave it significance far greater than could have been originally expected. Its provisions, as an indication of Italian policy and power and of the use of that power, are no less enlightening. These provisions fall under two chief heads that may be distinguished as national and imperial, the two overlapping or merging in the Adriatic.

Under the first head came the enlargement of the national territory. This was so designed as to achieve two purposes: the acquisition of what ethnically Italian territory still remained under Austrian rule, the Trento and Trieste slogan of long-standing nationalistic agitation; beyond that, the securing of a good strategic frontier which, going past the ethnic line, was virtually the line which in fact became the frontier of Italy from Switzerland to the Adriatic. There is one qualification to this, namely the town of Fiume, which the Treaty of London specified should be left to Croatia. The point would hardly be worth mentioning were it not for the extremely important events which wholly unpredictable (in 1915) circumstances were to associate with Fiume in 1919 and 1920.

Coming to the Adriatic, Italy was to acquire, on the eastern shore of that sea, roughly the northern half of Dalmatia and, in the south, Valona with an adequate hinterland for its protection. The Adriatic was to become an Italian-dominated sea, thus placing Italy in a favorable position for the future game of Balkan politics.

Beyond the confines of purely national territory and the adjacent Adriatic, Italy's imperial ambitions also appeared in the Treaty of London, but only in vague and ill-defined terms. The equilibrium of power was to be preserved in the Mediterranean, said the treaty, translating this purpose into the statement that, in the event of a partition of Turkey, Italy would be entitled to "a just share of the Mediterranean region adjacent to the province of Adalia." Also, if Britain and France should enlarge their colonial domains in Africa from the German possessions, Italy might "claim some adequate compensation" in the form of frontier adjustments between her existing East African and Libyan colonies and the adjacent British and French possessions.

Sonnino's policy, expressed in the terms of the Treaty of London, was rounded out by the subsequent agreement of St. Jean de Maurienne of April, 1917, concluded between Britain, France, and Italy, and "subject to the consent of the Russian government," which consent was never forthcoming, owing to events in Russia during that year. Russia was soon to eschew all participation in "wicked" imperialistic partitions. This agreement involved Italy's ratification of the arrangements previously made between her allies for the division of the Near East and defined her own zone of interest in that region, roughly the southwestern third of Anatolia including its chief port, Smyrna.

These wartime agreements were in the true tradition of Italian foreign policy during the preceding fifty years. In the framework of 1914 Europe, they were an expression of belief in the balance of power. Whatever the outcome of the war, the chief powers would continue to exist and to function as such; Sonnino would have been horrified at the thought of the complete destruction of the Dual Monarchy. Such possibilities were the later result of the duration and bitterness of the conflict; and Sonnino's shortcoming lay in his failure to grasp the new conditions which the conflict itself brought into existence. But in the context of 1915 his outlook was sound. Italy was taking advantage of a situation where her tight-rope-walking policy of the past fifteen years could bear fruit. The Allies had no love for the bargain; as Beckendorff, Russian Ambassador to London and signer of the Treaty of London, put it, "circumstances give a weight out of proportion to its [Italy's] real strength." Yet the Italian demands could hardly be called exorbitant: a good bargain, from her point of view, would be more apt as a description of the arrangement. Italy, and her spokesman Sonnino, entertained in 1915 no bloated dreams of grandeur, but a sober estimate of the burdens which her powers could carry. If anything, one might express surprise at the apparent lack of interest in colonial questions. But Sonnino had a colonial policy. If he failed to evince interest in the non-existent possibilities of East African and Libyan deserts, he pursued assiduously the more solid realities of the Near East. That, too, was sound, in the context of 1916, the time when he was negotiating the St. Jean de Maurienne agreement.

But it is equally true that Sonnino's policy lacked breadth of vision. Socialist utopias (especially when couched in the unrestrained terminology of their more violent exponents), the national aspirations of the South Slavs, were things which he despised or failed to understand, to be fought against or ignored depending upon the degree of their misguided strength. His shortcomings, and the consequent tragic failure that he was, came out in 1917 and after, when his inflexibility made him refuse to acknowledge that the world had changed. It would be interesting to speculate upon what the keen political sensitiveness of a Cavour would have done in the circumstances: obtuseness was not among his characteristics, and, while capable of playing the game of power politics with the best (or shrewdest), Cavour also had a place in his system for the force of aspirations whose aims cannot be measured in mere square miles of territory. One is tempted to venture the generalization that Italian policy in 1915 and after the war was merely the fruit of the pedestrian approach which had characterized the political life of the country since the completion of unification. It would be less than fair, however, not to point out that the agreements of London and St. Jean de Maurienne were typical fruits of a diplomacy which should be described as European rather than peculiarly Italian.

One more qualification must be made, and it is important. The vast majority of the masses, not excluding the socialist masses, among the initial belligerents felt that they were waging a war of self-preservation. However much we may have been conditioned by German policy and deeds then and since, it must be remembered that this feeling was no less genuine and strong in Germany than among the Allied populations. But Italy entered the war in 1915 with complete deliberation, having carefully weighed the advantages of neutrality versus intervention, bargained with both sides, and finally coldly espoused what promised to be the more profitable alternative. It was only natural that her former allies should look upon her behavior as treasonable, while her new ones felt that she had exacted the highest possible price that their plight would induce them to pay. Sonnino's cold and uninspired, if realistic, calculations, his very personal manner in fact, did nothing to mitigate these views. By no stretch of the imagination could Italy's intervention be called a defensive action, and she, or at least Sonnino, conscious, or perhaps self-conscious, of this fact, emphasized it by their behavior, looking upon her participation as in the nature of a separate private war, conducted alongside and so to speak on the margin of the main conflict, a state of affairs most accurately expressed by the unfortunate phrase *la nostra guerra,* our war. In the First World War, Italy had truly the unfortunate distinction of holding a unique position.

In keeping with this state of affairs, and as already indicated, the country was divided in 1915 on the issue of intervention. Once the government had decided to enter the war, there remained, despite the vocal interventionist propaganda, a delicate task of psychological preparation to perform. Neutralists on their side were not idle; they could count on substantial forces and Giolitti became their rallying point. In January, a much debated letter of his was made public, wherein he expressed the view that Italy might expect to obtain a good deal (*parecchio*) for her continued neutrality. It was an open secret that some negotiations were going on and that Germany was playing the role of intermediary in trying to bring about an understanding between Vienna and Rome. How delicate the home situation was may be judged from the course of events during the last days preceding Italy's formal declaration of war on May 23.

One of the provisions of the Treaty of London, which had been signed on April 26, was that Italy should take the field within not more than one month. The Triple Alliance was formally denounced by Italy on May 3. There remained to face Parliament which was to reconvene on the 12th. The task was delicate, for Giolitti's hold on that body was still secure. By this time, it may be said that interventionist opinion, fostered by the government in part, was stronger in the country at large than in Parliament. The meeting of that body was put off a week, but the ultimate test could not be avoided. Salandra's handling of the situation is a tribute to his skill. Giolitti was called in by the government and given full information on Italy's existing commitments to the

Allies. His reaction was one of anger, but he saw a way out: he would guarantee a large adverse vote in the Chamber, under cover of which the country would withdraw from the Treaty of London, a scheme which he presented to both Salandra and the King. The tenseness of the situation is illustrated by these two facts: on the one hand, Giolitti's arrival in Rome was greeted by a hostile popular manifestation; on the other, three hundred deputies personally left their cards at his residence as a token of their allegiance. Salandra met the dilemma by resigning. The move was a successful bluff; for if Giolitti was willing to guarantee a covering vote in the Chamber, prudent man that he was, he had no desire to assume the open responsibility of power in face of the temper of the country. Within three days, it was announced that Salandra's resignation had been refused, which meant that Giolitti's opposition had been withdrawn, whereupon the Cabinet continued in office and proceeded to carry out the country's obligations. Giolitti withdrew into passive silence and Italy's entry into the war terminated in effect his long domination of the political life of the nation.

The detail of these events in May, 1915, has been recounted at some length because of their significance. Salandra's maneuvering could successfully bridge a dangerous passage; it could not effect a real reconciliation of fundamentally divergent opinion, for the heritage of divergence was inherent in the manner of Italy's deliberate intervention. As if to emphasize the special position of the country within the conflict, when the government declared war on Austria-Hungary on May 23, it contented itself with severing diplomatic relations with Germany. It took a whole year before Italy's new allies could induce her to declare war on the latter country.

ITALY AT WAR

Of the military aspects of Italy's war little will be said. The fact of war was, in itself, a unifying force in the nation—up to a point. Ordinarily, victory might be expected further to enhance unity. That this was not the case was due to the circumstances of the war itself and to the peculiarities of the subsequent peacemaking, or attempt at peacemaking, as will be described presently.

Very soon after her entrance into the war, the fundamental assumption which lay behind Italy's intervention was shown to be false. This assumption consisted in the belief that, in the stalemate which had been reached in 1915, the weight of Italy's power would be sufficient to break the deadlock. The war was to be short, the paltry £50,000,000 credit provided for in the Treaty of London being an indication of the expected magnitude of the undertaking. The Italian declaration of war was to be synchronized with a Russian offensive in the East, but the plan went awry after some important initial successes in the Carpathians, and before long it appeared that nothing conclusive had been achieved. The insatiable war machine had an additional forty million bodies to draw upon for cannon fodder, a new front was created from Switzerland to the Adriatic, and the stalemate continued. It was a very difficult front, much of it in the high Alps, in a setting of natural grandeur, but truly more suited to the destruction of human life than to its preservation. There is no lack of irony in the observation that it takes the futile endeavors of war to plumb the depths of fortitude of which the human soul is capable. The armies bore their hardships well, as armies are wont to do. The command and the rear gave them inadequate leadership and support respectively.

Therein lies, in brief, the explanation of Caporetto, the sensational Austro-Hungarian breakthrough which seemed to threaten for a time the complete collapse of the Italian front. If the episode achieved greater international renown than comparable Russian, British, and French disasters, it is because it could be cited as confirmation of the low esteem in which the outside world held Italian military competence, a situation for which Italian diplomacy itself was in part responsible, and because of Italy's emphasis on the separate nature of her own war, again a fault of her diplomacy. However, the gap was plugged, largely by Italian efforts, although some French and British assistance was forthcoming. But foreign criticism rankled in the Italian consciousness.

At home, the result of Caporetto was a change in ministry and the formation of a union government which set about the task of reorganizing the unsatisfactory condition of the home front. Caporetto occurred in October, 1917. That year was one of weariness and depression for the Allied peoples; it was particularly so in Italy, less united from the start in the purpose of war. Giolittian and socialist neutralists of 1915 had been at best unenthusiastic; as the war and its attendant losses and costs kept mounting to undreamed of heights, their initial, if reluctant, passive acquiescence became disgruntlement and open criticism, verging at times on disaffection and defeatism.

But the year 1917 witnessed another event as well, of far greater import for the future. Caporetto and the October Revolution in Russia were simultaneous occurrences; the coincidence in time was a fitting expression of the fact that there was much in common between the causes of the two events. Russia, backward, atrociously managed by her leaders, and cut off from the West, collapsed into the complete chaos of revolution and withdrew from the struggle. Italy, less poorly directed, accessible to assistance from her allies, part of the western world, retrieved herself and carried on to the end. The Russian upheaval was destined to have far-reaching consequences and to exert vast powers of attraction on the western European masses. But, owing to the chaos which accompanied this upheaval and to the greater than ever separation between Russia and the West, these consequences were somewhat delayed. In the West, the defeatism of 1917 was followed by a rally, a rally which was in part a purely internal resurgence of domestic energies. The formation of the union ministry of Orlando was its outward symbol in Italy, similar to Clemenceau's accession to power in France, though the men are hardly to be compared. But the rally must in large part be credited to the other great event of 1917, which had more immediate and important consequences than the Russian collapse for which it more than compensated, the entrance of the United States into the war.

There would be little value in reviving here the pointless debate of who won the war, or trying to apportion the share in victory of the various Allies; but that it was the weight of American resources, fully thrown into the balance from 1917 on, which tipped the scales of victory may be taken as indisputable fact. The details of American military and economic intervention need not detain us. But what is important for the story being told is the impact of this intervention on the Italian position. This must be examined under two heads which, for convenience, may be called the military and the political.

As a consequence of the Russian collapse, the main strength of all the belligerents, Allies and enemies alike, was concentrated in the West; Balkan and Near Eastern diversions, important as they were, absorbed but a relatively small part of the war effort. The Italian front continued to be purely Italian and, partly because of its physical nature, remained relatively secondary in the larger picture of the war—in the eyes of the other allies at least. The American effort was thus naturally concentrated on the western front, and the bulk of the American armies, their headquarters and supplies, were located in France. Of the American presence in the conflict, Italy had little more concrete evidence than the token representation of a regiment. This fact, small in itself, must be remembered in conjunction with the American view of the various Allies. That Britain should loom largest on the American foreign horizon needs no explaining. However much modified in time, the American nation and culture are, in the last analysis, built upon a broad foundation that is British. Whether the British association was an object of admiration and pride, or of intense dislike and suspicion, there was in any case no need to make American consciousness aware of the existence of Britain. And Britain had, in addition, for over a century, filled the role of number one great power in the world.

France and her culture have been the object of estimates ranging from sound appreciation to humorous and foolish prejudice. But even without going back to the important eighteenth century connection, and leaving aside the not very meaningful platitudes about Washington and Lafayette, there was in 1917 the fact that, for Americans especially, the war was mainly fought in France. The largest armies in the field were French, as well as the greatest losses in manpower and the greatest physical devastation. So France, too, loomed large in the war. But of Italy little was known in America. Outside of an infinitesimal cultured and traveled minority, American acquaintance with things Italian was derived from a considerable, but recent and therefore unassimilated, immigration, drawn largely from those depressed and swarming masses of southern Italy which have been described in an earlier section, a source of cheap and exploitable labor. In so far as Italy existed at all for the bulk of the American people, the picture of her was a ridiculous distortion.

Italians at home, those at least who were aware of the situation, were sensitive to the unfair, but understandable, discrimination. Little was done to right the picture, and little could be done, for that matter, by way of official propaganda. But the fact was important, psychologically at least, which is why it must be emphasized: it served to stress the special position of isolation which was Italy's in the war.

Yet, more than ever, this isolation was dangerous and the consequences of it were soon to have their disastrous manifestation. For America—even though she was, before many years had passed, to make a futile attempt to escape and deny the fact—had rather suddenly become the greatest power in the world; her active participation in the conflict transferred this enormous power from the realm of the potential to that of the effective. In other words, America's voice and her views were, from now on, of capital importance.

America's position in the conflict was also unique. For all the subsequent disillusionment which developed in America over the results of the war, it is sound to assert that she entered the conflict in legitimate defense of self-interest. It is rather clearer in 1949 than in 1917 that this country, like Britain, has a stake in preventing the dominance of the European continent by a strong military power. But if the fact is clearer now, it was no less true thirty years ago. At the same time, it is also true, now as then, that this country is a stranger to the petty historic quarrels and rivalries of Europe and therefore can take, now as then, a more detached and fairer view of those differences. If, therefore, American intervention was not an exclusively altruistic crusade in defense of abstract principles of justice—degenerating as some would have it into pulling other people's chestnuts out of the fire—the subsequently much derided American idealism of 1917 was a very real force indeed. Quite genuinely, America wanted the destruction of German militarism and a lasting peace on the basis of a fair settlement.

It was therefore natural that the American intervention should place new stress on the ideological aspect of the war, in which respect its influence worked to the same effect as that of the Russian revolution, denouncer of imperialisms and their secret diplomacy. In an effort to hold the loyalty and bolster the morale of their own peoples, while weakening those of their enemies, the Allied governments were driven to the necessity of clarifying their war aims. Their record was mixed, for the defensive character of the war on their side had not prevented the conclusion of various agreements whose terms were not too consistent with the proclaimed purity of their motives. It was thus natural that the leadership in the formulation and exposition of Allied war aims should fall to America, both by reason of her power and of her lack of earlier commitments.

How did all this affect Italy? It created for her a peculiarly delicate situation in which the nature of her intervention and her isolation in the war were soon to bear bitter fruit. An opportunity was hers for a while but she muffed it. There were those in Italy (they may be called the true inheritors of the Mazzinian legacy) who understood this opportunity and wanted to take advantage of it. Such a man was Bissolati, for example, a moderate Socialist who had rallied to the cause of intervention and even accepted a ministerial post. Sonnino, however, in charge of the country's foreign relations, practical exponent of *Realpolitik* that he was, full of contempt for visionary idealism, was the last man to understand and appreciate the opportunity. The story which is about to be told is a prime illustration of the limitations of practical men in general, and of Sonnino's shortcomings in particular.

The focus of Italy's coming difficulties lay on the shores of the Adriatic where Italian nationalism clashed with Slav. The Treaty of London, as mentioned before, promised Italy certain territories of the Dual Monarchy inhabited by Slavs. It has been pointed out that, in the context of the Europe of 1914 and of the balance of power concept, the price promised Italy for her intervention was not unreasonable. The whole arrangement was predicated, however, on the assumption that Austria-Hungary would survive. But, as the war became protracted, and especially after the events of 1917, the Allies turned an increasingly attentive eye to the possibility of exploiting the disruptive force of the suppressed nationalities of Austria-Hungary.

The idea of forming a large unit comprising all the South Slavs of Austria-Hungary and their Serbian cousins was thus given a strong impetus; such a scheme inevitably brought into collision the aspirations of these South Slavs and those of Italy. And here came Italy's opportunity: she could come to terms with her new prospective neighbors by making certain territorial concessions to them. This would of course have meant a diminution of the promised benefits of her intervention. Obviously, such yielding does not come easily to any government. But a broad—and, for the longer run, one might even say wise and astute—statesmanship might have understood that for the relatively small price of these concessions (even assuming that no compensatory equivalent could be obtained elsewhere) far greater, if territorially and immediately intangible, benefits could be had: to say nothing of the definitive removal of the Austrian menace, the possibility was open to Italy of staking out a prior claim to a position of leadership in Central Europe and the Balkans.

There was indeed a momentary wavering when it seemed that the opportunity might be seized. Partly as an aftermath of Caporetto, there was held in Rome, in the spring of 1918, a so-called Congress of the Oppressed Nationalities of Austria-Hungary. Orlando, the Prime Minister, addressed and welcomed the delegates, although Sonnino would have nothing to do with them, and this high-water mark of Italo-Slav cooperation had no practical consequences. Sonnino held on to his pound of Dalmatian flesh and carried along with him the majority of his colleagues in the government.

Far more important than the Rome congress was the message which President Wilson had delivered to the American Congress three months earlier and in which he formulated the famous Fourteen Points. One of the dominant conceptions running through this statement of Allied war aims was the acceptance of the principle of self-determination, thereby giving recognition to one of the dominant forces of the nineteenth century. The power and prestige of America gave this pronouncement of her spokesman more than passing significance and the Fourteen Points were to play a vital role in the peace.

The Fourteen Points were not born, full-grown like Minerva from Jupiter's brain, out of President Wilson's mind; they were, for the most part, the condensation of much detailed and careful study. At the same time, they did not attempt, as they could not at the time, to lay down specific frontiers. Point IX, which dealt with Italy, stated simply that *"a readjustment of the frontiers of Italy should be effected along clearly recognizable lines of nationality."* Such a statement amounted to a flat repudiation of the Treaty of London. To be sure, America was not committed to this treaty any more than to any other arrangements made among the Allies prior to her intervention. There were clearly the makings of a controversy on this point: one solution would have to give way to the other, unless some compromise could be found. However, the issue was not met at the time and the war went on to its successful conclusion in the autumn of 1918.

When the time came for negotiating the armistices, the request of the Central Powers being based on the acceptance on their part of the Fourteen Points as the bases of peace, the issue had to be met squarely of whether or not the Allies would formally commit themselves on their side. Colonel House, gone to Europe for the specific purpose of elucidating this question, spent some days in close discussion with the chief Allied spokesmen at the end of October and the beginning of November. Save for a British reservation regarding the meaning of the Freedom of the Seas (Point II) and a French one on the scope of restoration (Point VIII), the Wilsonian program became the formally accepted basis of the forthcoming peace.

During these discussions, an unfortunate thing happened for Italy. Well aware of the inconsistency between the Fourteen Points and the Treaty of London, the Italians thought the time had come to protect their interests, which they endeavored to do by introducing a clarifying interpretation of Point IX. But, at this juncture, the special and isolated position which Italy had made hers during the war reappeared with a vengeance. Her allies, quite naturally, thought of Germany as *the* enemy, just as Italy had focused her attention on Austria-Hungary. This last country was, by this time, in process of disintegration with the result of emphasizing all the more the position of Germany as the sole enemy. House, on his side, while he put up a stiff fight to secure acceptance of the Fourteen Points by the Allies, was, in his wonted manner, anxious to avoid and minimize differences. The outcome was that, on the plea that Point IX did not bear on the conditions of the German armistice, the Italian reservation was brushed aside and Orlando committed the tactical error of not insisting upon it. There are issues which the mere passage of time will soften and resolve; there are others which it serves to exacerbate. Here was one which it would not be possible to avoid facing some time, and putting it off during the pre-armistice discussions among the Allies merely served to introduce an element of future confusion and a basis for recriminations. Technically, the question remained unanswered whether or not Italy was bound by the Fourteen Points.

In these circumstances hostilities came to an end in the autumn of 1918. It is a commonplace in 1949 to say that the problems of peace are greater than those of war. But the reason this is a commonplace is precisely because in 1918 there was a widespread feeling that victory had solved all problems, that the damage and cost of the war would simply be made good by the enemy; and there was also a colossal pressure to return to "normalcy" as soon as possible. This urge was only natural, and we have seen it manifested again in this country at the end of the Second World War. The fighting men, drafted civilians, were anxious to shed their uniforms, and they expected to return to their peacetime occupations finding the gratitude to which they felt entitled in the better world so often and so glibly promised by their leaders. These expectations were common to all belligerent countries, and, in varying degrees, they were destined to be frustrated in all. The degree of frustration was determined in large measure by the resilience of their respective economies, which depended in turn upon the extent of damage incurred, and by the resources available. The business of war had severely strained the economic and financial structure of all the European belligerents.

Of the chief European Allies, Italy bore the smallest loss. Her dead at 600,000 were two thirds of the British and 40 percent of the French. Her high birth rate made that loss even easier to bear. The devastation of her soil was incomparably smaller than that suffered by France, and her expenditures likewise were far lower than those of either the British or the French. But these economic losses only take on full significance when remembered in terms of existing resources. The poverty of Italy, despite what progress she had made, has already been stressed. Consequently, if the economic cost of the war was smaller *in absolute terms* for Italy than for any of the major allies, this was not the case of the *relative cost*. The greater relative drain on Italy's resources made the task of readjustment to peace a particularly difficult one for her. This difficulty was of course not immediately apparent upon the cessation of fighting; it was a factor which was to operate over a period of time.

It will be touched upon again, for it is an element vital to the understanding of what happened in Italy. It is mentioned at this point because it must be borne in mind as an important part of the background against which Italy was to conduct the peace negotiations to which we must now turn.

THE "MUTILATED" VICTORY

The role of Italy in the making of the peace may be summed up briefly as a continuation of the special position of isolation which had been hers during the war. The episode has been analyzed in ample detail and we shall be content to recall here those aspects of it which are relevant to the larger story.

Two things were paramount in the eyes of the government after the armistices had been signed. At home, the primary concern was the economic readjustment to peace, the handling of demobilization in all its multifarious aspects; politically, this meant trying to hold together the rather disparate team organized under the stress of the war emergency in 1917. This necessity was forever present in Orlando's mind; it harassed and hampered him during the rest of his days in office, until June, 1919, that is during the very time when the foreign situation demanded all his attention. The resignation in the preceding January of Nitti, one of the leaders of Parliament who had joined the Cabinet under the pressure of the wartime urge to unity, was the harbinger of a return to political "normalcy," if by this we mean the personal and party strife of peacetime politics.

The centrifugal tendency of internal politics was in itself a temptation to try to maintain unity at home by stressing the importance of agreeing on the position to be taken toward the outside world. That was the other great concern of the moment. In view of the sharply drawn issue between the Treaty of London and the American position, the problem of Italian foreign policy was clearly defined. The Italian reaction was still somewhat uncertain. The two antagonistic tendencies, which might be described for simplicity as the Wilsonian and the Sonninian, the New versus the Old, were both represented in the Italian Cabinet. Bissolati, heir to the Mazzinian legacy, was naturally attracted by the Wilsonian outlook; he was the chief advocate of a policy of conciliation toward the Slavs. He was so far successful at one time as to induce his colleagues to underwrite the statement that "Italy considers that the movement of the Yugoslav people for independence and for the constitution of a free state corresponds to the principles for which the Allies are fighting and to the aims of a just and lasting peace." This was in September; by the end of October, we have seen how Sonnino's views had become the official Italian position in the pre-armistice discussions. The showdown between the two irreconcilable tendencies could not be long delayed. It took place at the end of December with the result that Bissolati resigned from the Cabinet.

This resignation was almost simultaneous with the official visit that Wilson paid to Italy during the last days of the year and the first of 1919. As it turned out, Wilson's visit, which might have been a last chance to bridge a dangerously widening gap, merely served to add confusion to misunderstanding. The prestige of the United States and the importance of the personality of Wilson at this time cannot be overemphasized. In the eyes of the weary masses of Europe, the New World was much more than the final artisan of victory. For victors and vanquished alike, Wilson personified in a very real sense the promise of a new and better order and found himself raised as a result to a precarious Messianic height. Italy was no exception, and the popular acclaim given there as elsewhere to the American President was well calculated to nourish in him the feeling that he was truly the spokesman, not only of his country's idealism, but of the aspirations of the masses of humanity at large. Indeed this was true at the time. But his feeling when coupled with his latent American suspicion of the ways of the Old World fostered the fatal illusion, one of the causes of Wilson's undoing, that as a last resort, in a crisis, the masses of any country would go the length of ranging themselves with him against their own governments if need be. How this illusion was to be tested and shattered over the Italian issue, we shall see presently.

To the bulk of those in the seats of power in Europe, Wilson was in the nature of a novel specimen in the diplomatic fauna, to be handled therefore with circumspection. His program elicited responses ranging from incredulity to sneers, which latter, in the case of Sonnino, certainly constituted the dominant note. Orlando, less direct and more supple, could find the proper phrases that would still serve to befuddle and conceal the issue for a time. It was symbolic and in character, if odd by diplomatic protocol, that while in Italy Wilson should consult with Bissolati, however much the two were meant to understand each other. But it is also while in Italy that Wilson seems to have committed himself to acceptance of the Brenner frontier for Italy. Precisely how he came to do this we do not know with certainty. Unquestionably, it was a departure from "clearly recognizable lines of nationality" and, from the Italian point of view at least, if one departure could be encompassed, why not another? One is tempted to say, Shades of Yalta! The concession introduced a further element of confusion into the situation.

It was but a few days later, on January 11, that the same Bissolati, now free of governmental responsibility, attempted to expound in public his views on the Italo-Yugoslav difference. At the *Scala,* in Milan, where he was to speak, he was howled down by an aroused nationalistic mob. By itself the incident was not too important; its significance lay in the possibility to which it pointed of arousing national passion with the double purpose of using its pressure as a tool in foreign negotiations while at the same time diverting the country's attention from its internal difficulties. Nationalistic feeling, the force of which Wilson failed to take into his calculations for all his devotion to self-determination, had by this time begun in Italy to raise the cry, largely unknown until a short time before, for the city of Fiume. The role which this small city was destined to play very soon and for some time thereafter constitutes one of the strangest episodes in the annals of a troubled period.

Such, then, was the situation in Italy as the Peace Congress assembled in Paris in the middle of January, 1919. A government, none too secure at home, was preparing to face a most delicate situation abroad. The conduct of negotiations on the Italian side was essentially in the hands of two men, Orlando and Sonnino. In the close give and take of direct exchange, the role of personality can be of considerable importance; in the circumstances, neither man was a happy choice. Of Sonnino we have already spoken. As far as he was concerned, he and Wilson could come to terms in one way only: through Wilson's accepting his point of view— a most unpromising prospect. The best service Sonnino could render his cause would have been to keep out of Wilson's way. Orlando was a much more attractive personality; unfortunately, his whole tendency was to conciliate, procrastinate and avoid decisions, while the Italian problem had reached a stage where the passage of time could only hinder rather than facilitate its solution.

Even had they been anxious to reach this solution, the Italians were handicapped by circumstances. For one thing, all major decisions had to be put off in deference to Wilson's determination to see the League of Nations through before anything else. This done, quite naturally and inevitably, the German problem had priority over all others. To be sure, much of the basic technical work of the peace drafting was turned over to and settled by various *ad hoc* committees, final decisions only being left to the central committee of the chief political heads of the delegations.

This central body, the Supreme Council, had to be small if business were to be transacted with tolerable expeditiousness. It consisted at first of ten members, the Prime and Foreign Ministers of the five chief powers, the United States, Britain, France, Italy, and Japan. Before long, the Japanese having little direct interest in European matters which constituted the near totality of the Council's business, the Council of Ten was superseded by the Council of Four, consisting of Wilson, Lloyd George, Clemenceau, and Orlando. Quite accidentally, the very manner in which business was conducted served to emphasize Italy's isolation on the margin of the chief topics of discussion. It so happened that neither Wilson nor Lloyd George could handle the French language, whereas Clemenceau had a good command of English. In so small a body as the Four, it was obviously a great convenience to be able to indulge in direct exchange without the awkward and time-consuming resort to interpreters. Thus it happened that a good deal of discussion went on in English. But Orlando had no English; his command of French was good, though the use he made of that language was not always devoid of unintentional humor. As he had, besides, taken the position that he was willing for the most part to defer to the decisions of his colleagues in matters pertaining to the German question, there he sat, forlorn symbol of Italy's truly unique position.

The Covenant of the League once agreed upon, Wilson had to visit the United States to attend to pressing domestic matters; thus another month was consumed during which no important business could be settled in the Council. Much work was done during this time by the various above-mentioned commissions, but little on the Italo-Yugoslav frontier, core of the Italian problem, for the committee on Yugoslav boundaries had been specifically instructed to exclude that sector from its considerations. Upon Wilson's return to Paris, he was confronted with the issue of the French security demands. On the very sensible, yet in retrospect unfortunate, manner in which that difficulty was resolved—or dodged—at the time, we need not dwell here; the episode was a strain on the tempers of all who were involved in it, a strain which, for temperamental reasons, told most severely on Wilson.

It was April by the time the Council was at last ready to deal with the Italian question. If we ignore the accumulated flood of notes and memoranda, none more inept than the verbose and ill-conceived Italian memorandum of claims, this is how the matter stood at this juncture.

On the Italian side, Orlando was prepared to accept the only solution which seemed possible to him in the circumstances, namely a compromise. He was willing to give up the Treaty of London to the extent of yielding the Italian claim to the northern half of Dalmatia. But, in order to protect himself from the attacks to which such a concession would lay him open at home, he must have something to show in exchange for it. He thought he had found the terms of a reasonable *quid pro quo* in the equation Fiume-for-Dalmatia.

The case of Fiume must be explained briefly at this point. The current status of the city proper, or *corpus separatum,* under the Hungarian crown, dated from 1868. The population of this entity was a mixture of Italian and Slav in the ratio of about two to one. The suburb of Sušak, separated politically, but physically divided from the *corpus separatum* by the width only of a narrow stream, was almost wholly Slav. Taken as a whole, the urban agglomeration of some 50,000 was about equally divided between the Italian and Slavic elements. The surrounding countryside was, and is, solidly Slav. So much for the ethnic situation. Culturally, the Italian element was dominant, as it was along much of the Dalmatian coast, owing to urban concentration and tradition descended from the days of Venetian dominance. Italian had been the language used in the Austro-Hungarian navy.

The frontier promised Italy in the Treaty of London included the whole Istrian peninsula, reaching the Adriatic at the head of the gulf of Fiume, within a few miles of the city. This same treaty specifically excluded Fiume from the Italian claim. This was done in recognition of its economic significance as the chief port of Croatia and Hungary proper. These are, in brief, the facts about Fiume. Fiume had had no place in the traditional claims of Italian irredentism. But, during the war, there began to appear in Italy some literature which brought the town before the national consciousness; one could hardly speak, however, of any widespread agitation. It is at this point that Orlando took up the matter and made a number of mistakes. For one thing, the government gave encouragement to the nationalistic agitation for the annexation of Fiume; by the spring of 1919, this agitation had reached sizable proportions. This movement, and Orlando himself, sought to present the matter in the light of a case of self-determination. This was in part disingenuous for it ignored the fact that Fiume was a mere island of Italian population; that aspect of the situation was better calculated to antagonize Wilson than to appeal to him. The plea that Fiume had become a necessity of domestic politics, in the light of the government's own share in fostering the agitation for it, worked to the same effect.

The result was that the Italian case, as variously stated, in official memoranda, to Wilson, and in the Council, was open to a telling charge of inconsistency. This case amounted to a demand for the terms of the Treaty of London, partly on the strength of respect for treaty obligations (with some modifications in Italy's favor on the plea of strategic necessity), plus Fiume on the basis of self-determination. This was the manner at least in which the case was put, although, we must repeat, Orlando was hoping to effect a compromise in the end. Allowing for the difficult position that was his, the presentation was, to say the least, psychologically unfortunate.

On the American side, Wilson's position was clear-cut. He was not bound by the Treaty of London; he was indeed, on a later occasion, to make the unaccountable statement that he had no knowledge of that instrument. He felt, however, very strongly beholden to the principle of self-determination. Viewing Europe as a whole with a too serene detachment which failed to take into account its passions (had he not declined to visit the French battlefields lest his emotions be thereby unduly aroused?), the fact that the bulk of the new Yugoslav nation consisted of ex-enemies carried little weight with him by comparison with the aspect of the issue as a contest between right and wrong, strong and weak. All that was needed, therefore, was to ascertain the facts in the case. For this, he depended on his technical advisers, who served him faithfully. On that level, the issue was simple indeed. Wilson thus came to take his stand on the so-called American line. Not only was Dalmatia wholly denied, but even the Treaty of London line from Idria to the Adriatic was pushed to the west. This done, Fiume was no longer in the position of a bit of Italian territory adjacent to the national boundary, but denied inclusion in it. It appeared as the isolated ethnic island that it really was, and economic considerations therefore indicated that it should be attributed to Yugoslavia. On the basis of an examination of local conditions, the American solution could not be described as other than eminently fair. No one could deny that Fiume belonged with its Central European hinterland, and the total Italian population involved was very small—less than 25,000. Moreover, even the so-called American or Wilson line was not the result of uncompromising adherence to the ethnic principle (it would have been impossible to draw such a line in this case), but represented a compromise between ethnic, economic, and strategic considerations. It would have placed within Italy some 400,000 Croats and Slovenes, against whom might be counted the Italians of Fiume and Dalmatia. The American line was ineradicably identified in Wilson's mind with the idea of simple justice.

The position of the other interested parties may be stated briefly. The Yugoslavs, like the Italians, bombarded the Conference with elaborate memoranda of claims. But, far more skillful than the Italians, and more favorably placed, they announced that they were willing to accept the results of Wilson's arbitration. This position was psychologically the best that they could have taken. For all his rigid adherence to principle, Wilson was not impervious to flattery. The British and the French, involved through their signature of the Treaty of London, took the position that they of course recognized the binding character of their signature, but hinted that it was for Italy to decide which she preferred—the concrete advantages embodied in the treaty or American good-will—adding the consideration that the demand for Fiume exceeded the terms of the original agreement. Without love for that agreement, they were not averse to remaining on the sidelines and letting Orlando fight it out with Wilson.

Orlando had thus unwittingly maneuvered himself into an impasse. Fiume had by this time really become a necessity from the domestic point of view, to the extent that all Italian energies were focused on this comparatively insignificant item, with the loss of all sense of proportion and to the neglect of far more important questions. The repetition *ad nauseam* of the familiar arguments had no effect other than wearying the opponents. Wilson's temper had by now worn thin. On the plane on which the discussion was being conducted, there was no solution. Wilson was right in absolute terms, while the Italians felt that they were being singled out for the strict enforcement of dubious justice mainly because they were weak. Had not Wilson managed to make concessions to Lloyd George and to Clemenceau? Wilson's disgust and Sonnino's indignation were on a par. The well-meant, but ill-timed, intervention of some members of the American delegation made a bad situation worse, for it gave the Italians the impression that the Americans were divided (which to a point they were) and to Wilson the feeling of a sense of disloyalty among his own people which merely served to stiffen his resolution.

The outcome was the explosion which took place on April 24. For a few days prior to this date, the Italian question had absorbed the almost exclusive attention of the Supreme Council, until discussions between Wilson and the Italians had to be carried on through the intermediary of Lloyd George and Clemenceau who, in the last analysis, could see no virtue in an open break. Finally, on the evening of the 23d, Wilson resorted to the device which he had threatened to use, but had so far refrained from using, on other tense occasions. He gave out to the press a public statement of his position in what amounted to an appeal to the Italian people over the heads of their government. The device was novel as diplomatic procedure; it was the expression of Wilson's profound conviction in the unimpeachable justice of his position, coupled with the belief that the masses of the people could not fail to rally behind him—even against their own representatives—if only they were given an opportunity to have access to the truth. Such ideas represented, to say the least, a very oversimplified understanding of the processes of both psychology and history.

The incident was highly dramatic, but the explosion settled nothing. The Italian delegates reacted in the only way they could in the circumstances: Orlando issued a public statement of his own by way of reply to Wilson's appeal to public opinion and went home to secure the verdict of his own people in the form of consulting Parliament. The result could not be in doubt. Whatever the merits of the case, the manner of Wilson's challenge had raised a wholly different issue. Since after all the government issued from the Chamber, issued in turn from the country, it was that Chamber itself whose authority had been challenged. On that issue, it was bound to assert its own authority by giving the government a resounding vote of confidence.

But that, too, failed to settle anything. It simply meant that both sides stood on their positions, from which it was now more difficult than ever to retreat, since each had taken its stand in public. The orgy of nationalistic emotion unloosed in Italy was no weapon with which to coerce Wilson, on whom it made no more impression than did the bogey of a disgruntled Italy falling a prey to Bolshevism. Perhaps the danger of dissatisfaction, though not necessarily in the form of Bolshevism, should have been taken more seriously. Italy's British and French allies found a way out by taking the position that, as far as they were concerned, Italy could have the Treaty of London if she wished, but that her insistence on Fiume invalidated that bond. This amounted to throwing Orlando back on the horns of his dilemma. So, after a few days, the Italians were forced to the conclusion that, their withdrawal from the Conference having failed to intimidate others and gain any concessions for themselves, they stood to lose even more by continued abstention; explaining their departure as the mere wish to have their mandate ratified in the face of Wilson's challenge of its validity, they returned to Paris. Less than ever could they now yield on Fiume, and the continued search for compromises between Wilson and the Italians remained barren of results to the end.

The details of this story, interesting and dramatic though it was, would not have been worth recounting had no more been at stake than a squabble over a few square miles of barren Alpine land and the ownership of the small port of Fiume. Of that particular aspect of the matter, it will suffice to say that the deadlock could not be broken so long as Wilson persisted in exercising his power of veto over any settlement of the issue that did not meet with his approval. This he continued to do to the very end, with the consequence that the frontier between Italy and Yugoslavia was finally settled by direct negotiations between the two countries, but not until November, 1920, after Wilson had been removed from the political scene and America had embarked upon the attempt to realize the happy illusion that she could wash her hands of the quarrels of Europe. It may be said, in passing, that the settlement reached at the end of 1920 represented a compromise, not very good perhaps yet reasonable, if all the circumstances of the case are taken into account: Italy obtained the Treaty of London line, slightly modified to her advantage, down to the Adriatic; she gave up all claims to Dalmatia, save the city of Zara; and Fiume itself, without Sušak, became for a time a Free State.

But far more important than the details of the controversy and the settlement were the effects of the episode in Italy. They went deep. Most important perhaps was the test of power. Italy had of course no means of making America or Wilson bend to her will: the two powers simply are not and were not in the same category, even though Orlando was one of the Big Four in 1919. But, on the other hand, neither was Italy so negligible a quantity that she could be coerced into acceptance of a settlement that aroused her national will.

This arousing of the national will was the most regrettable aspect of the matter, the consequences of which may be said not to have yet been liquidated. And we must for a moment turn back to the Italian scene in 1919 in order to appreciate these effects. In the spring of 1919, Italy, like all the rest of the belligerent world, was in a state of restless expectation. The inevitable stresses of the readjustment from war to peace, economic and psychological, were particularly severe in her case. Her native resources being as slim as they are, it was not so much a question for her of "providing a world fit for heroes to live in" as of avoiding collapse. She was highly dependent on the outside world (primarily America, and Britain to a lesser degree) for the continued economic and financial assistance which the wartime pooling of resources had given her. We thus find her very anxious at the prospect of the termination of the wartime arrangements, just as in 1945 we saw in Britain a reaction of hurt and dismay at the American announcement of the termination of Lend-Lease. But, in 1919, the shoe was on the other foot for Britain, or at least she thought that it was, and the world had yet to learn the lesson of its economic interdependence in peace as well as in war. Britain, and America even more, were, in 1919, anxious for the speediest possible return to economic "normalcy," the lifting of controls and the reinstatement of the blessings of "free" competition, nationally as well as internationally. In addition to which it may be pointed out that the desirability of assistance is much easier to perceive for the recipient than for the giver of it, and that gratitude is a term of extremely limited usage in the international vocabulary.

The consciousness of inferiority and dependence, even though vague, is apt to manifest itself in what psychologists call compensation which, in this case, took the form of an oversuspicious and overassertive national sensitivity. Such facts as the Caporetto episode, advertised abroad where it was often taken as confirmation of the widespread belief in Italian military incapacity, worked to the same effect. That nationalists, sincere or professional, should get wrought up over Fiume was but to be expected. Far more significant and disastrous was the effect of Wilson's appeal on the most sincere believers in Italy in the things that Wilson at heart stood for. Even Bissolati had to take exception. Professor Salvemini, whose devotion to liberal ideals no one could question, likewise gave expression to bitterness and disillusion. As he wrote in *Unità:* "Not today but two months ago, and not only to the Italian people, but to all the peoples of the Entente, should President Wilson have addressed himself to recall them to a greater realization of the dangers that threatened peace. . . . Not from the Adriatic negotiations alone, but from all negotiations, should he have withdrawn in time, without ever giving up any essential point from the system of ideas on which the hope of the world was founded. . . ." These men did not draw back from criticizing their own representatives, but they were after all Italians, and they could see no justice in what appeared to them as discrimination against their country mainly because she was weaker than others. They felt all the more bitter from a sense of betrayal of their common ideals on Wilson's part.

Anger, bitterness, and disillusion make an unhealthy brew. The government which had unwisely abetted the nationalistic agitation, increasingly centered on the pinpoint of Fiume, could feel in April that it was gathering the fruits of its policy in the pleasing manifestation of popular and parliamentary support which it received. The display of unanimity was misleading, for the Roman holiday of flag-waving and shouting was by its nature a short-lived emotional outburst; like all emotional excesses it was followed by a letdown when the bleakness of reality had to be faced again. The foreign problem was left precisely where it had been before; confronted with her allies' determination to proceed with the German peace, without Italy if need be, Orlando and Sonnino had returned to Paris empty-handed at the beginning of May. Renewed attempts at finding a way out of the impasse need not be reviewed, for they were barren of results. America, Britain, and France were again wrapped up in the German settlement now being put through its final stages. On June 28, 1919, anniversary date of the Sarajevo murder which had set in motion the momentous train of events a long five years ago, an impressive ceremony saw the German delegates acknowledge the utter defeat of their country in the same setting where the birth of the German Empire had been proclaimed in 1871.

CONCLUSION

From the gathering at Versailles, Orlando and Sonnino were absent, their places being filled by a new set of Italian representatives. For, shortly after the events of April, the position of the government had begun to deteriorate. Shouting for Fiume and reviling Wilson may have been a pleasant pastime, but it did little to alleviate such concrete and immediate problems as a difficult food situation. Indeed, reviling Wilson and America might not be the best way to secure further economic assistance from them. It was thus an easy transition for the anti-foreign feeling to turn against the government which, in the last analysis, had failed to win Italy's case. The dissatisfaction came to a head in this same

Parliament which overthrew Orlando's ministry on June 19 by a seven to two majority. The succession was taken over by Nitti, who had been Orlando's Cabinet colleague until January, at which time he had resigned, partly with an eye on the succession when opportunity should offer. Italian domestic politics had made a very rapid return to "normalcy."

The very day after the signature of the Treaty of Versailles, Wilson left Paris on his way back to the United States, a fact symbolic of the common feeling that the main work of the peace gathering had been accomplished. Yet much remained to be done, for the German treaty, if undoubtedly the most important, did nothing to settle the confused situation in the rest of Central Europe. The signature of the German treaty itself and the near disbanding of the Peace Conference after June 28 once more emphasized the isolation of Italy. One of the victorious great powers, she had played a remarkably small part in the discussion and settlement of the great questions which had come up since the first meeting of the conference in January, ignoring most problems and foolishly allowing all her energies to be focused and largely wasted on the trifling issue of Fiume. It was not wholly her doing that things had taken an unexpected turn, but her statesmen certainly cannot be said to have given evidence of breadth of vision. Though a great power officially, she acted rather like a small one, one with an unusually narrow range of interests at that. And in the end she had not even succeeded in resolving that first of all problems, the definition of her frontiers.

No wonder, then, that the signature of the Treaty of Versailles elicited no great response in Italy. Rather she took of that treaty a detached and critical view, as of something with which she had little concern. The next settlement to be taken up, that with Austria, might have been expected to arouse greater interest. Yet that was hardly the case. The Austrian settlement was drafted during the summer months, and the treaty with Austria was signed on September 10 at St. Germain-en-Laye. The event went relatively unnoticed; understandably so perhaps, for little Austria, whose birth certificate this was, was a puny fragment of an empire great but yesterday, and the world was too wrapped up in the myriad difficulties of the aftermath of the war. Yet, this formal sanction of the disintegration of the Dual Monarchy was the registering in the book of history of the end of an epoch for a large section of the European world. Austria, and its heart, Vienna, had played a long role and filled a mission as the easternmost outpost of western civilization. But to the challenge of solving the nineteenth century problem of nationalism, its ancient machinery had been unable to rise. In the long struggle between Metternich and the Jacobins, the latter seemed to have decisively won: in 1919, Austria was both a national state and a democratic republic.

Italy might have been expected to respond to the significance of the occasion. For a century, her national life had been a long struggle in which Austria was the chief obstacle to her wishes. The tradition of enmity associated with the *Risorgimento* had been taken up again, despite the formal alliance, by the new nationalism and because Austria-Hungary had more recently become the chief rival of the eastward expansion of Italian interests. The opponent was not merely momentarily defeated, it had ceased to exist. By way of comparison, if we think of the traditional Franco-German rivalry, we may consider for a moment what the irretrievable disintegration of Germany would have meant to France. But Sonnino was not the person to rise to the occasion; the possibilities which were opened were too overwhelming for his narrow outlook and he preferred the mean legality which entitled his country to a few square miles of territory (he himself would have taken his stand on a strict interpretation of the Treaty of London, without Fiume)— insisting on his pound of flesh, as some put it.

The country likewise, deprived of adequate leadership—avowedly difficult to provide—concentrated on those few square miles of land (plus Fiume) and, introspectively, on the real enough domestic difficulties. Thus it came to pass that Italy emerged from the war, not with the elation of victory, but with a deep sense of grievance and frustration if not of actual defeat, and there arose the myth of the "lost" or "mutilated" victory.

Yet, in a sense, it may be said that the myth and the grievance corresponded to a reality, albeit not for the reasons that fed the popular discontent. For one of the results of the war was to bring out the deficiencies of Italian power, the real measure of which had been tried for the first time. This hitherto untested power had been magnified to proportions beyond its resources by the nature of the European balance which Italy had exploited with skill. Her intervention and the price for it in 1915 had been the fruits of this situation. But, as we have pointed out, 1915 still thought in terms of pre-1914. It had taken the unexpected stresses of a long war and the collapse of three empires to upset the picture radically. In 1919 there was no longer any equilibrium in Europe, and, as a consequence, Italian support could no longer command a very attractive price. That is why at the peacemaking Italy remained on the sidelines and maintained to a large extent the attitude of a demander dependent upon others. When it came to a showdown, the most she could do was to threaten withdrawal; but if her associates took the position, as they did in the last resort, that she could withdraw if she wished, the state of isolation lost its attraction. Only sterile disgruntlement remained.

The collapse of Austria-Hungary created in Central and Southern Europe a vacuum which might have seemed to open a new fertile field for Italian penetration. But there Italy ran into another difficulty and another influence. Across the Adriatic was a new and unexpected creation, the Kingdom of the Serbs, Croats, and Slovenes, upon whom the western Allies seemed inclined to look with favor. No serious effort was made at the time by those in power in Italy to conciliate the new Yugoslavia, even granting that it would have been, at best, a difficult task. Yugoslavia responded with justified suspicion and fear. She, like the other succession states which had benefited from the war, soon came to lean upon French support, a natural connection based upon an identity of interests in the preservation of the *status quo*. The Latin sister came to be the special focus of Italian resentment. Nor did the Latin sister give evidence in this case of tact or understanding. The bitter fruit took twenty years to ripen. Such was the Italy of late 1919. For three years she oscillated between convulsions of nationalistic exaltation and apathetic despondency until she gave up the struggle in favor of a novel course.

Part III

THE FASCIST EPISODE

Chapter V · WAS FASCISM INEVITABLE?

Sorrowful Italy allows her very victory to go unrecognized and to be of no avail.
(From the preamble of the Constitution of Fiume designed by D'Annunzio in 1920)

D'ANNUNZIO AGAIN

The Fiume Episode and Its Significance.—The Treaty of St. Germain was signed on September 10, 1919. Within two days of this signature the Italian and the world press blazoned headlines which, had not the world been shaken to its foundations by four years of war, might have caused it to shake with laughter. The occasion was the conjunction of those twin stars in the Italian firmament, D'Annunzio and Fiume. The conjunction was destined to have significance which the magnitude of the stars might not have led one to expect; for that reason it must detain us a while.

The place which Fiume had come to fill on the political horizon of Italy has been indicated in the preceding chapter, as well as the manner in which the course of events was distorted through the behavior of the various participants in the discussion of the Italian problem. The deadlock over Fiume between Wilson and the Italians continued after the former's departure from Europe following the signature of the Treaty of Versailles. Tittoni, the new Foreign Minister and head of the delegation which took over when Orlando made way for Nitti in June, 1919, carried on the weary discussion, bringing forward various suggestions, which all fell short of meeting with the American President's approval. This state of affairs had an inevitably unsettling effect in the city of Fiume itself, which was the scene of considerable agitation. In the city proper, or the *Corpus separatum,* the dominant Italian party was in the ascendant and clamored for annexation. But, in view of the rival claims of Italians and Yugoslavs, the city was subject to occupation by an inter-Allied force of British, Italians, and French. These last, moreover, were making use of Fiume as a supply base for their forces in Central Europe and the Balkans, and their friendliness to the Slavs did not make for good feeling toward them on the part of the self-appointed National Council of Fiume or of the more obstreperous League of Volunteers. It is not too surprising, therefore, to find some of these young enthusiasts, in the early summer of 1919, indulging in overt action against the Croat elements and becoming involved in affrays with the French, less than tactful perhaps on occasion. Despite some bloodshed, the episode was in the nature of a minor incident and was treated as such by the Council of Heads of Delegations sitting in Paris. A commission charged with the task of investigating the incidents brought in a report late in August. This report recommended among other things dissolution of the National Council and turning over the administration of the city to an inter-Allied commission which would maintain public order with the assistance of an American or British police force.

In 1919—as in 1946—America was loath to broaden the range of such commitments; it was therefore arranged that the British should take over on September 12. But at that point D'Annunzio made an appearance on the scene in the role of *deus ex machina*. With a small force of volunteers, some regular troops and others less so, he marched upon the city. On his way he was met by General Pittaluga who, as the result of the recent incidents and inquiry, had just superseded the former Italian commander of Fiume. D'Annunzio and Pittaluga went through the appropriate dramatic gestures, but their encounter was not altogether unfriendly, for the latter was unwilling to resort to the use of force. The result was that D'Annunzio was allowed to enter the city triumphantly at the head of his legions, taking over in the name of Italy.

In itself, the episode might have been dismissed as of little consequence. In the troubled aftermath of war, this was neither the first nor the last assertion of illegality; such happenings may be awkward, but are to be expected. But the affair had significance far beyond the local disturbance which it created, which is why it is being dealt with in some detail in this book. Locally, the stay of D'Annunzio in Fiume was highly picturesque, and on that level may be described as a contribution to the gaiety of nations. Some aspects of the performance remind one of the urbane game of war as played by earlier *condottieri*. Just as there was no bloodshed upon D'Annunzio's arrival, his departure after fifteen months was unaccompanied by violence. Once the government in Rome had resolved to oust him, a couple of shells from an Italian warship proved sufficient to prick the bubble of his grandiloquent declamations. D'Annunzio enjoyed his stay in Fiume. He was after all primarily a poet, and a genuine one for all the flamboyance and bombast he liked to make his daily fare. The situation for him was ideal, with a stage vaster than that given to most dramatists and he himself holding the center of it with ample room for the exercise of his exhibitionist propensities. Not devoid of personal courage, as his war record showed, he could and did give free rein to his poetic imagination applied to the political field. The result was interesting and will be examined in more detail presently. For the rest, his too heroic leadership kept the city in a state of turmoil; his innumerable proclamations to the city, to Italy, and to the world at large often make pleasant reading for their style; but none of this offered a real solution. When at last he declared war upon an ungrateful and unheroic Italy, a climax of humorless ridicule was reached. The more solid burghers who were anxious to go about their trade in peace were probably not sorry to see him go. To repeat, all this was local, picturesque, and in itself of minor importance.

But two aspects of the episode have significance far beyond the local scale of the stage on which it was enacted. First of all, it should be noted that if we wish to find actions comparable to the seizure of Fiume by D'Annunzio we must look to the newer countries in the politically unsettled part of Central and Eastern Europe. Korfanty moved into Upper Silesia and Zeligowski drove the Lithuanians out of Vilna; both instances were manifestations of the newly created Poland seeking to carve out for itself the largest possible place on the map. No little difficulty was experienced in getting the Rumanians to withdraw in Hungary to the line designated by the Council in Paris. But Italy was accounted no Poland or Rumania; she was supposed to be a major power with a functioning parliamentary system and a well-established central government. She herself had in fact taken the position that her high state of culture and political development precluded her undertaking the obligations embodied in the Minority Treaties and, on that plea, had signed no such treaties. But here she was the scene of an act of insubordination among her armed forces. The power that D'Annunzio commanded was wholly insignificant, and when the government in Rome decided to oust him, this was accomplished with the greatest ease; yet it took fifteen months before the government made up its mind to take this step.

The delay is in itself significant and constitutes an indication of the state of affairs in Italy. It is a measure of the strength, or weakness, of this presumably secure government. To be sure, the situation would have been awkward for any government, especially when we recall that the largely artificial cry for Fiume had been to a degree encouraged by Nitti's predecessor in office; to seem to oppose and thwart patriotic Italians in deference to interfering outsiders would have been an invidious position for any government to find itself placed in. But D'Annunzio could never have established himself in Fiume in the first place if the Italian forces in the city had resolutely barred his way. It is precisely because of the uncertain condition of the country that the armed forces, especially the higher ranks among them, could harbor doubts in their allegiance. Like the rest of the world, Italy in 1919 was faced with the multifarious problems of the aftermath of war. But, if we compare the Italian situation with that of her associates in the war, we find that it offered an illustration of the greater impact on the weaker structure, both economic and political.

It has been pointed out that Italy's contribution to the war, whether in casualties or wealth, was far smaller than the contribution of the French or the British, but that the strain imposed by this contribution only takes on its true significance when expressed in terms of the resources of the country. And Italy was far poorer and weaker, save in manpower, than her allies. That is why her representatives often took the position—understandable but unrealistic—that the fruits of victory ought to be shared in proportion to the contribution thereto of the various participants, not in relative terms to the contribution of each, but in terms of their own resources. That is why also, Italy, most dependent on the continued assistance of her associates, was most desirous to continue the wartime system of inter-Allied controls and pooling of resources. It is of interest to note, in passing, that in 1919 it was Britain and above all America which were most anxious to do away with these wartime arrangements, and most enlightening to observe how Britain, after the strain of the Second World War, has come to see the virtues of a position similar to that of Italy twenty-five years ago.

The greater economic pressure applied to the weaker political system which was Italy's serves to explain in her case the more acute form of the *malaise* which was, in varying degrees, a universal phenomenon. The interdependent aspects of economic, social, and political unrest, the general disillusion of the returning soldiery, finding at home a world highly different from what they had been led to expect—unlike the American veteran, the returning Italian soldier could look to a difficult time in making a living rather than to a bonus—created suitable conditions for a wide response to the proponents of panaceas and nostrums. That is one reason why the myth of the "mutilated" victory found such fertile soil in which to develop and why appeals to the emotions had a more than normal chance of success. D'Annunzio's picturesque and apparently bold gesture was just such an appeal. There was nothing irretrievable in the situation, and certainly Nitti had no sympathy with the gesture which meant nothing but embarrassment to him. A bolder man might have dealt with it summarily and with ease; in circumstances of flux such as prevailed at the time much indeed depended on the specific actions of individuals. But the timorous routine of halfway compromises, suitable enough to conditions of "normalcy" and peace, was more in the tradition of Italian political life. How even Giolitti, a far stronger personality than Nitti, failed to meet the test we shall see presently. Nitti sought to steer a middle course of compromise and let D'Annunzio perform in Fiume to his heart's content. Italy's allies, sympathizing with the government's difficulties, refused to take an alarmist view of the episode and did not press for a solution.

Thus the episode of D'Annunzio's adventure in Fiume, small enough in itself, was magnified to undue proportions and served as a focus and rallying point of much discontent that pervaded the country. Nationalistic emotion is one of the easiest passions to arouse; we have seen the reactions provoked in Italy by the decisions and later by the suggestions advanced in connection with the fate of Trieste since the end of the Second World War.

The Constitution of Fiume.—But flag-waving and patriotic oratory will not go very far to take the place of expensive bread. Nitti himself had come to office as the result of the discontent and letdown which followed the soon-dissipated unanimity of enthusiasm that had greeted Orlando after his clash with Wilson in the spring. The problem of Italy was primarily economic, with the inevitable political repercussions that economic difficulties have.

Here again D'Annunzio in Fiume was destined to play a curious part. His occupation of the city resulted essentially in a stalemate; if he was allowed to remain unmolested by the Italian government, he in turn failed to produce any concrete solution of the situation. Obviously, the Italian government could not simply annex the place, however often the city itself might proclaim this annexation; that would have raised too serious an international issue on a wholly different plane. As to the stream of proclamations and pronouncements that furnished the poet's facile pen with employment, if it served to keep the agitation alive in Italy, it also failed to elicit any definite response in terms of concrete action; it was useful in keeping the wound open while perhaps pouring a little salt into it. Failing to force annexation or to carry Italy along with him, D'Annunzio proceeded to organize a separate administration for Fiume. A new state was born; it would go alone on its proud way and have nothing to do with, save perhaps set a noble example to, the "sorrowful Italy" which in its timorous, democratic, and unheroic way allowed "her very victory to go unrecognized." Thus came into existence the so-called *Reggenza italiana del Carnaro* which, on September 8, 1920, proclaimed its independence at the same time that a popular vote ratified the constitution bestowed upon it by D'Annunzio. This curious, but interesting, document is worth recalling. Its importance must not be overrated, but it is an excellent indication of the tendencies and ideas which the confused gropings of the time brought to the surface. If it would be a distortion to see in this forgotten document, as in the whole Fiume episode for that matter, the beginnings of Fascism, it is nevertheless correct to say that these events reveal the presence of the seeds of which Fascism was born, while they themselves contributed a share to making the Italian soil receptive to the seed.

As might be expected, nationalism is stressed and exalted in the constitution of Fiume, a task to which D'Annunzio could devote himself with ease and delight. What is more important, and perhaps unexpected, is the strong egalitarian tendency which pervades the document. It might not mean much to find it stated that the government of the new state was to be "purely of the people," but the qualification that the basis of this government was "the power of productive labor" strikes a somewhat novel note in constitutional language. What is more, this note is not an accidental and expedient case of paying lip service; on the contrary, it is obviously central to the thought of the whole charter for we find it repeatedly and deliberately stressed. Thus we read that the state "amplifies and elevates and sustains above every other the right of the producers." The new constitution proclaimed the usual liberal freedoms of thought, press, and assembly, as well as the various rights of the citizen, but at the same time went on to say that "the state does not recognize ownership as the absolute dominion of the person over the thing, but it considers it the most useful of social functions," a nicely balanced statement into which, taken by itself, a variety of meanings could be read and which in practice was capable of extension in wholly divergent directions. But the intended meaning was perhaps clarified by the provision that "the sole lawful claim to dominion over any means of production and exchange is labor. Labor alone is master of the thing made most advantageous and most profitable to general economy." Consistently enough, there followed the conclusion that "incorrigible parasites who are a burden to the community" would not be entitled to the enjoyment of political rights. One might be tempted to ask whether D'Annunzio had gone Marxist. Perhaps it would be nearer the mark to say that, being no serious thinker, nor provided with firm belief in solid principle, his sixth sense made him aware of the general restlessness of the masses, which the war had greatly intensified, and prompted him, like the skillful orator who senses the mood of his audience, to reflect as much as to lead. Such an approach is suited to the demagogue and makes for popularity if not for clarity of thought. Times of stress, such as followed the conclusion of hostilities, create suitable conditions for an inordinate amount of muddled thinking, the very sort of thing in which we shall see Fascism excelling.

But there was even more to D'Annunzio's constitution of Fiume. The internal organization of the new state presented novel features, or at least an interesting combination of features, some new and some drawn from a forgotten past. "Three types of spirits and forces," proclaimed the constitution, "contribute to the founding, progress, and growth of the community: citizens, corporations, communes." Such language would not have startled thirteenth century Italians, but the concept was given a modern touch through the further statement that "only constant producers of the common wealth and constant creators of the common power are the real citizens of the republic." These true citizens were all to be enrolled in one of ten corporations. One is tempted to conjure the vision of a medieval soviet. But again, the corporative structure of the state turned out to follow lines of demarcation on the basis of social class rather than occupation. The communes, basic cells of the state, were granted the exercise of all the powers not specifically reserved to the central government by the constitution.

Finally, to cap the structure of government, a National Council, consisting of two houses, would exercise the legislative power. These two houses bore the names of Council of the Best, made up of representatives elected by popular suffrage on a population basis, and Council of Provisors, where representatives of the corporations would sit. The executive would be made up of a group of seven Directors, appointed yearly and functioning under the chairmanship of the Director of Foreign Affairs. To complete the cycle of historical allusions, there was a provision for the appointment by the National Council of a dictator for a renewable six-month term, in periods of emergency such as existed at the time the constitution went into effect. Considering the authorship of the document and the circumstances of its proclamation, it is not surprising to find in it also provisions for public works and for the general beautification of the city and of the life of its inhabitants.

Taken by itself, the toy state of the Italian Regency of the Carnaro might well be dismissed as a curious but unimportant freak. Increasingly scornful of timid Italy, D'Annunzio finally lost patience with her, gave his ego the gratification of a safe declaration of war, but, as mentioned before, yielded easily when, at the end of 1920, a show of force was made by Giolitti, who had in turn superseded Nitti at the head of affairs in Rome. Even the fact that the constitution of Fiume adumbrated a surprising number of the ideas and practices that Fascism was later to appropriate should not be regarded as a precedent of overwhelming importance. If the episode has been discussed at some length it is rather because of its significance as a measure of the conditions prevailing in Italy at the time. In times of confusion and stress, when men are dissatisfied with the present and weary of the past, novel, or apparently novel, solutions exert a greater than normal appeal. Seemingly inconsistent suggestions are not critically examined, but a premium is put on promises and nostrums, and the greater the promise the greater the appeal. Minor accidents of circumstance and personality, the attraction of the unknown in direct proportion to its seeming divergence from the drab and familiar past, can cause unexpected turns in the life of a nation. That is why, for instance, in 1919 and for some time thereafter, the Russian experiment exerted such a power of attraction on the disgruntled, suffering masses of Europe. If D'Annunzio's adventure had no immediate concrete repercussions beyond its local stage, its very occurrence was symbolic.

In such periods of stress and indecision there is also a premium on vigorous leadership. It does not perhaps so much matter in what direction this leadership may point so long as the direction is, or at least seems to be, clear; definiteness of assertion may in fact be far more effective and useful than clarity of thought or soundness of purpose. The easygoing pace of "normalcy," the assumption that the whirlpool of stirred discontent will of its own accord, if merely given time, resolve itself into the quiet flow of ordinary life, are not suited to such occasions. In these abnormal circumstances, what did the political life of Italy have to offer?

THE BREAKDOWN OF THE PARLIAMENTARY SYSTEM

Taken as a whole and viewed in retrospect, the four years that elapsed between the armistice of November, 1918, and the Fascist coup of October, 1922, present a picture of aimless floundering and of sinking into an ever deeper political morass. Orlando, who represented Italy at the peace, did not long survive his failure to elicit a solution. The excitement caused by the events of April, 1919, and the enthusiasm which greeted his gesture of defiance at the time merely served to increase the depth of disillusion when the futility of his endeavors had to be faced. In June, 1919, he had to relinquish office. His successor was Nitti, his erstwhile Cabinet colleague until the preceding January. It is an indication of the quality, and the weakness, of Italian political life that Nitti's resignation had been caused, in part at least, by too great a fondness for the traditional game of the pursuit of personal political advantage. The wartime "sacred union" had worn thin even before the peace was made.

Within these limits, Nitti was an intelligent enough man, albeit devoid of the determination and strength that the circumstances demanded. Sensing correctly that the difficulties of the home situation, mainly economic in nature, were more important and pressing than the irksomeness of an uncertain frontier, he stayed home and let his Foreign Ministers, Tittoni first, later Scialoja, look after the negotiations in Paris. Only at one time, at the beginning of 1920, did he take a leading part in the foreign situation. But whether in the foreign or the domestic field, his activity was equally barren of results. That he was faced, in both cases, with difficult conditions, no one would deny, but neither can it be denied that a policy of drift could only aggravate matters. This was especially true at home, for the abandonment of the wartime Allied economic and monetary agreements put a severe strain on Italian economy. Allowed to find its natural level the lira rapidly dropped to a fraction of its parity. Wheat imports could not be dispensed with and the device was used of subsidies in order to keep the price of bread accessible to the masses. But the makeshift expedient could only serve a temporary purpose while it put a further strain on the already shaky finances of the state. Nitti was not the person to produce a solution for a state of affairs which he merely allowed to continue. Tomorrow one would see. The immediate task was to navigate from day to day amidst the shoals of shifting parliamentary combinations.

This Parliament, it must be remembered, was old for, quite naturally, there had been no elections in Italy during the war. Not only was it old, but it was particularly out of date. It was a Parliament which, in 1915, had been more inclined toward neutrality than toward intervention. Salandra's skillful maneuvering at the time had saved the day. The task of conducting a major war with an unenthusiastic Parliament was no source of strength to the government or the country. Of necessity the neutralists had been driven to silence while the war was being waged; their leader, Giolitti, dominant figure on the political scene up to 1915, and still commanding an impressive following thereafter, had gone into virtual retirement for the duration. It is not surprising that the seeds of defeatism should have found congenial ground in the ranks of disgruntled Giolittian neutralists and of those who accepted the Marxist interpretation of the war. The awkward situation was resolved through the device of granting the government special powers. The device was legitimate enough and as such not peculiar to Italy, but the use of it had to be extended to lengths that verged on the unsound. To a far greater degree than her allies, who also gave their governments emergency wartime powers, Italy was governed by decree. The Italian Parliament seldom met during the war and when it did it was for brief periods and mainly in order to extend the duration of the emergency powers of the government.

It was this Parliament that Orlando and Nitti had to work with. The war now finished, the tendency asserted itself to return to "normal" politics, a tendency of which the behavior of Nitti himself was an example. But, at the same time, unable to agree upon some program, Parliament tended to solve, or rather put off solving, the issue of its responsibility through the device of continuing to grant the Cabinet powers to govern by decree. The responsibility for such a state of affairs cannot be laid at the door of specific individuals or parties, and while one may speak with truth of a failure on the part of Parliament to shoulder its responsibility, that statement contains after all little meaning. Parliament is not an entity with a distinct and separate existence, but the collection of its membership. What a situation of this kind reflects is rather the lack of sufficient tradition in the whole body politic of the nation, a tradition which is not so much the expression of national temperament as of historical development. Comparisons force themselves on one. No greater contrast could be found than that between this Italian parliamentary system and the British counterpart. Without embarking on a history of British parliamentarism it is worth pondering none the less on the remarkable evolution from the turmoil of the seventeenth century; through the Glorious Revolution; the astonishingly raw, yet normal at the time, corruptness of eighteenth century

British politics; the gross (by later standards at least) abuses that pre-vailed for a good part of the nineteenth century; to the contemporary quality and functioning of the present-day British Parliament. The end product is after all the result of a two-hundred-year-long process of evo-lution undisturbed by outside interference.

Coming back to Italy, her Parliament and her government in 1919, an election was at last announced that would give the country an op-portunity of expressing its views on the issues of the moment, far dif-ferent from those that had been central at the time of the election of the existing parliament. The election was of interest and importance, not only because of the changed conditions which it would reflect, but be-cause it was the first one to be held under the system of proportional representation which had just been introduced. This device might be thought particularly unsuited to the Italian political scene, all too in-clined to fragmentation. Yet the result might well be taken as indicative of progress. As was to be expected, the Socialists made impressive gains, emerging as the largest single group with over 150 representatives as against their former 50. Next to them, the newly organized *Popolari,* Christian Democrats or Socialists as we should now call them, under the leadership of Don Sturzo, emerged as a solid block of 101 deputies. Here, then, were two large groups, mass parties on a broad basis, with a substantial common area of agreement in the field of social policy; to-gether they controlled just half of the total parliamentary membership. Had they joined hands, the results might well have been fruitful and the history of the country might have taken a different course. The might-have-beens of history are numerous; what may be said of this one, however, is that it belongs in the realm of the possible, not of the wholly fantastic and unrealistic.

At any rate, the fact is that no startling innovations resulted from the elections. The difficulty lay in part with the internal problem of the Socialist party; for this party had gone before the country united on a platform which the influence of the early stages of the Bolshevik ex-periment in Russia had had an important part in shaping. But this unity was more fictitious than real, for a substantial portion of the leadership was in effect far more moderate than momentary expediency made it seem politic to aver. Within itself, it may be said that the Socialist party offered a replica of the shortcomings of the Italian political system as a whole: a lack of experience and responsibility, an undue tendency to yield to the political expediency of the moment, and a stress on the personal element. The gesture of these Socialists in walking out of the Chamber in a body upon the entrance of the King at the opening meeting of the new Parliament on December 1 was not so much a dignified assertion of principle as a manifestation of somewhat childish and irresponsible petulance. It was hardly suited to the difficult circumstances of the time unless the Socialists were in earnest about pressing their advantage of the point of creating a really revolutionary situation. That, however, for all their talk, they were not prepared to do. The gesture, not too important in itself, may well be contrasted with the smooth and dignified advent of a Labor government in Britain in the summer of 1945. This Labor government, taking office in circumstances of economic and political stress, not incomparable to those of 1919 Italy, backed moreover by an absolute, large, and enthusiastic majority, found no difficulty in accepting all the antiquated ritual that still surrounds the British monarchy. From a doctrinaire standpoint, such behavior may seem logically inconsistent, but the action is a good measure of the difference in the political experience and maturity of the two countries.

Despite the changed representation in the new Parliament, Nitti stayed on, largely for the reason that no one else would take his place. The new Chamber could defeat his administration, as in fact it did in the following March, and again in May. Nitti merely succeeded himself on both occasions. When he went out, in June, it was as the result of voluntary withdrawal rather than from an adverse vote in Parliament. This weakness at the top of the governmental structure, the negativeness of Parliament manifested by its inability to evolve a definite program and leadership, were ill calculated to enhance the prestige of the parliamentary system of government as a whole. That the system was inefficient no one could deny; that it was unsuited and decadent and that other solutions might be better adapted to the time and the circumstances, many could easily be led to believe and have since argued.

In order to succeed and capture the imagination, the new must assert itself with vigor. In default of this, the old must carry on. With the resignation of Nitti, the old had one more thing to offer: there seemed

nothing left but to turn back to Giolitti. Giolitti's dominance of Italian
political life has been explained before; his hold had only been broken
when, from his point of view and that his followers, Salandra had
managed to bring the country into the war against her wishes and those
of the parliamentary majority in 1915. Inevitably, as the result of the
war situation, Giolitti's star had gone into eclipse. His known opposition to intervention, the natural suspicion of defeatism which became
associated with his name, would have made it difficult for him to play
a role during the war. Nor did he try to. Despite his age, or perhaps
because of it, he could be patient and wait for the passing of the storm,
whose course he, unlike most, correctly predicted would be long. After
1919 he continued to wait, until he now found himself in the position
of the Grand Old Man, the last hope of the country. His age and the
experience of his long career in politics caused him to refuse to take
an overdramatic view of the situation and to proceed on the assumption
that the prevailing unrest could be handled in the manner of which
he was an experienced master. He had even been willing, while waiting
for his opportunity, to let his press contribute to the government's embarrassment by taking up the cry of most Italian Fiume. It is difficult
to visualize Giolitti feeling strongly about Fiume, but after all it must
be remembered that he had been the one to lead the country into the
Tripolitan adventure.

At any rate, Giolitti assumed the Prime Ministership in June, 1920.
The condition of the country must have reminded him of that which
confronted him in 1904, in the early days of his personal "reign," and
he set about handling it in much the same way as he had then. The thing
to do was not to meet discontent with an unreasonable attempt at
suppression, but, on the one hand, to alleviate its causes if possible, and,
on the other, to let those forces of discontent overplay their hand. Nitti's
weakness had encouraged disregard for the law. Strikes were frequent
and numerous, violence went unpunished, the general atmosphere offered an inducement to all manner of groups to take the law into their
own hands. Within three months of his assumption of office Giolitti
was confronted with the episode, ever since famous, of the occupation
of the factories. Sitdown strikes have become a familiar enough phenomenon and we no longer necessarily read into them revolutionary

implications. That was precisely Giolitti's reaction. Rather than make a heroic stand on the defense of the sacred rights of property, he preferred to let the strikers find out what they could do with the factories and let at the same time an increasingly large portion of the general public become dissatisfied with, hence turn against, this callous assertion of rights on the part of one section of the body politic against the whole.

To a considerable extent, it looked as if Giolitti's appraisal of the situation were correct, for the episode of the occupation of the factories in the autumn of 1920 was, for Italy, in the nature of a climax after which the temperature of the patient began to descend again toward normal. From Giolitti's point of view and understanding of the working of politics, things turned out even better than might have been expected. For it was in part owing to this episode of the occupation of the factories by the workers that in the following January the Socialist party found it impossible to maintain any longer the uneasy cooperation between the divergent tendencies within its ranks. The cleavage between Reformists and Revolutionaries, in Italy as elsewhere, antedated the war, but the Russian Revolution and the unsettled conditions of Europe in the immediate aftermath of the war had the effect of forcing the Socialists to take a definite stand on the issue of immediate tactics. The result was that the Italian Socialists split into three groups: what may be called henceforth the Socialists proper definitely espoused the cause of gradual change; this group contained the ablest of the party's leadership, who did not believe in the possibility of successful revolution; at the opposite extreme, the Communists definitely allied themselves with the Third International and Moscow, whose bidding they were then, and have been ever since, willing to do with unquestioning faith. A middle group that called itself Maximalist continued in uneasy cooperation for a time with the moderate wing of the party. At any rate, the convention of January, 1921, was the last in which the various Socialist factions sat together. A measure of the strength of the extremist tendency in the country may be gathered from the fact that in the convention of the Italian Confederation of Labor, held the following month, the Communists received some 15 percent of the vote.

All this was perfectly satisfactory to Giolitti who thought the time opportune to make his hold once more secure by announcing a general election. This was done in May. Giolitti's plan was to lead a coalition of all the scattered tendencies other than those represented by the Socialists and the *Popolari*. Things being what they were, he was willing to co-operate with the Nationalists, although his foreign policy of severe retrenchment was hardly calculated to appeal to this group. Even the new, boisterous, but little known and at the time seemingly unimportant, Fascists—of whom presently we shall have more to say—found a place in his calculations. The orderly process of law enforcement being at somewhat of a discount, it might be useful to have the services of a group of young enthusiasts willing to practice the persuasive tactics of breaking an occasional socialist head. This would not be a sanctioning of wholesale illegality and violence, but, if done on a limited scale, would merely serve to right the balance. The election over, this largely insignificant and inchoate group could be either tamed or dismissed and political life would resume a more sedate course. This may have seemed an eminently reasonable calculation, highly practical if unprincipled, but in the political philosophy of a Giolitti high principle was not a thing to stand or fall by; it was rather one of many tools that might be used on suitable occasion.

Whatever may have been the reasonableness of these neat calculations, the results of the election belied their accuracy. For if the combined Socialist factions lost some ground, they still had 135 representatives in the Chamber; together with the *Popolari* who picked up a few additional seats, the two groups, as in the previous house, controlled nearly half of the total membership. The new Fascists emerged with 35 members, not an impressive number; they elected to seat themselves at the extreme right wing of the Chamber and confined themselves to a position of intransigeance and the use of obstructionist tactics. To that extent, they could collaborate with the Communists, which was fitting enough, for since both extremes agreed that the parliamentary system was decadent and incapable of answering the needs of the time, it was natural that they should do their best further to discredit this system. *Les extrêmes se touchent,* as the French saying goes, and this unplanned but effective, though temporary, cooperation of outwardly irreconcilable extremes has repeated itself on more than one occasion, not least successfully in Weimar Germany.

It was not Giolitti's way to go down fighting in battle. If his plan had miscarried in April, 1921, time might yet prove him right. To attempt to continue in office was out of the question. His eminently sane foreign policy of retrenchment, as in the Near East and Albania, and of moderate compromise with the Yugoslavs, a policy which would appeal to the forces of the Left, held little attraction for the opposite side of the Chamber upon which Giolitti would have liked to depend. Even the liquidation of the issue with Yugoslavia at the end of the preceding year, though ratified by a large parliamentary majority, had been severely attacked and commanded little enthusiasm. The very reasonable, but somewhat awkwardly contrived, commitments of his Foreign Minister, Sforza (the insignificant issue of the delta of the Recina between Fiume and Sušak) left a bad aftertaste and was easily open to attack because of its lack of frankness. So Giolitti resigned in July and went back into retirement.

But if Giolitti was not equal to the emergency, who else could be? It has been said before that he was the last hope of a system unable to stand the strain that circumstances had put upon it. The fifteen months that elapsed between Giolitti's resignation and the March on Rome remind one in some ways of the decline of the Merovingian kings. The pace was slower in the eighth century and led to the imperceptible substitution of one dynasty for another. The faster tempo of the twentieth century compressed the period of uncertain wandering which ended in the advent of a new political system.

Giolitti, however, had not quite given up. His succession was taken over by Bonomi, the same Bonomi who was destined to reappear upon the scene after the collapse of Italy and the downfall of Fascism in the Second World War, one of those Socialists who had been ousted in the party purge of 1912. He governed by the tolerance of Giolitti's following and when that support was withdrawn after a few months he inevitably fell. At that juncture, Giolitti's old tactics failed once more, for the *Popolari,* with whose support he might have formed a government, did not prove amenable to the sort of deals that had been customary among the more personalized groups earlier in existence. The role of Don Sturzo in exercising what was tantamount to a power of veto on that occasion has been the subject of much controversy. After painful and protracted negotiations, Facta, a diluted Giolitti, succeeded in organizing a Cabinet. Facta might be compared to Chilperic III, last Merovingian king, whom Pepin had quietly shorn and put away in a monastery. Facta took office in March, 1922. Defeated in July, the political vacuum was such that no one could be found to succeed him. He stayed on for another few months until, figuratively speaking, the more vigorous legions, or hordes, of Mussolini, sent the whole Italian parliamentary system into the limbo of innocuous monastic retirement.

CONCLUSION: THE "MARCH ON ROME"

The episode of the March on Rome has been many times recounted. Briefly it must be recalled for it meant a parting of the ways for Italy. There was no violence nor any very sensational outward manifestation of radical change; in most respects, Italians went about their affairs at the end of October, 1922, in no wise conscious that a great change had occurred in their lives. This was because the change, though revolutionary, was affected with smoothness. What happened was that Mussolini and his Fascists, in the face of the complete stalemate of the government in the summer and autumn of 1922, had come to the conclusion that what would have seemed fantastic dreams a year or two earlier now had the possibility of becoming reality.

If large-scale illegality were to be resorted to, it could be countered in two ways. The government might assert with firmness its determination to maintain order; but in view of the record of the past two years so radical a change of direction as this would have necessitated was hardly to be expected. There was another way, which, while no permanent solution, might have served to keep Fascism from power. Illegality can be met with illegality and violence countered with violence. The Fascists and the various groups of Marxist persuasion had for some time been fighting it out in the streets. If the various Socialist groups had come together, the following they commanded was after all far greater than the number of Fascists. But, as said before, Italian Socialism presented a smaller edition of the divisions that finally brought the whole Italian parliamentary system to grief. There was indeed an attempt at rallying the forces of organized labor when a general strike was called in August for the express purpose of protesting against the Fascist danger which by this time was showing signs of threatening the political system at its very center. Since there were only 35 Fascist deputies in Parliament, they could obviously hope to achieve nothing by constitutional means. But the general strike was a failure, enhancing by its very failure the magnitude of the danger it had been intended to dispel. The result of the failure was a further cleavage in Socialist ranks; the reformist group and the so-called Maximalists finally put an end to their uneasy partnership, fundamentally for the reason that the leaders of the former tendency were coming to the conclusion that tactics of mere obstruction were fruitless, if not dangerous, and that they ought therefore to bolster the tottering system by giving it the support of their active participation in the responsibility of government.

Given time, this change of heart on the part of some of the Socialists might have been sufficient to save the day. But time was not granted. It has been said with truth that, during this period, there were in Italy two governments: the legal government, completely paralyzed, incapable of rousing itself to govern; and the Fascist organization, increasingly taking matters into its own hands, with complete headquarters established in Perugia. The Fascists were acting with complete openness. The large congress they held in Naples on October 24 was the prelude to final action. Their cohorts began to move on Rome from various points of the compass. There was drama in the situation, but also not a little windy bombast and possibly innocuous gesturing *à la* D'Annunzio. At the eleventh hour, Facta roused himself sufficiently to submit to his Cabinet colleagues a decree instituting martial law. To this measure they consented, even though it was generally understood that the current administration could not carry on. There were thus two sets of negotiations being conducted at the same time in an attempt to answer the two questions: how handle the immediate Fascist threat? who could organize a government? In the circumstances the King refused to sign the proclamation of martial law, thereby intervening in the situation in a manner exceeding the usually accepted bounds of constitutional prerogative. Why he thus interfered, the extent of the responsibility which he thereby assumed, and the motives which prompted him to this unusual action are things which have been debated ever since and will continue to be argued. That Victor Emmanuel III has never been a strong personality is certain; for that very reason, he had been careful up to this time to play with strict correctness his self-effacing constitutional role. Knowing the conditions of his Cabinet, he may well have been influenced by the advice of the military who, as a group, were more sympathetic to the Fascists than otherwise and therefore of doubtful dependability. What end could be achieved by futile bloodshed? The Fascist cohorts might be easily enough dispersed, but the result of such action would have been wholly negative, prolonging the existence of the political vacuum without solving the central problem of finding a government that could govern. At least such considerations seem plausible.

Be that as it may, martial law was not proclaimed, thus relieving both the Fascists and the army of the awkward dilemma which would have been theirs had they been ordered to fire upon each other. The situation was resolved through what might be called a not untypical Italian *combinazione*. There was no revolution, there was no *coup d'état* in the accepted sense. Quite simply, Mussolini was given by the King the mandate to organize another Cabinet. Some of the conservative and moderate leaders of Parliament, Salandra for example, were in favor of taking the Fascists into the government and so advised the Crown. But, taking advantage of the timidity and hesitation which prevailed at the center, plus the confusion created by the "March on Rome," Mussolini, from the distance of Milan, played his cards astutely and won. He would accept the King's mandate, but only on his own terms. This was finally granted and Fascism slipped into power.

Could things have been different? Undoubtedly they could. At the crises of history, accidents and personalities can play a crucial and decisive role. Had there been someone willing to act vigorously on October 28, the Fascist cohorts might easily have been dissipated into the bubble of wind that in large part they were; but there was no Bonaparte in Rome willing to use a whiff of grapeshot. Had the Socialists, or enough of them at least, been courageous enough, not so much to fight the Fascists in the streets, as to be willing to assume the responsibilities of government, the old system might have survived the crisis and through a new lease of life adapted itself to continued existence. But the Socialists would, or could, do neither this nor display sufficient cohesion to organize a successful general strike.

This also must be said. Times of stress put a high premium on reckless individuals who are willing to capitalize on confusion. Mussolini was precisely such a man and we shall see the wonderful confusion of his unscrupulous thinking, well designed to appeal to the most disparate elements. The process of slowly and honestly restoring order from confusion is an undramatic one by comparison, one that will have little attraction for the weary, disgruntled mass of the people. In the painful, but inevitable, readjustment from war to peace, the Socialists were a powerful pole of attraction. Their failure may be understandable, but the fact remains that they botched their opportunity. Mere obstruction in Parliament was too easy. Such tactics are not a program of government; to the discredit of existing government and institutions they, consciously or otherwise, contributed a goodly share. Giolitti's smooth methods also proved unequal to the stress of a situation which could not be assessed in the terms of pre-1914. Not to have understood this was his great failure. It is no wonder that Parliament fell into greater disrepute than ever and that in the ensuing political wilderness more and more people should find themselves attracted by the sort of thing which D'Annunzio had stood for in Fiume and which Fascism was to take over. There was nothing inevitable about the advent of Fascism to power in October, 1922, but in view of the background of political life as it had been conducted in Italy since she had become one, this advent may also be called a perfectly logical consequence. The self-abdication of Parliament was a good measure of how the members of that body themselves considered this to be the case.

Chapter VI · OPPORTUNITY AND OPPORTUNISM: FASCISM COMES OF AGE

I make this appearance as a purely formal act of courtesy. . . . I decided against pushing my victory too far. I could have exploited it to the end. I could have made this hall, dark and grey, a bivouac for my squads. (From Mussolini's first speech in Parliament after he became Prime Minister, November 16, 1922)

These are bold words. Did they correspond to any reality, or were they a mere flight of Italian oratorical fancy? And first of all, who were these Fascists and their leader?

For those who take a deterministic, or more specifically a Marxist, view of the course of human events, the Fascist episode represents a passing phase, or temporary aberration, the last stage in the evolution of a decaying social and political order, what may be described as nineteenth century liberal capitalism. In their view, this last convulsion of the dying past is foredoomed to failure, if indeed it does not hasten the demise of the order the beneficiaries of which think to retrieve what can be saved of the old by espousing the cause of Fascism. Such an interpretation is indeed the reason why the revolutionary Marxists, the Communists, were able for a time to look upon the advent of Fascism with equanimity, on occasion in fact to assist it in hastening the process of breaking down the bourgeois liberal state. This interpretation contains elements of truth, but elements only; like any single key to the development of history it is apt to open distorted vistas when used to predict the future. According to this same Marxist view, which has in fact permeated deeply the thought of the last hundred years, personalities are of minor importance; it is the great forces of historic development which determine the course of events, and the circumstances of any particular moment allow the appropriate individuals to become the tools of these ineluctably moving forces. Perhaps if there had been no Caesar or Napoleon, others would have played their roles and Rome and the French Revolution would have followed their appointed courses in identical fashion. In our own day, had there been no Lenin, one may believe that the Russian Revolution would have occurred in any case and followed the course that it has pursued after it first occurred. Or had there been no Churchill, perhaps Britain would have risen in any case to her emergency in 1940. Perhaps.

Pascal's quip, "if Cleopatra's nose had been longer, the face of the world would have been changed," aptly expresses the opposite extreme view. Allowing for the role of deep-rooted forces and the necessity of suitable circumstances, one may well argue that but for the able and ruthless determination of Lenin the Russian Revolution would have been a vastly different thing, had it been at all successful at the time; one may be also warranted in thinking that, after Dunkirk in 1940, less bold (or less rash) men than Churchill might have taken the views— less justified in restrospect, but, in the context of the time, more reasonable—of a Pétain. Had that been so, we should now in all likelihood have a very different world indeed. Battles *are* of importance at times, and they *can be* won or lost by men. We shall doubtless continue, and with justification on the whole, to give a large place in our history books to the names of Lenin and Churchill, to cite but two from the contemporary scene. At crucial times of crises individuals do play an important role.

For all the fitting ignominy that accompanied his exit from the earthly scene, Mussolini was one of those individuals that played such an important role. The title of *Duce* by which he was most commonly referred to was also the most fitting appellation. Italian Fascism cannot be divorced nor conceived apart from his personality, and nothing could have been more appropriate than the title *Mussolini's Italy* of one of the better books on the Fascist regime.

THE CONSISTENCY OF MUSSOLINI

Often as it has been done, we must therefore pause, if only for a moment, to consider the man and his career. Curiously enough, it should be added, for all the voluminous literature of which he and his movement have been the center, there exists no adequate biography of him, at least not of the most important part of his work.

Born in 1883, near Forlì, in Romagna, that section of Italy where a tradition of republicanism and violence is perhaps strongest, he was a product of the end of the nineteenth century. His antecedents were similar to those of his future counterpart—and nemesis—north of the Alps. Like Hitler, he came from poor parents though not illiterate peasants, his father being a village blacksmith, his mother an elementary schoolteacher. His father was an adherent of the ideas which had for some time begun to agitate the European proletariat, a Socialist, and the name Benito—of Mexican derivation—which he bestowed upon the future *Duce* was symbolic of the nature of the gods that he worshiped; his mother's deity was less unorthodox, she being a devout Catholic. The combination that was Mussolini's parentage was nothing unusual in the Italy of the time, or of later times for that matter. For a young man of ability and determination, escape from his native milieu was possible though not too easy. Italy was a democratic state, but that basic element of a democracy, equality of opportunity, was hemmed in by many qualifications in practice. Italy was not America with its open spaces and prodigious rate of growth beckoning to the ambitious young. The quality of the formal education that Mussolini obtained may be estimated from the fact that, in 1901, he received a normal-school diploma. Thus he stood at the opening of the century with the prospect of becoming a schoolteacher, a prospect neither brilliant nor inspiring, especially in view of the status of the Italian educational system in those days.

He did in fact teach school, for a brief term in 1902 and for a little longer during the interval 1906–8, but the decade of his twenties may be described as a period of wanderings, both physical and spiritual. Not so much the latter perhaps, outwardly at least, for, given his antecedents and his own makeup, his reaction may be described as the normal reaction of a young man of spirit in the circumstances. Critical of the society in which he found himself, he too became a convinced adherent of socialist doctrines. And, not being given to tergiversation by temperament, he espoused the more violent variety of the doctrine which believed in the necessity of revolutionary upheaval. The cleavage between the reformist and revolutionary tendencies of the movement, if not yet formal, was nevertheless already at work, in Italy as elsewhere. This decade served to complete his education, not so much in a formal way as in the more concrete, and, for a future man of action, more valuable, sense of gaining knowledge of the world that is and of its workings. Always a man of action rather than of thought, he nevertheless was attracted to ideas and read widely. During this time his peregrinations took him to Switzerland and to the Tyrol, then under Austrian rule. In Lausanne he was arrested for vagrancy, from Berne he was expelled for revolutionary agitation; the same treatment was meted him in Austria-Hungary. Meanwhile he had evidently attracted sufficient notice to warrant the police of his native Forlì keeping a record of his activities—not a badge of too great importance, however. In his own country, during this same period, he had minor brushes with the law, belatedly serving his military service in 1905–6 after having been declared a draft dodger for failing to report when due, and later receiving a brief prison sentence in 1908 for threatened violence in connection with labor organizing.

This period of uncertain wanderings was not wasted time, for, while it lasted, Mussolini may be said to have gone through an important process of clarifying and crystallizing his ideas and at the same time considerably enlarging his horizon beyond the narrow confines of provincial activity. This formative phase may be said to have ended around 1910 when he became editor of the weekly *La lotta di classe* (The Class Struggle) the name of which is sufficient indication of the tendency which it represented. Simultaneously, he was leader of the Socialist federation of Forlì and later in the year addressed the national Socialist congress at Milan. An enlightening comment is the view he took of himself, expressed in these words dating from the same year 1910: "Within myself, I recognize no one superior to myself." Mussolini was then twenty-seven.

From this point on, he continued to behave like an orthodox Socialist of the revolutionary variety and his rise in the party was rapid. To the episode of the Tripolitan War he reacted with consistency. Here was a typical imperialist war, and a probably unprofitable adventure to boot (which was true enough), in which the workers had no stake and no cause to shed their blood. Nationalistic emotion was being exploited and misled, and, appropriating the French Hervé, Mussolini too asserted that "the national flag is a rag that should be planted in a dunghill." In view of all this, the war should be opposed, by physical means if necessary; under his prodding, Forlì was one of the few places in Italy where violence did occur, in the form of an attempt to prevent the passage of troop trains. For his share in these proceedings, Mussolini was arrested and, despite a not unskillful, if legalistic, self-defense, was sentenced to a one year prison term, subsequently reduced to five months, at the end of which he resumed his editorial work.

The episode had served to enhance his prestige and to spread his fame. Four months after his release from prison he assumed a position of leadership at the national congress held in Reggio Emilia. On that occasion, as spokesman of the revolutionary tendency, his oratory won the day, culminating in the expulsion of the Right wing moderates in the party, among them Bissolati, the special butt of his attack. His victory was further confirmed by his becoming a member of the party's executive committee. Later in the same year 1912, he became editor of the official party organ, *Avanti*. Mussolini was definitely rising to a position of eminence in Socialism. It may be noted that already at this time he had nothing but scorn for the Giolittian wide extension of the franchise and that he showed no love for Freemasons, whose expulsion from the party he demanded at the congress of Ancona two years later. Quite consistently also, he was enthusiastic about the events of the famous "Red Week" which alarmed the country just before the outbreak of war in June, 1914.

This outbreak of war confronted Mussolini with a major dilemma. According to the orthodox Marxist view, the interpretation of the war presented no difficulty, but in the original belligerent countries, national feeling proved stronger than ideological conviction for the majority of Socialists: regarding the war as a defensive one, they accepted its necessity and behaved primarily as Germans, Frenchmen, Russians, or whatever their national allegiance might be. It was easier to retain a detached view in a neutral country such as Italy: Italian Socialists, including Mussolini, were in favor of "absolute neutrality" as the formula went at the time. However, even Socialists could see revolutionary possibilities in the fact of war and, for that reason, contemplate its occurrence with equanimity, if not with satisfaction. Mussolini, a restless temperament, for whom action, even for its own sake, always had a great appeal, would be attracted by such a prospect. From this, it might not be too difficult a step to taking a friendly interest in the idea of war. His rapid evolution and about face have been told in the preceding chapter. By autumn, when the war had clearly developed into an at least temporary stalemate, he began to talk about "relative neutrality." Unable to convince his fellow Socialists, the result was his resignation of *Avanti's* editorship followed by his expulsion from the Milan section of the party in November. By this time, Mussolini had become an outright interventionist; he had founded the *Popolo d'Italia,* in which he vigorously advocated Italian participation in the war.

Yet, if his evolution was rapid, his position was not altogether clear; it may be said in fact that the process of finding himself which seemed to have come to an end some years earlier was reopened by the fact of war and was destined to continue until the opening years of the next decade. Mussolini, whatever the party might do, still considered himself a Socialist at this time, although this by no means led to a rapprochement with men like Bissolati, another ex-Socialist, who also supported the war, to the extent in fact of eventually finding his way into the Cabinet. Mussolini's position was a lonely one, expression of the fact that for all the demagoguery and playing to the gallery of which he was capable, he remained at all times very much of an individualist. He could indeed go with the crowd, but only at the head of it, never as a follower. In the circumstances, there was no possibility of his playing a prominent political role in the war, for the duration of which he continued in the part of a lone wolf.

The end of the war created unexpected conditions. There is no need to describe again the role of the Socialists, their divisions, the ineptitudes and missed opportunities which characterized their behavior during the years of the immediate aftermath. Mussolini still continued to play a lonesome role and, to all outward appearances, an unrewarding and unpromising one. The example of Moscow did not appeal to him, although logically, in view of his revolutionary position, it perhaps should have. The reformist position, gradually drifting toward the acceptance of governmental responsibility, he found, temperamentally, even less congenial. He made, however, one correct judgment. Whatever else might be said of it, and whether or not one consider it ripe for revolution, the situation called for determined leadership and a willingness not to be bound by the grooves of the past. This Mussolini sensed and was willing to face, albeit in a still groping and uncertain way: "If one examines the programs of the various parties, the old as well as the new, one sees that they are all alike. . . . What makes a difference between parties is not their programs, but their point of departure and their ultimate aims" (*Popolo d'Italia,* 18 March 1919).

Rationalizing in somewhat obscure fashion, Mussolini argued that Italy's entrance into the war in May, 1915, had been a real revolutionary act, a triumph of the higher interest and will of the nation against a reluctant Parliament. The Socialists by their opposition to the war had taken an essentially reactionary position. It was the right of those who had favored the war to assert their leadership and continue the revolution, and Mussolini called a meeting for the 23d of March, which day may be taken as the formal birthdate of the Fascist movement.

The adjective Fascist and the noun Fascism are in themselves not very enlightening, being derived from the Italian *fascio,* which means bundle. The appearance of *fasci* was a common occurrence in Italy, indicating merely the formation of a group banded together in the pursuit of a common aim, political, economic, or other. At the outset, there was no such thing as Fascism in the subsequent sense, but simply a call on Mussolini's part for the gathering of people imbued with the same ideals and purpose. What these ideals and purpose might be, one would have been hard put to say after attending the small gathering which listened to Mussolini on March 23. He himself said that he would not go into details and made much of the need of fighting "neutralists" of all parties. The most specific part of his statement dealt with the foreign situation: professing opposition to all imperialisms, Italian as well as others, he nevertheless asserted Italy's right to Fiume and to Dalmatia. The nationalistic strain is in fact the only one that emerges clearly at this point; for the rest Mussolini's hands were not yet in any way tied.

The beginnings were modest, but the example of Milan was imitated and *fasci di combattimento* began to form at various points in the country. When time came for the elections, the vague statements of March 23 were elaborated into a more definite program, which it is worth quoting in full. Under the date of August 28, 1919, the Central Committee of the *fasci* issued the following proclamation:

ITALIANS!

Here is the national program of a healthily Italian movement. This movement is revolutionary, because it is neither dogmatic nor demagogic; it is definitely new because unprejudiced.

It is our purpose to realize the value of the revolutionary war above all things and all people.

As to the other problems, bureaucratic, administrative, juridical, educational, colonial, etc., we shall deal with them when we shall have created the ruling class.

In order to accomplish this we want:

For the political problem

a) universal suffrage, with regional lists and proportional representation, and votes and eligibility for women.

b) lowering of the voting age to 18; of eligibility for deputies to 25.

c) abolition of the Senate.

d) convocation of a national assembly for a period of three years, whose task it shall be to establish the form and constitution of the state.

e) formation of national technical councils for labor, industry, transportation, social hygiene, communications, etc., elected by the professional groups and the trades, endowed with legal powers and with the right of electing a general commissioner with ministerial rank.

For the social problem we want:

a) the immediate promulgation of a state law to establish the eight hour day for all workers.

b) minimum wages.

c) participation of workers' representatives in the technical management of industry.

d) entrusting of these same proletarian organizations (when morally and technically worthy of it) with the management of industries and public services.

e) rapid and complete organization of railway workers and all the transport industries.

f) a necessary modification of the pending bill for disability and old age insurance, lowering the proposed age from 65 to 55.

For the military problem we want:

a) institution of a national militia with short periods of instruction for exclusively defensive purposes.

b) nationalization of all arms and explosives factories.

c) a national foreign policy designed to give value in the world to the Italian nation in the peaceful competition of civilization.

For the financial problem we want:

a) a heavy extraordinary tax on capital of progressive character that shall have the form of a real PARTIAL EXPROPRIATION of all wealth.

b) confiscation of all the property of religious congregations and abolition of all episcopal allowances which constitute an enormous burden on the nation for the benefit of a few.

c) revision of all contracts for war supplies and confiscation of 85 percent of war profits.

ITALIANS!

Italian Fascism in its new national life wants to continue to realize the value of the great soul fused and tempered in the great cement of war; it also wants to keep united—in the form of an anti-party or super-party—those Italians of all persuasions and of all the productive classes in order to sustain them in the new inevitable battles which must be fought to complete and realize the value of the great revolutionary war. The *Fasci di combattimento* want that the sum of sacrifices accomplished may give to Italians in international life that place which victory has assigned to them.

For this great work all must join the Italian *Fasci di combattimento*.

To much, if not nearly all, of this, any Socialist could have subscribed. At this time, it is true to say that Mussolini's social views had not undergone any essential change; his chief quarrel with the Socialists came from their different views on the matter of participation in the war. But that went back to 1914 and, the war now over, was a dead issue on which to fight elections. Mussolini may still be described as a Socialist at this time. Certainly the proposals just outlined could have no appeal for conservatives. But there was no question of his going to a Socialist Canossa and rejoining the ranks of his former associates; they distrusted him and he, for his part, showed no desire to do so. What was meant by "realizing the value of victory" was not made sufficiently specific and, when it came to posing as a patriot, there were others with older and better proprietary claims to that attitude. While there is a definite patriotic or nationalistic strain in the appeal—the only aspect of it to which a Socialist might take exception—it is rather vague, certainly by comparison with the specific demands dealing with matters social and economic.

Mussolini was therefore very much of a lone wolf and without any appreciable influence. D'Annunzio's gesture in Fiume appealed to him and he announced his support of it in September, 1919; the nationalistic component of his thought was becoming increasingly clear. But at the general elections of November, running as a candidate for Parliament in Milan, he was ignominiously defeated with a bare 6,000 votes. The year 1919 did not therefore appear as very promising or fruitful; the searching for position must continue. Fascism at this stage was a broad movement of somewhat uncertain tendencies, not a political party.

But the elections produced no improvement of the political situation of Italy, a state of affairs which continued to be reflected in the same impotence of government that has been described earlier, an impotence which was largely responsible—whether under Nitti's weakness or Giolitti's mistaken astuteness—for the amount of disregard for law which characterized the Italian scene at this time. Fascism, though still young and weak, also began to resort to the tactics of violence in the form of attacks and raids on Socialist establishments and persons. There was a distinction, however, between Socialists and workers, and the episode of the occupation of the factories in 1920 did not evince either anger or condemnation on Mussolini's part. In fact, if the workers were able to insure better production than the employers there was no reason, according to him, why they should not take the place of the latter. Meanwhile *squadrismo,* the tactics of direct action by Fascist bands or "squads," assumed a growing part in the development of the movement. The police and the army, often reviled and attacked by the "Reds," were not loath to have on occasion the assistance of such voluntary allies, and the government's neutrality in the conflict thus helped the formation of a sympathy growing into an eventual tacit alliance between the Fascists and the armed forces.

This actual behavior of the Fascists, their willingness to use violence against the elements of the Left, whatever the socialistic tinge of their language when speaking of social and economic problems, is what rallied to them a substantial support from the middle class. The phenomenon need not surprise us and we have seen it repeated in Germany where the same group provided some of the stanchest support of the Nazis. The middle class, whether independent shopkeepers or professionals with fixed incomes, highly individualistic and largely unorganized, hence unable to protect its interests in the same manner as the workers, was to a large extent bewildered and frightened by the circumstances of the time. It saw its social status as well as its possessions menaced by forces which it did not understand; but the behavior of the workers, their strikes, their demands for compensations, backed by a powerful organization, were easy to perceive.

Among these people the sort of talk was rife that one hears in times of unsettled economic conditions, during inflationary periods for instance: the workers were receiving too high wages, and asking for more; their demands were unreasonable and selfish; they thought of nothing but their immediate interest regardless of the effects upon the community as a whole; the government was pusillanimous and unable or unwilling to maintain either order or a proper balance. In the resentment born of such thoughts, the Fascists seemed to many like saviors; if they, too, resorted to illegality and violence, the adoption of such tactics was forced upon them, so they claimed, by the default of the established law-enforcing agencies of the state. The episode of the occupation of the factories gave a great boost to this type of thinking—or feeling—and correspondingly enhanced the prestige and the hold of the Fascists. The result was in some respects curious, for, whatever his shifts, one thing about which Mussolini never changed his mind from the beginning to the end of his days was his contempt for the unadventurous, security-seeking, property-worshipping bourgeois. Here was a reservoir of potential allies which, if too numerous, might threaten to annex the movement. The youth of this class, however, not yet saddled with the responsibilities of later life, could respond to the display of vigor and enthusiasm and to appeals couched in terms—however fallacious or misleading—of selfless idealism.

There was another election in May, 1921. Mussolini, on the plea that Fascists never refused facing any battle, decided to enter the parliamentary contest. The appeal issued in April is still quite vague in its content, but it stresses definitely the welfare of the commonwealth as a whole, the necessity of intensifying the development of the scant economic resources of Italy, and while still speaking of peaceful expansion, stresses the right to this expansion—in the Mediterranean and the Atlantic. The Rapallo settlement with Yugoslavia had already been accepted by Mussolini, but, in spite of this fact, Dalmatia was not renounced. For that matter, Mussolini had already said that, while treaties ought to be respected, they could not be expected to freeze the *status quo* for time everlasting—an eminently reasonable statement, but one capable also of aggressively elastic interpretations.

Out of the election the Fascists emerged with 35 representatives, a small figure in itself, less than 7 percent of the total membership of the house. At the same time, in view of the fact that they were a group of recent formation, this represented rapid growth. Depending upon circumstances and the course of events, the movement, as it seemed at the time, could just as well peter out as develop into something of importance. Mussolini himself was elected. Giolitti's share in bringing about the success of the Fascists should not be forgotten, nor the fact that less than 60 percent of the electorate exercised their right at the polls.

Fascism—and Mussolini—were approaching the crossroads. What use would be made of their parliamentary representation? One thing may be mentioned again, namely the fact that the Fascists sat at the extreme right of the Chamber; in other words they emphasized above all else their enmity to the "Reds" and if they continued to stress their contempt for a Parliament of which they were part, it must not be forgotten that, in their contention, that Parliament, like the whole state, was dominated by a virtual dictatorship of the Left. One thing of interest which happened at this point—indicative of Mussolini's hesitancy—is the fact that he favored a truce in the tactics of violence. He pressed the point so far as to make an agreement between his own followers, the Socialists, and the General Confederation of Labor, a move which met with much opposition in Fascist ranks. This proved to be, however, one of those occasions where he was capable of asserting his leadership and he emerged stronger as the result of squarely meeting the test.

At this time also, in November to be exact, the movement formally transformed itself into the National Fascist Party, on the occasion of a congress that was held in Rome. In the address that Mussolini delivered before the congress he stressed again the national ideal: "we begin with the concept of Nation. . . . The dream of a great humanity is founded on utopia." He professed himself an economic liberal: "In economics we are avowedly anti-socialist. . . . The ethical state is not the monopolistic state, the bureaucratic state, but the one that reduces its functions to the strictly necessary." This did not mean robbing the mass of the benefits it had gained; quite the contrary, for a nation the bulk of whose people are ignorant, unhealthy, and poor is not a healthy nation. He did not think that Fascism could find an adequate model in the constitution of the Regency of the Carnaro, although that charter had in it a spirit which Fascism could make its own. Having also paid tribute to Crispi as the only statesman of vision that United Italy had produced, he closed with this appeal: "This, O Fascists, is our oath: to love every day, ever more, that adorable mother which is called Italy." On the constitutional question he dodged artfully: admitting that he had said the "tendency" of Fascism was republican, he argued that this was only a general statement looking to an indefinitely remote future and by no means intended to raise an immediate issue.

Where did Mussolini stand? As before, the national component is fairly clear, indeed becomes clearer, but on social and economic matters widely divergent interpretations were still possible. Into what he said could be seen no more than a paternalistic state *à la* Bismarck, or perhaps of some earlier vintage. There was no question, however, that the Left were enemies and the discussion of the constitutional issue certainly had all the earmarks of an olive branch proffered to the monarchy by the erstwhile revolutionary firebrand. In view of all this, at any rate, it is not surprising that the Nationalists in particular and the conservative groups in general should look with favor upon the untried and unpredictable, but perhaps rising, force. How accurate their calculations, we shall have occasion to see.

Shortly thereafter the truce with the Socialists was denounced and the Directorate of the party gave a definition of what the party was and stood for: "We are a voluntary militia placed at the service of the nation. We shall be with the state and for the state whenever it will show itself a jealous guardian, defender and expounder of the national tradition, the national feeling, the national will, capable of imposing its authority upon all. We shall substitute ourselves for the state whenever it displays itself incapable of facing and combatting without disastrous indulgence the causes and the elements in internal disintegration of the principles of national solidarity. We shall align ourselves against the state whenever it might be in danger of falling into the hands of those who threaten the life of the country. Italy before all, Italy above all."

And finally, in connection with the formal organization of the political party, a more detailed and elaborate statement of its program and organization was prepared and issued at the end of 1921. Mussolini's own preface to this document, tracing the evolution of the party from March, 1919, was an essentially sane, balanced and moderate exposition, wholly devoid of grandiloquence, threats, or bombast, well calculated to make one believe that the ballast of statesmanlike responsibility had entered the makeup of the former socialist agitator. Often as the document has been used, its importance warrants a somewhat detailed analysis.

As fundamental, the Fascist credo proclaimed that "the nation is not the mere sum of living individuals nor the tool of parties for their ends, but an organism comprising the indefinite series of the generations of which the individuals are the transitory elements; it is the supreme synthesis of all the values, material and non-material, of the race."

"The state is the juridical incarnation of the nation. Political institutions are effective forms in so far as national values find expression and protection in them." And furthermore it was asserted that "in the present moment of history the predominant form of social organization in the world is the national society and the essential law of the life of the world is not the unification of these various societies into a single immense society, mankind, as the internationalistic doctrine would have it, but the fruitful, and desirable, peaceful competition among the various national societies." These views are basic.

As to the state, "it should be reduced to its essential functions of political and juridical order" with the consequence that the powers and functions of the Parliament should be curtailed; problems which had to do with the activity of individuals in their capacity of producers should be dealt with by national technical councils. These views led to the unorthodox—by the standards of existing economico-political categories hitherto in existence—advocacy of such things as the eight-hour day, social legislation in regard to accidents, disability and old age, workers' representation in industrial management, management of public services by competent workers' organizations—all measures which may be broadly classified as socialistic—and at the same time the turning back to private management of those enterprises which the state had shown itself unable to run efficiently, particularly the railroads, and even the postal and telegraph service.

On the score of social and economic policy, the party took what might be called a middle-of-the-road position. Thus, its program stated that "the state recognizes the social function of private property which is at once a right and a duty." D'Annunzio's constitution of Fiume was being quoted almost verbatim. But, "when confronted with the socialistic projects of reconstruction on the basis of collectivistic economy, the National Fascist Party places itself on the ground of historic and national reality which is not committed to a single type of agricultural or industrial economy but favors those forms—whether individualistic or of any other type—which insure the greatest production and the highest welfare." Such language reminds one of much that has been said in a country like France after the liberation, to cite but one among many possible illustrations, about nationalizing certain fundamental industries while at the same time preserving a "free sector" in the economic life of the nation.

As to foreign policy, there too, the Fascist program made use of moderate and responsible language. There was not even talk of Dalmatian claims, but a broad assertion of Italy's position as a Mediterranean power and as the bulwark of Latin civilization. There was, however, a clear repudiation of international ideals, of whatever origin or color, strengthened by the assertion that "Fascism does not believe in the vitality of, or the principles which stand inspiration to, the so-called League of Nations, in view of the fact that not all nations are represented in that organization and that those which are represented in it are not on a footing of equality."

In this wise did Fascism enter the year 1922. The events of that year, culminating in the March on Rome at the end of October, have already been rehearsed and need not detain us again. The aims and purposes of Fascism and its leader were not, however, altogether settled from the beginning of the year. The first six months, in fact, until the first fall of Facta, were a period of seeming hesitation during which Mussolini toyed with the idea of being content with a purely constitutional, parliamentary role. But the size and nature of the parliamentary representation of the party soon showed the futility of this notion. The possibility of leading a coalition of various groups in the Chamber also had to be adandoned; nor did the prospect of drab "normalcy" hold much appeal for the more obstreperous Fascist deputies, tactics of obstructionism and disruption being far more congenial to them. The result was that, after the end of the first Facta administration, and especially after the failure of the attempted general strike—a failure to which the Fascists made a substantial contribution—the course was definitely set for the seizure of power, by violent means if necessary. Mussolini gave at this time a good illustration of his flexibility: his unqualified acceptance of the monarchy was just what was needed to remove whatever qualms the army may have had on the score of these upstarts in politics. At the beginning of November, Mussolini was the King's Prime Minister and, what is more, the position had become his on his own terms.

It was a long way to have traveled during the space of ten years, and, to all outward appearances, as thoroughgoing a *volte face* on the part of the ex-revolutionary Socialist as one could wish to find in historical annals. The monarchy was accepted and Socialism was now the greatest enemy; what greater inconsistency could be shown? And yet, for all the undeniable change of position, was the change mere opportunism designed to serve ends of personal self-seeking? The existence of this element cannot be ignored and, on the level of personal, psychological, explanation one can see in Mussolini's evolution a considerable degree of consistency. The man was by nature a leader rather than a follower, and wherever he happened to be his tendency was to push to the fore. Courage and determination he possessed in large quantities and he was quite capable of undergoing the trials of a long wandering in the political wilderness as had been the case from the time he had become an interventionist in 1914. But if he could stand alone, his ego was large and he was also possessed of a quick sense that made him apprehend the deeper significance of the change wrought by the war while others were content to chew the cud of outworn shibboleths and formulas. The demagogue was a large part of him, but he was also endowed with a keenness of apprehension that manifested itself in a flexibility that made him realize when and how to appeal to the mob and when to resist the rasher and less farsighted elements among his followers. In terms of personality Mussolini was quite consistent.

But if he was intelligent, intellectual honesty was alien to his makeup. Ideas he could grasp and understand, but, like men, they remained for him tools rather than ends in themselves. His handling of Socialism is typical. With the theoretical Marxist interpretation he played fast and loose and can rightly be charged with betrayal. But, after all, why were large sections of the mass socialistic? Undoubtedly, less because of a theoretical view of history and an abstract analysis of social forces than because of specific promises and concrete hopes of betterment of their material lot. Which, incidentally, has been a source of strength but also of great weakness to Socialism, for what remains of theoretical interpretations if these material benefits can be attained in other fashion? And we have seen the large component of promised social benefits that the early Fascist program contained. For that matter, Mussolini was bold enough to acknowledge that he could change his position and even to boast that he would not be bound by a narrow regard for petty consistency.

ADAPTATION TO CIRCUMSTANCES

But the lack of solid theoretical foundation was also bound to produce confusion and uncertainty. In 1922, Fascism could mean all things to all men. As is often the case with political theory, rationalization after the event, Fascism therefore was primarily an uncertain, opportunistic, and unpredictable response to circumstances which, beyond a doubt, were not those of peaceful "normalcy." Briefly, therefore, we must survey its course of adaptation to these circumstances, after which we shall see the philosophers erecting a system on the basis of what had taken place and dignifying it with the apparatus of theory and ideas.

Victor Emmanuel may have stretched a point when he declined to sign the proclamation of martial law demanded by his ministers, but Mussolini's accession to the premiership had taken place within the framework of constitutional practice. If any question of legality still remained, the voluntary acquiescence of Parliament must set it at rest. For, as mentioned before, in appointing Mussolini to office, the King had followed the advice of parliamentary leaders. Nor will it do to argue that the Fascist show of force frightened these men into accepting a result that they would otherwise have rejected. A sufficient number of these leaders and of their following were quite amenable to the experiment.

They thought, in fact, that Fascism might be tamed by the responsibilities of power and that by accepting it they could play a moderating role while escaping from the impasse of parliamentary impotence. Nor did such calculations at first seem to be necessarily mistaken. For, if Mussolini would only take office on his own terms, he seems to have been uncertain just what to do with power and, in the ministry which he proceeded to organize, Fascists did not even hold a majority of the posts. When he first appeared before Parliament in his new capacity, he issued the warning quoted at the head of this chapter. Ominous sounding words, but how seriously were they to be taken? "I decided not to push my victory too far" contained a threat of more drastic action in the event of recalcitrance, but could also be interpreted as the proffer of an olive branch. Parliament voted confidence. But such acquiescence under the stress of undoubtedly unusual circumstances could hardly be expected to produce a real change of heart among the deputies—a passing storm had to be ridden, many thought—any more than the sudden acquisition of power could be expected to produce a thoroughgoing change of heart and behavior in a large sector of the Fascist membership, for whom the chief stress had been on direct action, violence, and disregard for the established forces of the state.

Mussolini was too intelligent to believe that the methods which served the end of achieving power could be used in the continued exercise of it; not if the state were to be strong and life within it orderly. He proceeded therefore with relative moderation, perhaps not fully appreciating, himself, the real nature of the forces that had been unleashed. Thus we find that, in 1923, in an attempt to curb the more unruly elements of the party, those who saw in its triumph little more than a pretext for personal gain or the venting of private revenge without fear of the law, there was organized the Fascist Militia, whose role in the service of the state (hence of order) was emphasized, a role further stressed by the outward symbol of an oath of allegiance to the Crown. The success of the attempt was definitely qualified; there were many, among them, local bosses—*rases,* as they came to be known, from the name of local Ethiopian chieftains—whose understanding of statesmanship did not extend beyond the use of brute force. Nor could they be controlled easily, for the *Duce's* hold upon his followers at this time was not yet what it was later to become.

On the parliamentary side, a compromise of sorts was effected. Parliament would continue in its function, but in order to avoid a recrudescence of the confusion into which it had foundered, a new scheme was devised for the election of its members. The so-called Acerbo electoral law, named from its sponsor, was aimed at obviating the shortcomings of the multiparty system as it had been operating in Italy. On the plea that this multiplicity of parties, with the attendant necessity of coalitions, was responsible for the governmental deadlock—a plea not without foundation—the scheme was hit upon of producing a solid majority through the device of allocating two thirds of the seats in the Chamber to that party which polled the largest popular vote, provided that were at least 25 percent of the total. This was the direct antithesis of the system of proportional representation to which Italy had just been introduced.

The law was passed by the same Parliament, not until considerable pressure had been put on the *Popolari* to obtain their consent, but passed it was in accordance with constitutional practice. Thereupon elections were held, in April, 1924, and the results were eminently satisfactory to the Fascists, whose list secured the electorate's overwhelming endorsement. How free the election was is arguable, for the Fascists did not refrain from the use of the sort of persuasion in which *squadrismo* had become adept. Nor should the fact be overlooked that they had at their disposal the use of all the state machinery; but that, if we recall how Giolitti had perfected the art of "making" elections, was hardly new in Italy. It should also be pointed out that the Fascist lists included many names long familiar to the Italian electorate, conservatives or conservative liberals rather than outright Fascists, who were willing, however, to support the existing administration in office. At any rate, as the result of the 1924 election, Mussolini was assured of a presumably reliable support in the Chamber instead of being subject to the bane of perpetually shifting personal bargains and *combinazioni*.

But the transformation had been brought about with much less speed and thoroughness than was to be the case ten years later in Nazi Germany. If the Fascists had a dependable majority of their own in the Chamber, a substantial core of opposition still existed in that body which did not hesitate to make its complaints loudly heard. It is at this point that events took an unexpected turn. One of the most vigorous critics of the regime was the deputy Giacomo Matteotti, a leader of the reformist Socialists. At the end of May, 1924, he delivered a particularly violent diatribe against the government; shortly thereafter he disappeared and his body was eventually found in a woods near Rome. The final word on this assassination has not yet been written, but, whatever the precise events, it was clear almost from the beginning that the deed was the work of Fascists and also that persons high in the administration were implicated. This was a new development, and the reaction, in Parliament and in the country at large, was profound. It was one thing for Fascist squads to fight it out with their opponents in the streets; but many who could tolerate such tactics on the plea of abnormal times or through fear of the "Reds" drew the line at political murder as an instrument of government. Rather than being stilled, the opposition grew louder than ever; those in Parliament, Socialists, *Popolari,* and some liberals, manifested their disapproval by refusing to participate any longer in the deliberations of the house; they withdrew to form the so-called Aventine opposition. Throughout the country, the press was loud in denunciation which the passage of time and the official whitewashing of an unconvincing trial did not still. Even some of the conservative supporters—not themselves Fascists, though elected on Fascist lists—men like Salandra for example, abandoned the fold.

The second half of 1924 was a period of deep crisis for the new, semi-constitutional system that was Fascism at this time. This was the last occasion on which the forces of legality might have recovered their hold on the state. Had they known how to unite and had they been able to produce some clear leadership that would show the way to determined action, the situation might yet have been retrieved. But, as in the past, counsels of timidity and division continued to prevail, and the initial grand gesture of withdrawal flattened out into innocuous talk. That in itself, however, was not enough to dispose of the crisis of the regime or to allay the widespread unrest which might have led to mere disintegration and chaos.

But at that point, Mussolini's action saved the day, for himself, for Fascism, and (Fascists would say) for Italy. He did essentially two things. While naturally denying direct guilt for the assassination, he presented himself before Parliament and the country as accepting moral responsibility for it, following this with the implied question: What do you propose to do about it? The boldness of this stand turned the tables against the ineffectual opposition, which could indeed talk but had neither men nor plans to supply a workable answer to the question. But this was not all. He turned to his followers also and, using as an object lesson the crisis which had been brought on, demanded a strict adherence to discipline and obedience to leadership, if for no other reason than for the common good of all members of the party. This bold gamble—the sort of thing which appealed to Mussolini and at which he was most adept—was highly successful. As a consequence, the Matteotti affair had the double, and unexpected, effect of strengthening Mussolini's control of the party and the hold of the party on the country, which in turn meant Mussolini's personal hold. From this time on we may begin to think of Italy as being governed under the personal dictatorship of Mussolini. If there was still some pretense at preserving the outward shell of the constitutional framework of the state, in actual fact Fascism set about conquering the state and molding it to its ends.

THE CONQUEST OF THE STATE

Even this conquest, however, was a gradual process. Indeed, fundamental statutes continued to be enacted to the very end of the life of the system, but it may be said that by 1929 the Fascist state had emerged in full bloom; the years 1925–26 were particularly fertile in legislation. How this was done and what the product meant may best be examined under two heads which may be regarded as answers to two questions: first, how to acquire control and consolidate the hold on the state; second, how to retain this hold. As there would be little point in undertaking here a minute analysis and description of the detailed workings of the Fascist system—a task which has been done many times—only those more salient and significant features which gave it its true significance will be considered.

The first question evidently deals in the main with matters constitutional. Outwardly, there was no attempt to write a wholly new constitution, or even to modify the existing *Statuto* dating back to 1848. The retention of this instrument did not hamper the institution of change for it was more in the nature of a theoretical declaration of principles than a document of the kind that is the American Constitution, for example. The monarchy was retained and the position of the Crown under it remained essentially what it had been hitherto; Victor Emmanuel would continue in his self-effacing role, perhaps a little more self-effacing than ever. The preservation of the formal position of the crown was to be of use when the end came in 1943.

The plea was used that the constitution, rather than being undermined, was, in fact, being restored to its original intent which the parliamentary annexation of all power had distorted. The contention was fraudulent, however, for what took place was not the establishment of equal and independent powers *à la* Montesquieu, but a complete reversal of the situation. Instead of a Prime Minister, there was now to be a Head of the Government, the new appellation symbolic of the new functions of the office. For—and this is the heart of the matter—as the result of legislation enacted at the end of 1925 and the beginning of 1926, the Head of the Government was to be *no longer responsible to Parliament, but to the Crown alone.* This legislation, in addition, conferred upon the newly defined executive virtual powers of ruling by decree. Mussolini was still head of the Cabinet, as any prime minister is, but his position in the Cabinet was no longer one of primacy among peers; it was definitely that of arbitrary ruler, the ministers were responsible to him alone, and he did in fact on many occasions effect "changings of the guard," thorough reshufflings of personnel and portfolios, without benefit of either Crown or Parliament. Of these portfolios, he himself held a variety and a considerable number at once. His power was in essence irresponsible and dictatorial.

Yet Parliament continued in existence. The fundamental constitutional legislation just mentioned was in fact put through by this same Chamber elected in 1924, or rather by the Fascist rump of it augmented by whatever members of the Aventine opposition elected to do penance and return. This same house lived out its normal five-year term. In keeping with the new order of things, an election, or rather a plebiscite, was held in 1929. Neither the old system of proportional representation nor the Acerbo law were now used. Instead, out of a list of 1,000 names submitted by various bodies, professional, syndical, and so on, 400 were chosen by the Fascist Directorate and submitted to the electorate with the simple alternatives of approval or rejection. Appropriately, the voters were given a choice of tricolored ballots for the affirmative and of blank ones for the negative, all under the watchful eye of faithful Fascists. The result was the only thing that it could be under the circumstances; about 1.5 percent of the voters—and some 8.5 million out of a possible 9.5 exercised, or were "induced" to exercise, the right to vote—registered opposition. This near unanimity was even improved upon on the next occasion, in 1934. All this will appear farcical and largely meaningless to the American elector. What it meant was that the state was securely in the hands of a party, or clique, and that Parliament had been reduced to an insignificant role. While it continued to meet—far more frequently and for longer periods than the German Reichstag after it had gone through a similar transformation—its function is quite comparable to that of the German counterpart. This should be added, however: there is no way, of course, of knowing what the outcome of a "free" election would have been, but there is little reason to doubt that, had the election been free, the Fascists would have been overwhelmingly endorsed. To a very great extent, the Italian people were, either enthusiastically or apathetically, in favor of the regime. Of the senate little need be said. Largely amenable from the start, the high rate of mortality among its elderly life-appointed members made it a simple task to have it thoroughly fascistized within a few years. Thus degraded, Parliament became thoroughly unimportant, reduced to the function of a rubber stamp. Of its final transformation in 1938 we shall speak presently.

Controlling the state at the top was essential but hardly sufficient, and this same period witnessed the process—less dramatic but not less important—of fascistization of the whole administration and civil service. Here again, the existing framework was maintained. The prefects had always been the chief cogs in the administrative machinery of the state; they continued in that capacity, and their subservience to the regime was rather the continuation of a tradition of long standing than an innovation in Italian political life. With the double purpose of increasing centralization and tightening the political controls, the old-time *podestà,* henceforth to be appointed by the central government in place of the formerly locally elected mayors and councils, were revived in the communes; in the larger cities alone did a municipal council survive. The judiciary likewise was annexed and its independence curtailed.

But in any regime, however dictatorial, there are bound to be limits to the extent of personal control and the making of decisions of higher policy, if for no other reason because of the complexity and quantity of business to be handled. Such regimes, therefore, usually have a body wherein this higher policy is framed. In the case of Italy, this body was initially the Central Directorate of the Party which evolved into the Grand Council of Fascism. Not until 1929 was the existence of this organ regularized by a law which made it a regular part of the governmental machinery. The Grand Council was the body in which policy was debated and settled; it consisted of the most important personalities in the party, and the various inevitable tendencies within its ranks were represented in it and openly discussed. This was the nearest thing to free debate that existed in the Fascist system, wholly comparable to the Politburo wherein the policy of Communism is framed. In this body was real power situated. But if debate could be free, and at times heated and acrimonious in the Grand Council as in the Politburo, in both cases the cardinal tenet of discipline prevailed. Personalities, rival factions, and cliques are bound to play a great part in such an inner sanctum, always with the qualification that a smooth and solid façade must be presented to the outside world. Mussolini probably dominated the Grand Council to a greater degree than Stalin has dominated the Politburo, largely by reason of the greater discrepancy in his case between his own personality and those of the other members of the group. In the inner council of Fascism there was no individual of the caliber of a Trotsky or a good many other since-eliminated Bolsheviks; the Grandis, the Farinaccis, and the Cianos were on an incomparably lower level, as the result of which Mussolini's own leadership asserted itself from beginning to end in the Grand Council. It was the Grand Council that was also entrusted with the task of providing for the succession to the *Duce,* obviously a function of crucial importance. As it was, the issue never presented itself, the nearest thing to it being the palace revolution that was attempted in July, 1943, under conditions that spelled disaster for the whole regime.

NEW TECHNIQUES OF POWER

The machinery of the state was thus securely in hand. But if Fascism never spoke in quite so fantastic a fashion as Hitler with his promise of 1,000-year duration, neither did it look upon itself as a transitory phenomenon; rather it claimed to be the harbinger of a new era destined to indefinite duration; in human terms, to permanency. It was therefore necessary to provide for self-perpetuation and the future. The core of the provision aiming to this end was the party which, duplicating the state in all its organs, tended increasingly to merge itself with and gradually master the state. The comparable evolution in the Soviet Union would be enlightening to trace. That is why the Grand Council, primarily a party organ, did not attain constitutional status until as late as 1929, and this formalization itself was indicative of the increasingly closer identification between the party and the state.

Thus Fascist Italy, like Communist Russia, presented the spectacle of two parallel sets of institutions: the old state structure retained in its existing form, but fascistized in Italy, and alongside it, at all levels, the corresponding organs of the party. Mussolini's own dual capacity was symbolic of the setup, for he was at once Head of the Government and leader of the party; the common appellation of *Duce* being an apt description of this latter capacity. He stood at the apex of a pyramid which, through the successive echelons of the party secretariat, the eleven member National Directorate, the federal secretaries, the provincial leaders, reaching down to the cells of the local *Fasci,* constituted a solid hierarchy, highly centralized and rigidly controlled from the top. Needless to say, this duplication of functions was useful in providing patronage for deserving, if not always necessarily competent, adherents and served to fasten the hold of the party on the state. While the two sets of functions were kept distinct, their connection was close, particularly at the top, as exemplified by the position of Mussolini and the Grand Council; the secretary of the party was appointed by Royal decree. Thus came into flower in Italy that remarkable contribution of our age to the art of government, the one-party state. The same duplication occurred with the armed forces, for Fascism had its own army, the Militia, plus a variety of special bodies which made the country resplendent with a large number and selection of uniforms. All of which, party and Militia, had to be provided for and did not serve to lighten the financial burden of the nation.

Two more things must be mentioned, both logical developments, to round out the picture of the new techniques of power. Opposition could not, of course, be tolerated, and the apparatus of suppression was carefully nurtured. Especially after 1925, the still considerable freedom of expression which had hitherto existed largely disappeared, until, going the length of issuing minute directions for what news should or should not be given in the press—even details as to the manner in which headlines were to be displayed on the printed page—Fascism made the Italian press the same nauseating tool of propaganda that it is under any similar totalitarian regime; prostitution is a polite word to describe the result. For any recalcitrant individuals unable to see the light of the new day, the inevitable secret police, the little-spoken-of but none the less important, if euphemistically named, O.V.R.A. (*Opera volontaria repressione antifascista*), the Special Tribunal for the Defense of the State, and the small islands which served as concentration camps were always available. The most that can be said of all this is that Italian repression was considerably milder—or less efficient—than the German and Russian varieties; but the intent, purpose, and techniques were the same in all three cases.

The apparatus of suppression to enforce uniformity is an inevitable concomitant of any totalitarian system. But that is not enough. If the system looks to premanency, it must undertake the molding of the minds of future generations. Quite rightly from its own point of view, Fascism therefore lay great stress on the process of indoctrination of the young. It is a measure of the importance attached to the control of education that one of the first moves of the newly established regime, in 1922, was to entrust the philosopher Giovanni Gentile, generally sympathetic to the cause, with the drafting of a reform of the Italian educational system. Gentile's plan was essentially put into effect, first by himself, then by his successors after his ruffled philosophical sensibilities had caused him to resign his post at the Ministry of Education. Here again, the general framework of the previously existing system was retained, but it was permeated with the dominant undemocratic tendency of Fascism. The chief purpose was the creation of a dependable elite in place of the formerly prevalent humanistic approach aiming at the disinterested cultivation of the mind. Technical studies were least affected, save that the time and energy devoted to the learning of the new doctrine did not serve to raise professional standards. Greatest stress, soundly again, was placed on the lower levels of education, for thus the broadest masses would be reached and because the young mind, relatively unarmed with critical faculties, is most amenable to indoctrination. A thorough job was done of rewriting textbooks.

Alongside control of the schools, there was an elaborate attempt, again similar to those of the Nazis and the Russians, to regiment youth, enrolling young people from the age of six on into a succession of organizations (Wolf Cubs, *Balilla,* Young Fascists) whose general purpose it was to instill into young minds the ideology of the system while training young bodies in preparation for presumably martial deeds. The somewhat qualified success of this endeavor was more a measure of lack of efficiency than of the lack of purpose of Fascism.

At this point, in the matter of education and control of youth, the Church is likely to become particularly interested, for it, too, believes in the overwhelming importance of early conditioning. The Catholic Church and an authoritarian system like Fascism have here a point of contact and a point of divergence. The Church is also built on the authoritarian principle, hence can sympathize with it—so long as it is not used for purposes inimical to its own. Mussolini, former atheist, early accepted the view that the influence of the Church in Italy should be used as an asset instead of becoming a source of opposition. In keeping with this sensible view, he succeeded in procuring a settlement of the long-standing dispute between the Vatican and the Italian state. The Lateran accords of 1929 were in the main a success for the Italian state —and a feather in the Fascist cap. The Pope spoke of Mussolini in unusually kind terms. But the Church, for all its authoritarianism and approval of the principle of obedience, cannot in the last analysis compromise on that fundamentally central tenet which asserts the sacredness of the individual person. On the whole, relations between Fascism and the Church remained satisfactory rather than the opposite, despite the existence of a rabid anticlerical tendency in the Fascist fold and the friction which arose over the activity of Catholic organizations. It was not long after the conclusion of the 1929 agreements that the Vatican had cause to complain of encroachments on the part of the regime; but the quarrel was not pushed too far; the Church, more easily than Fascism, could bide its time, and, in a deeper sense, remained a potential source of opposition. At least it kept alive within its fold, even though unostentatiously, ideas which, in the long run, could not but be inimical to Fascist totalitarianism. We have seen a comparable role played by the various Christian Churches in Germany, and in both countries these churches have been important rallying points after the collapse of the respective regimes.

THE IMPORTANCE OF ECONOMICS

But all the apparatus of suppression, regimentation, and indoctrination, added to the effective control of the political and administrative machinery of the state, would be operating in a vacuum if the economic life of the nation were in an unsatisfactory or at least not orderly condition. Whether one accept the Marxist view or look upon it with horror, to recognize the importance which economic factors have assumed in our day is merely to accept an incontrovertible platitude. And indeed a large component of the condition of uncertainty and dissatisfaction which had created the atmosphere wherein Fascism could become established had its roots in economic unrest reflected on the political scene. The early platform of Fascism had accordingly devoted considerable attention to matters economic, and Mussolini, it must never be forgotten, used to be an ardent Socialist. Just precisely what content should be put into these early Fascist pronouncements no one knew at the time. What was known, however, was that, however much Mussolini might call or consider himself a true Socialist and charge his former comrades with betrayal, the fact was that the Fascists were in effect fighting the Socialists with great conviction and that they sat at the extreme right in the Chamber. It was easy from this to infer that they represented the forces of order, to which statement indeed they themselves subscribed, and this in turn could be translated into conservative bias. When they took office, the Fascists did have the support, political and financial, of the large moneyed interests of the country who thought they were making a shrewd long-term investment.

The early activity of Fascism in power may have served to bolster such expectations. Strikes disappeared and the finances of the state were set in order within a fairly brief space of time. But the Fascists had views of their own, or at least they developed such views, on the subject of the proper functioning of the economic life of the nation. Mussolini had for some time proclaimed that the concept of the class struggle was out of date and generally detrimental to the welfare of the common-wealth. The concept of corporations, suggested by D'Annunzio in Fiume, was revived and perfected. Looking at the matter from the point of view of the national community as a whole, it was claimed that capital and labor had a common stake rather than antagonistic inter-ests. Thus it was argued that all persons concerned with, let us say, the maritime activity of the nation had a common interest in the smooth, efficient, and successful functioning of that enterprise, hence should cooperate to that end.

Thus began to evolve what came to be known as the Corporate State; its emergence was gradual, for, while a Ministry of Corporations was set up as early as 1926, the National Council of Corporations only ap-peared in 1930, and the Corporations themselves did not come into existence until 1934. In 1926 was issued the Law Concerning the Disci-pline of Collective Relations, and the year 1927 saw the promulgation of the Charter of Labor, a document of prime importance which con-tains the essence of Fascist economic thought. Enlarging on the ideas just stated above, the Charter proclaimed that "the Italian Nation is an organism endowed with a purpose, a life and means of action *trans-cending those of the individuals, or groups of individuals,* composing it." And further, "the legally recognized occupational associations en-sure legal equality between employers and workers, maintain discipline in production and labor and promote the betterment of both." Most enlightening was the additional statement, which closely followed the Fiuman constitution of 1920: "The Corporate State considers that, in the sphere of production, private initiative is the most effective and valuable instrument in the interest of the Nation." Private ownership was thus definitely endorsed, but this endorsement was immediately qualified by the declaration—or warning—that "the private organization of production is a function of national concern, the organizer of the enterprise *is responsible to the State* for the management of its production. Collaboration between the forces of production gives rise to reciprocal rights and duties. The worker, whether technician, employee or laborer, is an active collaborator in the economic enterprise, responsibility for the direction of which rests with the employer." And, lastly, to clarify the precise role of the state in the situation, "State intervention in economic production arises only when private initiative is lacking or is inadequate, or when state political interests are involved. The intervention may take the form of control, of assistance, or of direct management."

As it finally emerged, the Corporation which was the instrument through which these views were to be implemented was to consist of three units: a federation of employers; an employees' syndicate; governmental representation to safeguard the interests of the state. There was still considerable room for interpretation in all this, and much would depend upon the manner in which the philosophy was applied in practice. It could turn out to be no more than a device for the composition of labor-management disputes with the state in the role of fair, impartial arbitrator; or it could be a mere subterfuge which, under the guise of impartiality, would in reality place control in the hands of either management or labor depending upon which controlled the state. We are touching here upon a very crucial point, one of the reasons for the appeal of much that went with Fascism to widely different, even violently antagonistic, groups, hence one of the sources of the prevalent current confusion which has made it possible for the word Fascism, just as for the word democracy for that matter, to be hurled about indiscriminately. Taken by itself, the idea that what we have come to look upon as the classical method of solving labor-management conflicts involves waste and harm to the community is reasonable enough. From this, it is an easy, logical, and natural step to seek other less harmful methods, and the state appears immediately as the obvious intervening agency. But in reality this approach begs the question, for it leaves unanswered the all important issue: Who, or what, is the state?

This is one of the central problems of our time, but in one form or another, Fascism's contribution—and such it may be called in the sense at least that Fascism has compelled a facing of the problem—is very much alive. Nor could it be otherwise, for the passing of Fascism in a specific place has not eliminated the problem which is pressing and world-wide. Its manifestations crop up everywhere. To cite an illustration culled from a wide variety of possible choice, we have seen the Vichy regime in France attempt to set up a corporate state to the accompaniment of much that was absurd and unviable. Vichy was a sickly abortion, a passage through limbo, that has gone down in suitable ignominy, but the forces and groups that fought it most vigorously in France do not reject all aspects of its economic thought, largely derived from Italian Fascism. Nor is it without interest to read the following passage in an open letter to President Truman in the year 1946: "Neither labor nor management should seek to dominate the industry; the good of the industry must dominate each. Finally, what is good for the industry will in the last analysis be determined by what is good for the nation as a whole." Lest one think this is part of the manifesto of a neo-Fascist organization, it may suffice to point out that the name of Max Lerner appeared among those of the signers of the document.

But to return to Italy and Fascism, what counts is the manner in which the above-mentioned concepts were used. A detailed survey of its legislation and practice in the economic field would show that, on balance, Fascism was more favorable to ownership, management, and capital than to labor, despite an unquestionable stress on social legislation and the general welfare of the people. But to say this is to tell but a part of the story, and not the most important part at that. For what happened, and was probably unforeseen by either conservatives or Socialists, was the emergence of the state in a novel capacity, an entity in itself, distinct from and above either capital or labor, both of which were subordinate to the new Leviathan. This control of the economic life of the nation was but the counterpart of the general supremacy of the state which manifested itself in the other aspects of its life.

This raises at once the question: To what end? Had all this control been merely directed to greater efficiency and the common material welfare, much might have been said for it. That is indeed the aspect of the matter which opponents of Fascism who yet favor the retention of certain aspects of its economic policy have in mind. And this, in passing, touches upon the fundamental issue of the interrelation between economic and political theory and practice: the connection between economic and political liberalism on the one hand, between economic and political totalitarianism on the other. This is no place to enter that larger debate; it will be enough at this point to emphasize that, with Fascism, economic control and regimentation was but a tool, an adjunct to a higher end, the greater power of the state. At this point things may be said to have gone wrong, for this power of the state could not remain an end in itself, and the dynamic policy of Fascism has the logical and inevitable consequence of an aggressive foreign policy. That constitutes a story in itself which will be traced in subsequent chapters. As far as the internal economic policy of the regime was concerned, the ultimate effect, as in the case of Germany, was the adoption of the policy of economic self-sufficiency, or autarchy as it has been called. This was an unfortunate, if inevitable, turn, particularly so in the case of Italy, one of the most poorly endowed by nature among the more important nations. The world economic crisis of the nineteen thirties gave considerable impetus to the tendency, thereby further deepening the vicious circle of the crisis. Much was done in Italy, to the accompaniment of the usual Fascist fanfare of advertisement; land reclamation and the battle of wheat did achieve a fair success, to the extent that Italy became nearly self-sufficient in the production of that vital staple. Great efforts were made to develop whatever meager and low-grade coal deposits existed in Sardinia and Istria. Increasingly, such endeavors were bound to be uneconomic, and the improved statistics of production were poor compensation for the real cost to the country. Neither the standard of living of Italians nor the finances of Italy were improved during the thirties, and all the costly efforts and sacrifices could not in any case bring Italy within sight of the proclaimed goal of self-sufficiency. Attempts of this nature in the case of a country with the resources of Italy are a mere *reductio ad absurdum*—unless the gamble of successful aggression should return dividends commensurate with the risks of the investment. We, who have nothing to gain by war, should not forget that the belief that war cannot pay was not universally accepted.

The twenty-two corporations into which the economic activity of the country was parceled out were brought into existence by the law of February, 1934, and the whole system was climaxed by the abolition of the Chamber of Deputies in 1938 to be replaced by a new body, the Chamber of Fasces and Corporations, apt symbol of the recognition of the importance of economics in the life of a modern nation. The idea that the state should have a political body where representation is no longer on the traditional basis of geographic or territorial distribution, but on the basis of the various aspects of its economic life, the corporations if one wishes, is one which is very much alive at the moment. It is one indeed for which, under the proper circumstances, there is much to be said. The espousal of it need not be equated with the advocacy of Fascism, but the fact remains that it was an important aspect of the Fascist system.

CONCLUSION: THE PHILOSOPHERS AT WORK

As Mussolini himself said: "Fascism was not the nursling of a doctrine worked out beforehand with detailed elaboration; it was born of the need for action and it was itself from the beginning practical rather than theoretical." This stresses one of the cardinal points of difference between Fascism and Communism, a doctrine growing out of a well thought-out philosophy. We have traced in an earlier section the uncertain beginnings of Fascism, adequately reflected in Mussolini's own groping hesitations, and stressed the element of adaptation to circumstances. The factor of opportunism always remained strong with Fascists, but during the period from 1925 to 1929 a system had nevertheless taken shape. During this same period, various intellectuals who had either belonged to the movement from the beginning or had subsequently been attracted to it, undertook the task, partly rationalization, of formulating a consistent doctrine as a theoretical basis for Fascism. Outsiders, too, have theorized at length on the nature and roots of Fascism, until a wide body of literature, of very varying quality, has grown around the subject. There is no intention in this survey of giving an elaborate and detailed presentation of the philosophy of Fascism, but merely, with selective treatment as often emphasized before, of picking out the more salient among the relevant factors that may serve to answer the query: What is Fascism? just as the sketch of its vicissitudes has been an attempt to supply an answer to the question: How did Fascism come to be and to gain control of the Italian state?

The ablest theorizers of Fascism in Italy came in the main from the Nationalist camp. From the foundation of the movement in 1919, a strong and consistent thread of nationalism runs through Fascism, and it was fitting that the small, but on the whole talented, group that constituted the Nationalist party in the Chamber of Deputies should be the first to merge formally with the Fascists, not long after Mussolini's accession to power. These Nationalists were more than mere irresponsible rabble-rousers; they had an organized and thought-out *Weltanschauung*. At the opposite pole from the extreme Marxists, they nevertheless agreed with the latter in their dislike of and contempt for the liberal, parliamentary, democratic state. If their criticism was telling, that was because it had certain solid foundations, owing to much confusion that had come to prevail, and still does prevail for that matter, in the democratic state. The doctrine of the equality of men is a noble ideal, as much democratic as Christian, so long as its true meaning is kept clear, in the sense that is of equality before the law, equality of opportunity, or such like interpretations. No one, to be sure, has ever seriously asserted the equality of endowment among individuals, and there would have been little point in combating such an absurdity. But Nationalists —and Fascists—attacked what they contended were the demagogic results of the spread of the egalitarian doctrine, and their attack was on solid ground when it pointed to the performance of democratic politics —Italian politics in particular—as illustrated in the management of the state: the above-mentioned degeneration into rival parties, factions, and cliques combining or squabbling over the control of this state for narrow reasons of selfish advantage, wholly oblivious of, when not antagonistic and harmful to, the general good of the commonwealth as a whole. The extreme Right agreed to a surprising degree with the Marxist interpretation of the role of the bourgeoisie and the bourgeois state: a useful role in the nineteenth century when it had served to break down the former feudal structure, but a role which had served its usefulness and had been superseded. The ideology which had attended the process of the triumph of the bourgeoisie they looked upon as sham, and as a consequence they were at one in their contempt for this bourgeoisie and the timid virtues which it had exalted. But, at that point, Right and Left parted company, for if the Marxists looked forward to an extension of the egalitarian process, their antagonists insisted upon stressing as fundamental in human nature, hence as essential in the structure of human society, the fact of inequality: it was the difference between the stress on mass and on class. This remains to this day the fundamental and irreconcilable cleavage between Fascist and Marxist, however much in actual practice the two may have produced increasingly less distinguishable results.

It was an easy step to proceed from these views to ideas about the nature and relationship of society, the state, and the individual. Passing over "the more or less decayed corpse of the Goddess Liberty," to use Mussolini's own scathing phrase, society could only be organized and function successfully if the direction of it were in the hands of an elite. This organization and functioning of society was the task of the state, which became identified with society, and, since any international ideal was considered utopian, with the national state. Fascism did not escape the influence of the principle of self-determination, that most important nineteenth century force which may be said to have obtained its highest consecration in the settlements issuing from the First World War. The national state then was the highest expression of social evolution to the present. The nation, in addition, and as already mentioned, was not the mere collection of its living members at any one time, but the sum total of past, present, and future generations, thereby exalted into an abstraction immeasurably higher than any of its members.

The effect of such an approach on the position of these individual members can be one thing only: the complete and total subordination of the individual to the good of the nation—at any one moment, to the state. Thus the state became supreme. Such ideas were not new and much has been written about their filiation. The name of Machiavelli inevitably comes to mind, and the Fascists unquestionably drew inspiration from his doctrine. The controversy over Machiavelli will continue to attract the attention of the politically minded, but there can be no question that he has been a profound influence on Italian political thought and that he did exalt the state. But there is no need to go back to the Renaissance for precedent and historic support. The absolute rule of the enlightened despots could also be a model; a Frederick of Prussia or even a Bismarck have their place in the line of development in which Fascism is but an episode. These figures were naturally enshrined in the Nazi hall of fame, but Italian Fascism, in so far as it had German roots, derived rather from the Hegelian influence passed on through its Italian idealist disciples. There were even those who argued, as in the Germany of the first half of the nineteenth century, that real liberty could only exist in a strong state; the argument was somewhat tortuous and fine spun, but it is what made it possible for the philosopher Gentile to rationalize his acceptance of the new system and induced a temporary hesitation in Croce at the beginning. Gentile and Croce soon parted company, however.

For, after all, philosophers' abstractions can be used to confuse as much as to enlighten, when translated into the application of practical politics; more important are the actual doings of the system, especially in a regime with so large a component of opportunism in its makeup. Having talked high-sounding phrases about the nation, a more concrete question was, who would control the state? This control was to be in the hands of the elite, which again by itself is confusing. There will always be an elite, however much demagoguery we may indulge in, but the real issue is, who constitute this elite and how is it to be recruited? We hear much on that score in our democracy, though we like to eschew the use of that particular noun and prefer to talk in terms of leadership and the training therefor. The Fascist solution was simple and in practice amounted to making the will and the power to rule the ultimate criterion of the qualification to do so. Considerable stress was laid on the fact that any state, at any time, must in the last analysis rely upon force for self-preservation, that this reliance upon force is legitimate because inevitable, and that in the absence of opposition was to be found the real meaning of consent. Much of this was mere quibbling, for while the central tendency of democratic liberalism has been consent obtained through rational persuasion (hence the vital significance of the classical democratic liberties), Fascist leadership relied from the start, and continued to rely, on violence and on the whole apparatus of suppression and indoctrination which has been described earlier. Consent obtained through the administration of large doses of castor oil was indeed a novel contribution to political methods. This must be said, however, that after the regime had become well established, the necessity for the use of suppression was relatively small, a state of affairs largely due to the existence in Italy—as anywhere for that matter, albeit in varying degrees—of an overwhelming mass that is essentially apolitical.

Thus there is a whole Fascist literature (much of it nauseating and not a little perverse, for with skill it distorted into wrong channels an appeal to essentially nobler emotions) devoted to the exaltation of violence as an outward manifestation of the vitality of this strong state and its members. We can trace there the influence of Georges Sorel whose *Reflections on Violence* gained a rather wider hearing in Italy than in its country of origin. Interestingly enough, Sorel was no conservative nationalist like his countryman Barrès who could see the virtues of war as "a whiplash on the energy of the nation," but belonged to the opposite extreme of the political spectrum. Sorel's ideas had appealed to Mussolini the revolutionary Socialist, while Barrès had been a source of inspiration to Italian nationalists. It was perhaps appropriate, if not devoid of irony, that the two should now meet in Fascism. All of this had naturally its appeal to the young, and Fascism was untiring in its stress on youth. But more significant than the exaltation of violence was the emphasis on the hierarchical structure of party, state, and society and the stress on discipline. Most appropriately, the walls of Italy displayed with ubiquitous insistence the slogan *Credere, Obbedire, Combattere* (To believe, to obey, to fight).

However, in the last analysis, of greater importance than the theorizing about Fascism and the tracing of its philosophic roots from antiquity through Machiavelli, to Hegel and others, is the cardinal fact of opportunistic flexibility. Fascism, like National Socialism, was born of a response to existing conditions and circumstances. In this respect, the Teutonic version of the same product is far more appropriately named. Probably the most important single development of the last century in the realm of politics has been the appearance of the industrial proletariat.

The introduction of this new element into the body politic has been the result of scientific and technological progress which has had at the same time the effect of raising the standard of living and increasing the literacy and the political consciousness of the mass. It was inevitable that such a powerful force should assert itself, and this assertion by and large took the form of the growth of Socialism. The basic reason for the success of Socialism was the fact that, reduced to its simplest expression, it promised these masses an alleviation of their often unwarrantedly unhappy lot. This was all on the material level, and, appropriately, Socialism was materialistic and rejected with scorn values other than material. "Religion is the opium of the people" is the tersest expression of this view. This narrowness, in the long run, is a source of weakness, for the platitude remains true that man does not live by bread alone. Yet this materialistic stress was inevitable, both because the prevalent *zeitgeist* of the period, resulting from the truly amazing progress of science, was mechanistic and materialistic in its outlook, and because also to talk "higher values" to people on the borderline of physical existence has an inescapable connotation of cant. In the seemingly stable society of pre-1914, Socialism reached its heyday, although, even before that time, it had begun to show signs of internal stress. The war subjected that stable society of Europe to unexpected stresses that shook all values, material as well as moral. In a country like Britain, with a greater margin of safety in the economy of the nation and a deep-rooted tradition of flexibility of political adaptation within a seemingly fixed constitutional framework, the shock could be absorbed and the old practices and values of democratic tradition maintained.

Not so in Italy, where the same system outwardly prevailed as in Britain. In Italy that system was young, an alien importation without roots in the past. It jogged along, after a fashion, during the times of peace and "normalcy" and might indeed, if granted a continuation of those times, have taken root. But essentially, the shock of war and the problems of its aftermath proved too much for it. To Mussolini's credit, he understood or sensed the new situation. However opportunistic, irresponsible, and perverted Fascism may have been, it furnished the nation with a "myth" that the general strike could not. Hence the unholy alliance so aptly described by the name National Socialism. The very confusion of the old values that the name implied was the source of its success, for, in the groping futility of the surrounding atmosphere, it could mean all things to all men.

One more thing must be said at this point, which is in fact one of the reasons for the writing of the present essay. The Fascists themselves emphasized that Fascism was not an export article—in the earlier period at least. Many believed them, not least in the western democracies, where a good many liberals, genuine or otherwise, while convinced that such a phenomenon could never be duplicated in their own countries, argued that, after all, in view of the peculiar circumstances of the Italian scene, it was not surprising, if not indeed the best thing for Italy. The mistake is understandable in view of the existence of those special conditions which have been analyzed; but the mistake also represented a failure to realize that some of these conditions might be duplicated elsewhere and to understand the fundamental nature of a problem which is in reality universal. And that is why, in passing, if the overthrow of Fascism in Italy was desirable it was, in a sense, of secondary importance, and also why the endeavor to legislate Germany into denazification is largely futile and foolish. Fascism cannot be killed in such fashion; potentially, it exists everywhere and the home ground is where its seeds need most watching. The only successful antidote in fact is to go behind Fascism, outward manifestation that it is, to the roots, that is, to the problems that made its emergence possible. So long as these remain, Fascism remains as a potential threat, less in the might of arms, now destroyed, than in the hearts of men.

Chapter VII · ESSAYS IN POWER

The fundamental orientations of our policy are as follows: the Peace Treaties, good or bad as they may be, when once they have been signed and ratified, are to be executed. A State which respects itself can have no other doctrine. But treaties are not eternal and not irreparable. They are chapters in not epilogues to history. To execute them means to test them. If in the course of execution their absurdity becomes manifest, that may contribute a new fact which opens up the possibility of a further examination of the respective positions. (From Mussolini's speech in Parliament, November 16, 1922)

THE FOREIGN POLICY OF FASCISM (to 1935)

The Inheritance of Nationalism.—Whatever else may be thought of Fascism, its inner qualities and nature, there can be no doubt about its dynamic character. Once in control of the state, to what use would it put the power of the country? Talk there had been in floods, but, as always, the correspondence between promise or desire when out of office and the realization of these after the responsibility of power has been assumed remained an open question. The outside world could not but remain uncertain. Would the new regime attempt to conduct an aggressive, perhaps an irresponsible, foreign policy, or would it seek to consolidate its hold upon the country and build up its strength with an eye to some indefinite future? Or could its outward assertiveness be mere talk? The answer to these questions depended upon the nature of the regime and the program that it meant to enact. And the answer was all the more difficult to foresee because of the large element of opportunism in the Fascist makeup.

It may be well at this point to consider for a moment the background, for the foreign policy of nations is apt to be possessed of a remarkable degree of consistent continuity in its fundamentals, regardless of shifting administrations and even of revolutionary changes within the body politic. Ever since Italy had become one, her policy had been characterized by a shrewd understanding of the relation between ends and means, in the sense that those in charge of the conduct of this policy had been well aware of the limitations of the resources at their disposal and had wisely pursued aims consistent with the extent of her power. Up to the end of the war, the Crispian episode had been the only exception to this sane policy and the Crispian dream of empire had ended in abject failure. Even in that case, it might be debated whether Crispi had demanded of the country an effort which she was unable to furnish or whether he had been merely guilty of levity in making inadequate preparations for an undertaking which need not have exceeded her capabilities. The possibility of an Italian East African Empire was not, in the nineties, in the realm of unqualified fantasy. However that may be, with the possible exception of that episode, sane moderation may be said to describe the quality of Italian foreign policy before Fascism.

So long as Bismarck had dominated the European scene and skillfully manipulated the threads of its diplomacy, Italy was with him, just as she was on friendly terms with Britain. The Mediterranean agreements of 1887 gave apt expression to this state of affairs. Italy's alliances served to protect her from any possible French danger—assuming that there was one—and to minimize the likelihood of a dispute with Austria-Hungary. With the passing of Bismarck and the too rapid growth of German power—the central fact responsible for the change from German dominance to a system of rival alliances—Italy had not been long to perceive the virtues, from her point of view, of the newly established equilibrium. Aware of her own limitations, she correctly judged that her best chance lay in taking a not too clearly defined position between the two rival camps, even though she formally continued to adhere to one of them. The Triple Alliance was duly renewed as late as 1912, but neither her allies nor the members of the Entente entertained sanguine illusions about what she might do in the event of a conflict.

The war had given her an opportunity to capitalize on the position into which she had maneuvered herself, and the behavior of Austria in 1914 had facilitated her task. Coldly, she had calculated her chances and used her position to the best advantage. The Treaty of London, which has been discussed earlier, was the fruit of her consistent policy. And it should be noted that this master work of Sonnino was in the tradition of moderation and balance. For Italy this arrangement represented a good bargain, and Sonnino exploited with skill the situation arising out of the military stalemate between the Central Powers and the Entente. Even if the bargain be considered a hard one—a view toward which the Entente powers were inclined—it certainly could not be said to represent unreasonable hopes: Italy did not propose to destroy Austria-Hungary but merely to displace that power's predominance in the Adriatic, and in addition to extend her influence in Asia Minor. Sonnino was quite content with these prospects and was not to be lured by the will-of-the-wisp of grandiose African projects.

The failure of his statesmanship did not stem from the program carefully laid out and which he tenaciously pursued to the end, but rather in his inability to appreciate the nature of the forces unleashed by the war, forces which found their concrete expression in the American intervention and the Russian Revolution. The peculiar position in which Italy found herself at the peace table, especially as the result of the former event, was totally unforeseen. It might well be argued that it would have been the part of wisdom and higher statesmanship for the Italian leaders to espouse the Wilsonian program wholeheartedly, even though it is unlikely that such a move would have placed their country in a position of leadership in a world founded on a purported New Order. Possibly Britain or France might have achieved this status of leadership in Europe; Italy's power was not sufficient. Even so, in view of the limitations of this power, one may feel that the Bissolatian policy of so-called renunciation would have paid better dividends than the Sonninian insistence on the letter of a law which was being superseded. It is well to recall that, in the midst of this dilemma, Orlando sought to effect a not unreasonable compromise. His failure was due as much to his weakness as to adventitious accidents of circumstance and personality over which he had little control.

The outcome, once the smoke of verbal battle had cleared, represented an equilibrium of forces, of which the extent of Italy's power was one of the components. If very different from what had been envisaged by Sonnino during the war, the result was by no means unfavorable to her; for if the Dalmatian pound of flesh had been whittled down to Zara and a few islands, the defeat of Germany and the disintegration of the Dual Monarchy opened up for Italy very large possibilities indeed in the Balkans and in Central Europe. It was perhaps the very magnitude of the prospect that proved too much for the sane but narrow, and supposedly realistic, outlook which had become the tradition of the *Consulta*. Looked at from a different angle, one might say that Italian policy, too long geared to the minute niceties of a delicate balance of power, was unable to make the drastic readjustment demanded by the complete, if momentary, destruction of this balance.

In any case, these just-mentioned accidents of circumstance and personality, reflected in the course of the peace negotiations as they affected the Italian aspects of the settlement, were responsible in large measure for the prevailing disappointment and frustration which were Italy's reaction to her share of the fruits of victory. Italy had neither the specific territorial advantages she had hoped to acquire, nor any position of leadership, nor even any friends: her relations with her neighbors, old and new, were made up in equal parts of reciprocal recrimination and suspicion. In one respect Italian opinion may be said to have retained its sanity and moderation: some of the most detached judgments on the general quality of the European settlement as a whole, free alike from the French obsession of fear, the Anglo-Saxon "guilty conscience," and the German acrimony, were voiced in Italy.

The difficulties of the domestic situation had the combined effect of increasing the feeling of frustration and of minimizing the importance of foreign affairs, save in so far as an occasional attempt was made to distract the attention of the Italian people from the former by laying stress on the latter. But, in general, during the years immediately following 1919, the Italian electorate showed itself primarily concerned with its more pressing domestic problems, with the consequence that the foreign policy of the successive governments was one of weakness and retrenchment. Once again, it should be emphasized that such a policy of abdication was essentially an accurate expression of existing power.

The sharpest focus of dispute, the frontier between Italy and Yugoslavia, was finally disposed of, through the efforts of Giolitti and Sforza, by the Treaty of Rapallo of November, 1920. This settlement secured for Italy the line of the Treaty of London, slightly modified to her advantage from Austria to the Adriatic, the Dalmatian town of Zara and some islands; but she renounced any other claims on the Dalmatian mainland. The settlement was open to criticism, mainly on ethnic grounds, criticism which the argument of strategy did not adequately answer. The whole question was to be reopened and settled anew (for the moment), as the result of Italy's role in the Second World War; but, in the context of 1920, the arrangement may be described as a not unreasonable compromise. Giolitti and Sforza were genuinely anxious to liquidate the whole unfruitful quarrel and to establish friendly relations with the new Kingdom of the Serbs, Croats, and Slovenes. They drove D'Annunzio out of Fiume, and the absurdly overinflated problem centering on that town was disposed of—temporarily as it proved—through the creation of the Free State of Fiume.

Sforza's policy was sound, but the manner in which he entered into understandings with the Slavs to exclude Porto Baros and the delta of the Recina from the territory of the Free State furnished ammunition with which to attack Giolitti's government. Giolitti in fact resigned shortly after the unenthusiastic ratification of the treaty in the Italian Parliament. In view of the temper of Italian opinion, Giolitti and Sforza had conceded about as much as was possible. The evacuation of Albania during this last tenure of Giolitti was another aspect of the policy of retrenchment—or abdication. The same spirit had presided over the Tittoni-Venizelos agreement of 1919, an agreement which looked to the eventual cession of the Dodecanese islands (save Rhodes) to Greece. This agreement was, however, denounced by Sforza.

Asia Minor had been the chief focus of Sonnino's attention and to it he had largely sacrificed the possibility of colonial acquisitions in Africa. This hard-won concession, though endangered during the peacemaking in the spring of 1919, was substantially implemented in the Treaty of Sèvres of the following year, although that settlement deprived Italy of the valuable port of Smyrna. But Venizelos' skill in displacing the Italians from Smyrna merely proved that he had overreached himself: the Treaty of Sèvres, which was signed by an impotent Sultan, rather than marking the end of Turkey was the sign of her rebirth.

This is not the place to tell the story of the rise of Kemal and his preparations in the interior of Anatolia. The fury of the new nationalist Turkey vented itself mainly upon the luckless Greeks. Kemal did not acknowledge the Sèvres settlement, but instead won recognition for his new Turkey in 1923 in the fresh Treaty of Lausanne, which obliterated Greek as well as Italian and French claims in Turkey proper. In his successful fight, Kemal was assisted not a little by the fact that the Allies, the British and the French in particular, had fallen out among themselves over this issue. In these events, Italy played a passive role, neither supporting the Greeks as Britain did, nor the Turks as did France. Wisely on the whole, she accepted the emergence of the new Turkey and let her claim to southern Anatolia lapse. But if this was undoubtedly wise, it was also a manifestation of the same policy of retrenchment, and this was more marked in the case of Italy than with Britain or France, for unlike these powers, Italy had no compensating colonial advantages or mandates elsewhere. In passing, it is worth recalling that this result was largely brought about by the fact of Sonnino's exclusive concentration on Asia Minor—a sound policy in 1915-17 we repeat—and the subsequent and largely unforeseeable (again in 1915-17) circumstances of the peacemaking of 1919. And this contributed a share to the feeling of frustration over the whole peace settlement for, if it is not true that Italy was excluded from colonial compensations in 1919, the fact remains that, even though she acted wisely in withdrawing from Asia Minor, she did in the end emerge without any compensations worth mentioning outside Europe. Frustration and resentment could easily be turned against former allies, even though these allies could hardly be held responsible for Italy's own decision in regard to Asia Minor, the main field of her imperial interest during the war.

The largely aimless governments that succeeded Giolitti, wholly wrapped up in the effort to survive amid the stresses of the domestic scene, could hardly have been expected to pursue a vigorous foreign policy. We have traced the activities of the Fascists during this period of postwar uncertainty. The attention of the country was mainly focused on its internal pains of readjustment; the Fascists, like other groups, spent the greater part of their energy on the discussion of these same domestic problems and their proposed solution of them in the form of direct action aimed at the groups of the Left, but they, and Mussolini in particular, were not slow to perceive and capitalize on the possibilities of exploiting the discontent produced by the foreign policy of abdication. Having cheered D'Annunzio in Fiume, they proceeded to espouse a vigorous nationalistic program and appropriately effected a merger with the small, but able, group of Nationalists in Parliament. From this coalition they reaped the advantage of securing what came to be some of the most capable theorizers among their ranks. In this fashion, the revival of nationalism which had taken place during the first decade of the century bore fruit, its exponents now arrived in the seats of power under the wing of the Fascist alliance. Which brings us back to the question raised at the beginning of this chapter: bearing in mind the inheritance of nationalism as an important part of its makeup, and the immediate background of the confused aftermath of the war behind it, we must proceed to examine Fascism at work in the domain of foreign policy.

The Italian Drang nach Osten: Italy in the Mediterranean.—Under whatever regime, the Mediterranean must remain the foremost region of Italian interest. The Treaty of Lausanne of 1923 which undid the effects of Sèvres for Turkey was one of the first international acts in which Fascist Italy was called upon to participate, hence a valuable test case. But the situation in Anatolia had conclusively taken shape before the advent of Fascism. However much Italian nationalism may have objected to a policy of renunciation in Asia Minor, in the circumstances it would have been mere irresponsible foolhardiness not to recognize the *fait accompli*. Fascism, always priding itself on its "realism," therefore accepted the Lausanne settlement. Its policy in this quarter may be described as one of cutting losses. Following Sforza rather than Tittoni in this particular respect, however, Italy secured final and unencumbered title to the Dodecanese with the small island of Castellorizzo. The value of this possession is wholly strategic as there has never been any question of its economic importance or of its overwhelmingly Greek character. The population, which had welcomed rather than opposed the original Italian occupation in 1912—a relief from Turkish rule—was by this time definitely hoping to rejoin the Greek motherland. Fascism did as much as could be done at the time in asserting the continuance of Italian interest in the eastern Mediterranean. But this was rather stopping a retreat than an aggressive move in itself. What form this Italian interest might or would take remained therefore an open question and would depend upon the future course of the regime. The new Turkey, itself highly nationalistic—though not imperialistic—could not but be sensitive to the presence of Italy in the Dodecanese and, especially in view of the past record of Italian attempts in Asia Minor and of the unknowns in the Fascist makeup, remained suspicious of a possible revival of Italian imperialism. The subsequent assimilation of the Dodecanese to the metropolitan administration and the establishment of a strong naval base in the islands could only confirm the mistrust and guarded suspicion of Fascist Italy's intentions which continued to characterize the Turkish attitude, even despite a relaxation of this feeling during the years around 1930.

The question of the Dodecanese involved likewise the relations between Italy and Greece. The ink was barely dry on the signatures of the Treaty of Lausanne before these relations were to provide a more telling test of Fascist methods and intentions in the foreign field. Italy and Greece had another point of contact in Albania and, despite her withdrawal from that country, Italy could hardly disinterest herself completely from developments across the Strait of Otranto. The southern portion of Albania, also known as Northern Epirus, had been contested between that country and Greece and, in 1923, an international commission representing the powers was in process of delimiting the Greco-Albanian frontier on the ground, in accordance with a decision of the Conference of Ambassadors two years earlier. While engaged on this work, General Tellini, Italian member of the commission, and three of his assistants were murdered in the neighborhood of Janina on August 27. In that not too orderly part of the Balkans there might be some doubt as to the origin of those responsible for the crime; but the Italian reaction was very similar to that of Austria-Hungary on the occasion of the Sarajevo murder, and a harsh ultimatum was delivered to Greece. Was Mussolini, like Berchtold nine years earlier, determined to use the incident as a pretext, regardless of the merits of the case, to assert his position in the Balkans and to retrieve the ground given up by Giolitti? Greece reacted in very much the same way that Serbia had in 1914, accepting most of the Italian demands, but taking exception to those she deemed injurious to her honor and sovereignty. Wasting no time in negotiations, an Italian naval squadron was dispatched to the island of Corfu which, after a needless bombardment, was occupied on August 31. The next day the Greek government brought the case to the attention of the Council of the League of Nations, then in session in Geneva, under Articles 12 and 15 of the Covenant. Simultaneously, the Conference of Ambassadors demanded an inquiry of the Greek government, which responded by submitting in advance to any decision of that body. Mussolini on his side was determined that he would not accept any League interference, threatening to make the occupation permanent. In the face of this confusion of authorities, the issue was peacefully resolved though not squarely met. Acting upon an informal recommendation of the Council of the League, the Ambassadors decided that Greece should deposit 50,000,000 lire—the amount of the indemnity demanded by Italy—pending final adjudication. Despite the fact that the guilty parties could not be apprehended, the Conference of Ambassadors, alleging Greek negligence, ordered the sum to be paid to Italy, whereupon Mussolini declared himself satisfied and Corfu was evacuated at the end of September. To what extent the Fascist government, barely in control for a year, still felt itself too weak to defy public opinion abroad and British pressure in particular cannot be ascertained. What is certain is that the incident left a bad aftertaste. The League hardly came out of it with credit, and the Fascists, even though they compromised in the end, created the impression that they were willing to resort to strong-arm methods and unilateral action in disregard of such international organs as the League.

Curiously enough, while the passing of time did not completely allay these suspicions, neither did it confirm the fears that had been engendered. For a considerable time, Fascism, while growing ever more strongly entrenched at home, seemed to give the lie in action to the belligerent talk in which its adherents continued to indulge. This is well illustrated by the relations between Italy and Yugoslavia. In view of the background which has been analyzed earlier, it might have been expected that the two countries would be bitter enemies. Indeed their relations can hardly be said to have been cordial: while the cry for Italian Dalmatia often resounded in Italy, deep suspicion was the inevitable response across the Adriatic. Fiume, that original apple of discord, did not long prove a source of continued difficulty. It soon became clear that the Free State set up by the Treaty of Rapallo was not a successful or even a viable creation, for it remained the scene of local agitation and coups while Sušak and the Delta continued under

Italian occupation. In somewhat brusque, though not unreasonable manner in the circumstances, Mussolini cut the Gordian knot in 1923 and a final settlement was effected the following year. The whole Adriatic issue was not reopened, as might have been feared, but Yugoslavia acquiesced in the annexation of the Free State to Italy and Mussolini agreed to accept the terms of Rapallo for the rest, including Sforza's commitments in regard to the Delta, even though he described this agreement as "a lamentable transaction." In view of the problematic nature of Fascism and of such manifestations as the Corfu episode, this could be considered as at least moderate behavior.

Taking the outwardly unexceptionable position that treaties are not eternal, that they are expressions of a situation in existence at the time of their making, and that therefore they ought to be susceptible of modification under changing circumstances, but that once signed their provisions ought to be loyally lived up to, Mussolini seemed bent on a thoroughgoing liquidation of the quarrel with Yugoslavia. The annexation of Fiume by Italy was followed by the conclusion of a five-year Pact of Friendship and Collaboration between Italy and Yugoslavia, and the following year, 1925, witnessed the drawing up of the so-called Nettuno Convention designed to implement this collaboration in the domains of economic and cultural relations. But this agreement was destined to be the high point of cordiality, for the resentment of Croat and Slovene deputies was sufficient to block ratification of the Nettuno Convention in the Skupshtina; when it was eventually ratified by Belgrade three years later its possible psychological value had evaporated. This last event was a measure of the failure to overcome the deep-rooted differences between the two countries, differences which had manifested themselves meantime in rivalry over the same Albania, point of contact between Italy and Yugoslavia as well as between Italy and Greece.

During the year 1925 Albania had been the scene of some typical Balkan intrigues, which resulted in the displacement of Monsignor Fan Noli by Ahmed Zogu. This personage, who was later to elevate himself to kingship, once he had made his hold on the country secure, was successful in his initial bid for power owing in part to machinations directed and assistance received from Belgrade. But, once in control, he quickly came to the conclusion that greater benefits could be derived from across the Adriatic than from his immediate territorial neighbor. Albania consequently became the client of its Italian paymaster. The position of Italy toward that country may be described as willingness to purchase political dependence at the price of subsidies in the form of uneconomic investment. The arrangement, for a time, was equally satisfactory to Mussolini and to Zog and it might well be argued that, economically, it was rather Albania that exploited Italy than the reverse; by strict business standards, the security of the Italian investments would be considered flimsy. What ultimate or ulterior motives Italy may have had in such an arrangement were not, for a long time, apparent. It is interesting that, as late as 1938, a sober student of Italian policy could write: "that Italy ever nurtured the dreams of territorial expansion in the Balkans attributed to her by Italophobes is most improbable" (Macartney and Cremona, *Italy's Foreign and Colonial Policy, 1914–1937*). Belgrade could hardly entertain the same confidence that Albania was not the thin end of the wedge of eventually more extensive Italian penetration.

But Albania was but one point of contact between Italy and Yugoslavia. The relations between the two countries must be considered in the broader framework of the whole European scene. Inevitably, Yugoslavia was one of the states interested in maintaining the advantages she had derived from the war, a state therefore favorable to the preservation of the *status quo* as expressed in the peace settlements issuing from the war, and first and foremost of the territorial *status quo*. This interest found expression in her participation in the Little Entente, an alliance directed mainly against Hungarian revisionism, and in her joining France as the chief defender of the established order. It was some years after the peace before Yugoslavia formally entered the French camp; a Treaty of Friendship and Alliance between the two countries was initialed in 1926, the year, be it noted, of the Pact of Tirana which established the position of Albania as an Italian client. The Franco-Yugoslav treaty was signed in Paris in November, 1927, and within two weeks a treaty of defensive alliance between Italy and Albania was concluded. Officially, these events were unrelated, and formal protestations to this effect went to the length of Mussolini's acknowledgment of the correctness of the Franco-Yugoslav connection. But the resentment voiced in Italy was a

truer measure of the real state of affairs. In actual fact, the anti-Italian
motivation was highly secondary, if present at all, as far as France was
concerned, for France was naturally and correctly interested most of
all in the German situation. But the fact remains that the alliance
would tend to bolster Yugoslav confidence in resisting real or imagined
Italian encroachments.

What has been said of Yugoslavia and the reasons for her connection
with France applies similarly to those other countries which had the
same general interest in preserving a *status quo* that they found advantageous to themselves. This meant in brief the succession states of
Central Europe which had emerged as allies by the end of the war;
and thus, very naturally, there came into existence the so-called French
system of alliances, the central core of which was the military and
financial power of France. As a way to maintain the peace, this system
had many advantages, for, allowing for its shortcomings, it was essentially unaggressive. The consequences of its breakdown have shown
how frivolous and shortsighted was the criticism of it, especially in the
English-speaking world which has suffered grievously from its demise.
There is no denying, however, that those alliances served to boost French
power, beyond its own intrinsic measure one may say, and to institute
what has been erroneously called French hegemony on the Continent.
That the former enemies should have no love for the arrangement goes
without saying, but what is of especial interest from our point of view
is that there was no place for Italy in the French system of alliances.
For, in the destruction of the power balance in Europe, Italian policy
had been robbed of its most effective lever. France indeed would have
welcomed Italian adherence, but neither would nor could pay the price
of it; nor is there reason to believe that, whatever the price and had the
price been paid, this adherence would have been either lasting or dependable, for the simple reason that national interest would always
make Italy sympathetic to any possibility of reestablishing the balance.

The Espousal of Revisionism: the Four-Power Pact of 1933.—That
is the real reason for the sane and detached view of the peace settlements
taken in Italy. Italy was, in the last analysis, in favor of the restoration
of German power—up to a point. Much for the same reason, Fascist
Italy, both because she was Fascist and because she was Italy, looked

with an indifferent, or skeptical, eye upon the League and all its works: there was too much French influence in the League, hence too much stress upon the League as an instrument for the preservation of the *status quo*. Even the Locarno agreement, flattering as it was to national pride by making Italy a guarantor of the Franco-German frontier, was entered into with reluctance and partly because it would have been even more awkward to be left out of an agreement among the great powers.

But, even after Locarno, the prospects of a restoration of German power were dim and distant in the middle twenties. Italy, therefore, found herself blocked by French influence almost wherever she looked: a weak Germany was the cardinal tenet of French policy, which had had the corollary of making French clients out of most of the succession states. There was indeed but one place to turn and that was toward those countries whose interest was in the main opposed to that of the victors, the former enemy states. It would have been imprudent to espouse too soon and too vigorously the German cause, but there remained the smaller countries of Austria, Hungary, and Bulgaria toward all of whom Italy came to turn her sympathetic attention. Among these, Hungary was by far the most vocal and convinced exponent of the demand for revision of the peace settlements—especially in their territorial aspects—and it was natural that she, among others, should fall in the Italian camp as Italy became more definitely a revisionist power. As early as 1927, a Pact of Friendship was concluded between the two countries.

The Italian espousal of revisionism was a gradual process. Mussolini's statement in November, 1922, quoted at the head of this chapter, to the effect that "treaties are not eternal" was indeed unexceptionable. In the context that accompanied it, it could only be described as eminently sane, almost an obvious platitude in fact; but this same context gave no clue to the position that Italy might eventually take in the matter. In actual practice, Fascism had to consolidate itself at home first, and during the early years of its rule was neither bellicose (if we omit the Corfu episode, untypical of this period) nor apparently very much concerned with treaty revision. But it was also clear that Italy was not irrevocably wedded to the *status quo,* and the statement of 1922 served notice that she felt free to decide at any moment that new conditions created a demand for revision of it. The subject was taken up again by Mussolini in a speech before the Senate on June 5, 1927, in much the same outwardly calm and reasonable vein as in 1922. But from this time on the theme recurred with increasing frequency and insistence in Fascist pronouncements, which is why the year 1928 is often given as the date of Italy's espousal of revisionism.

A little later, in 1930, treaty revision was coupled with an attack upon the League as it had been operating. "Revision of the peace treaties," said Mussolini, "is not a predominantly Italian interest; it is a European interest, a world interest. This possibility of revision ceases to be something absurd and unrealizable from the moment when it is envisaged in the very Covenant of the League of Nations. The sole absurdity lies in the pretense that the treaties are immovable. Who violates the Covenant? Those in Geneva who have created and wish to maintain in perpetuity two categories of states, the armed and the unarmed. What equality, juridical or moral, can subsist between an armed and an unarmed man? How can the pretense be maintained that this comedy is to endure to eternity, when even the protagonists themselves are beginning to be weary of it?" Very reasonably and rather skillfully put, one must admit. We must put off for a while the analysis of the fundamental flaw in the Fascist position.

In 1930 the world was fast becoming engulfed in the depths of economic crisis. The correlation between the impact of this crisis and the rise of the Nazi party in Germany is too well known to need elaboration, though it would be an incorrect oversimplification to see in the former the exclusive cause of the latter. There is no need to discuss the connection between these events, or the similarities and differences between Nazism and Fascism; suffice it to recall that in January, 1933, the Nazis came to control the German state. The accession of Hitler to the German Chancellorship and the manner in which Nazism took control of the German state, far more thorough and rapid than had been the case with Fascism in Italy, changed the whole European picture in the first months of 1933. Mussolini was not slow to react to the new situation in which he saw an opportunity for leadership and for personal and national advantage, while the slow-moving chancelleries of the democratic nations, handicapped in addition by divided counsels at home, were trying to make up their minds as to the real nature of the new phenomenon which had emerged on the political horizon of Europe.

Mussolini's reaction took the form of his proposed Four-Power Pact, a proposal which has not received sufficient attention. It is worth studying in some detail for it constitutes an excellent and typical example of the sort of thing that Fascism stood for and thus goes a long way toward revealing the true nature of that system, even though the Four-Power Pact of 1933 was essentially a stillbirth.

The general situation at that time must be recalled briefly. Two long and inconclusive debates had been going on in Geneva almost ever since the end of the war. They were largely Franco-British debates, in the last analysis different aspects of the same fundamental issue which may be summed up as the issue of security versus disarmament. They represented also essentially irreconcilable, though honest, differences of opinion. Reduced to its hardest core, the difference amounted to this: France, in her fear founded on historic experience, would not divest herself of the advantage accruing from German disarmament, save in exchange for solid guarantees, whether in the form of an Anglo-American reinsurance as proposed in 1919 or through a clarification and strengthening of the League's powers of assistance to a victim of aggression. Britain, likewise conditioned by historic background, by her traditional island safety, plus reliance on the balance of power, argued that the very inequality of armaments was a factor preventing the restoration of confidence, hence of security. Give us security and then we shall disarm, said the French; disarm first and security will follow, retorted the British. In one form or another the two sides kept reiterating the same idea everlastingly. The debate could obviously lead nowhere on that basis and the disarmament conference, which incidentally met at last in the inauspicious atmosphere of 1932, could not but be a failure. Germany had withdrawn from it, having taken the position—effective as a debating point—that what she was primarily interested in was not either armament or disarmament as such, but equality of rights with others.

Simultaneously with the disarmament debate, went on the argument over the powers of the League, which the French would have strengthened while the British balked at increasing the range of their commitments. The economic distress of the early thirties hardly created an atmosphere of confidence and good-will in which to conduct the debate. Little was left by then of the so-called spirit of Locarno. As Mussolini himself put it, with his aptitude for neat phrase: "the label on the bottle remains, but the contents have evaporated." Even the Hoover moratorium which had led to the abandonment of the impossible attempt to collect reparations had been so handled that the benefits of this step were lost in the recriminations to which it gave rise.

What Hitler would do was, in 1933, not clear to most people or governments. Many thought the Nazis' bark might prove worse than their bite. Had not the Fascist regime proved quite tractable for the most part in its dealings with other nations? It could hardly be expected, however, that the new Germany would prove more amenable than the old. How then deal with it? Mussolini lost no time in producing an answer, and invited the British Ministers who were in Geneva in March, in connection with the futile discussion of disarmament plans, to come to Rome to discuss it. This is the origin of the Four-Power Pact. The proposal consisted of a few brief articles, the first two of which reveal the essence and the spirit of the project. Article 1 stated that

The four western powers, France, Germany, Great Britain, and Italy, undertake to carry out between them an effective policy of cooperation, in order to ensure the maintenance of peace in the spirit of the Kellogg Pact and of the "no resort to force" pact, and *undertake to follow such course of action as to induce, if necessary, third parties, as far as Europe is concerned, to adopt the same policy of peace.* (Italics added.)

The full significance of the italics was brought out in the second article which went on to elucidate that

The Four Powers confirm the principle of the revision of treaties, in accordance with the clauses of the Covenant of the League of Nations, in cases in which there is a possibility that they will lead to conflict among the states. They declare at the same time that the principle of revision cannot be applied except within the framework of the League and in a spirit of mutual understanding and solidarity of reciprocal interests.

Less important, but significant nevertheless in the context of the time, were the next two articles which read as follows:

Art. 3. France, Great Britain and Italy declare that, should the Disarmament Conference lead only to partial results, the parity of rights recognized to Germany ought to have an effective import, and Germany pledges herself to realize such parity of rights in a gradual manner, as the result of successive accords to be taken between the Four Powers, in the normal diplomatic way.

The four powers pledge themselves to reach similar accords as regards "parity" for Austria, Hungary, Bulgaria.

Art. 4. In all questions political and non-political, European and extra-European, and also as regards the colonial sector, the Four Powers pledge themselves to adopt, within the measure of the possible, a common line of conduct.

On the face of it, the proposal seems reasonable enough, and it is not surprising perhaps that the Labor Prime Minister of Britain should have been favorably impressed and should have spoken approvingly of it in Parliament. But, in effect, what was the real purport of the scheme? The first thing to be noticed is that, despite the diplomatic verbiage and the homage paid to the League, it was tantamount to a destruction of the foundations of that institution, for it aimed at bringing into existence a four-power directorate of Europe. Such a concept was not novel: Metternich's Quadruple Alliance, Tsar Alexander's Holy Alliance, and the Concert of Europe itself were, in one form or another, expressions of the same idea. Fascism had always prided itself on its realism and held in contempt the egalitarian principles of 1789, whether applied to individuals or among nations. In its eyes, the League was an utopian undertaking, founded on a denial of the realities of power and of life itself. Starting from an approving acceptance of the fact of power, it was logical, from the Fascist point of view, to place this reality at the base of any constructive suggestion. The most that Mussolini would do, not to arouse needless antagonism, was to pay lip service in his proposal to the League and to the Pact of Paris. The fact of power can certainly neither be denied nor dismissed. But we run here into an irreconcilable divergence of outlook between the Fascist or totalitarian and the democratic view. The latter, while not denying the fact of power in the domain of international relations as in others, seeks at least to mitigate its evil effects; hence the League and the spirit of the

League. This democratic approach is difficult; its results are highly imperfect in their search for compromise, and therefore open to easy criticism. The Fascist has the advantage of outward simplicity, and the vice of fundamental hopelessness in the future.

But there was more to the Four-Power Pact than this ideological difference, important though that was. If the four-power directorate which was envisaged had come into existence, the result would have been a complete rearrangement of the power situation in Europe; for how would matters stand among the Big Four? Germany could not do other than use the new situation to free herself from the disabilities resulting from defeat and endeavor to regain her own position of power; in this attempt she would inevitably run into French opposition born of French fear. But France would be but one among the four. Britain, whatever her motives and the soundness of her understanding, was not over-sympathetic to French power; her "guilty conscience" would dispose her to give much credit to German good intentions. Most of all, Italy would be able to resume her former position of fence-sitting—or selling her services to the highest bidder—and thereby enhance her value and prestige and possibly gain concrete advantages for herself. Mussolini's whole background and outlook would allow him to entertain fewer illusions than the British about the true significance of the restoration of German power. But he was willing to play the game and run the risks. In the last resort, if Germany should become too obstreperous, she could still be put in a minority of one among the Four. There is a simple test of the sincerity of Mussolini's apparently reasonable talk about revisionism in the fact that he always made it clear that revisionism might apply to others but in no circumstances to Italy: the independence of Austria, the acquisition of the Southern Tyrol, and the frontier with Yugoslavia were established facts, irrevocable decisions, about which he could expatiate with fervor, even calling to his aid the sanctity of the signature on a treaty.

It is clear from the foregoing that the chief price of a four-power agreement would have to be paid by France, from which it follows that the project might be expected to have held little attraction for that country. Yet France did not meet the proposal at first with an unconditional *non possumus.* There were others, however, who felt free to speak plainly. When the great powers have differences among themselves, there is always a danger that they may succeed in coming to terms at the expense of some smaller and weaker country without their charmed circle. This in fact may be said to have been one of the traditional ways in which they have avoided clashes among themselves. Historically speaking, it must be remembered that the principles of self-determination and of the rights of small nations are of very recent acceptance. The small countries are well aware of this, and, coming from a Fascist source especially, the phrase "undertake to follow such course of action as to induce, if necessary, third parties, as far as Europe is concerned, to adopt the same policy of peace" was a cause of serious alarm to them. This alarm was voiced most unequivocally by the Permanent Council of the Little Entente whose Foreign Ministers were in Geneva at the time Mussolini's proposal was made. We need only consider the dates March 18, when the British statesmen were in Rome, and March 25, when the Little Entente statement was issued, to appreciate how prompt and definite the reaction was. While welcoming the idea of collaboration among the powers, the Little Entente could not see that "the cause of good relations between the different countries is served by agreements which, it seems, had for their aim the disposal of the rights of third parties," and went on to express the "most explicit reserves concerning the eventual conclusion of such agreements." Belgium and Poland reacted in much the same way as the Little Entente countries.

Thus the minor partners in the French system of alliances were quick to perceive a potential threat to themselves in the Four-Power Pact. How right they were, five years would be enough to show, for the Munich Pact of 1938, which will be discussed in some detail in the next chapter, was nothing but the Four-Power Pact in action. France, despite Daladier's hasty declaration of "full sympathy" for the project, could not but look askance at the scheme. Her position was embarrassing for, in view of the German situation, she certainly did not wish to weaken her alliances but was also anxious not to antagonize Italy.

The result was that she took the initiative in proposing modifications of the original draft. Her suggestions became the basis of discussion and, after some brief exchanges, were essentially embodied in the final text of the treaty which was signed in June in Rome, after the Little Entente had been pacified by French reassurances. The heart of the change lay in Article 2 which in the revised and final version stated that

> In respect of the Covenant of the League of Nations, and particularly articles 10, 16 and 19, the High Contracting Parties decide to examine between themselves, *and without prejudice to decisions which can only be taken by the regular organs of the League of Nations,* all proposals relating to methods and procedures calculated to give due effect to these articles. (Italics added.)

The meaning of this is all the clearer when we recall that, while Article 19 of the Covenant stated that the Assembly of the League might "advise the reconsideration . . . of treaties which have become inapplicable," Article 10 stressed the preservation of the "territorial integrity and political independence of all members" and Article 16 made the resort to war by a member in disregard of its obligations under the Covenant "an act of war against all other members."

In 1933, then, Mussolini's attempt to institute a four-power directorate of Europe was blocked. The seemingly small change in Article 2 which, in the final form of the treaty, stressed the *status quo*-preserving aspect of the League did the exact opposite of what Mussolini had intended, namely to stress the revisionist Article 19 while paying innocuous lip service to the League in general. As it was finally agreed upon, the Four-Power Pact was little more than another meaningless reassertion of loyalty to the League, and signing it had no value other than that of a face-saving device for Mussolini, who had taken the initiative in the matter. He himself was too intelligent to be taken in by the verbiage and not to realize that he had failed. But, for all its failure, the attempt itself had considerable significance: it was a warning signal, the more urgent when we take into account the existence of Fascism in Italy and the coming to power of the Nazis in Germany, that the forces of change were issuing a challenge to those of conservation.

Two things must be stressed here. First, that these forces of change were prompted by motives of selfish gain and interest, as is borne out by Mussolini's attitude toward revisionism where it might affect Italian interests adversely. Second, that these same forces of change were essentially reactionary and retrogressive for they were issuing a challenge to the *real* forces of change, despite all the talk about youth, vigor, and the future so prevalent in Italy and in Germany. For change does not consist so much in the preservation or the alteration of some relatively secondary aspects of an admittedly imperfect *status quo* as in the acceptance of a novel outlook in the relations of nations among themselves, the endeavor in brief to substitute in those relations some rule of law for the anarchy which has so far prevailed.

How deep the issue goes is shown by the difficulties in which our present world is floundering in an attempt to reconcile the two approaches. The United States is not, to the extent that it was in 1919 at least, the exponent of the rights of small nations. From the necessity born of circumstances, mainly not of our choosing, and also because of a deeper realization of the extent of our involvements, we are placing greater stress on the element of power—our own and that of others. This decision has been reflected in the present constitution of the United Nations, most specifically in the veto arrangements in the Council. The arguments for the veto are strong, and this is no place to consider their pros and cons. But the effects of the use of the veto are already apparent. The problem is even more difficult than may appear on the surface, for it is not simply a question of devising skillful compromises. Compromises are necessary, but no amount of diplomatic verbiage, however clever it may be, can resolve the distrust born of radically antagonistic outlooks, the totalitarian and the democratic. We are faced with the far more subtle and difficult problem, laden with imponderables, of effecting a reconciliation between essentially divergent states of mind. The central problem of the League, the problem of subjecting power to law among nations, is still with us, wholly unresolved.

The Irresponsible Use of Power.—It was fitting and proper that the challenge to the whole philosophy that lay behind the League idea should come from Fascist quarters, for, quite honestly and sincerely, Fascism did not accept this philosophy. For reasons largely national the Italian attitude toward the League, even before the advent of Fascism, had been one of skepticism. Fascism retained this skepticism and emphasized it. In actual practice, it was not averse to a certain amount of cooperation with the League and could see possible advantages to be derived in its dealings with other powers, supporters of the League, from the known fact that Italy did not consider herself irrevocably wedded to membership in that institution. With the passing of time, and especially with the increasingly obvious futility of the disarmament discussions, Mussolini came to lay more and more stress on the need to reform the League if it were to survive at all. In many respects the point was well taken and served to bolster the belief in the fundamental reasonableness of Fascism.

But this seeming reasonableness was in reality fraudulent, for when it came to the real core and purpose of the League, the submission of power to law, Fascism was not with the friends of the League. The Corfu episode, small as it was by itself, was highly significant in this respect, a true measure of the real Fascist attitude: on a fundamental issue of national interest and power, Mussolini would brook no interference from the League. The later Abyssinian adventure, fraught with more serious consequences, was at bottom a reassertion of the same position. On this score Fascism ever remained consistent and true to itself.

As early as 1923, to go back no further, at the time of the Corfu episode, Mussolini had expressed himself in these words before the Italian Senate:

> In my opinion the Corfu episode is of the greatest importance in the history of Italy, because it has put the problem of the League of Nations before the public opinion of Italy in a way which no number of books could have done. Italians have never been very much interested in the League of Nations; they believed that it was a lifeless academic organization of no importance. . . . In point of fact, the League is an Anglo-French duet; each of these powers has its satellites and its clients, and Italy's position, so far, has been one of absolute inferiority. The problem may be stated in these terms: should Italy leave the League of Nations? Speaking generally I prefer rather to be inside than out.

This is as apt a statement of the Fascist position as was ever made, and from this view Mussolini never deviated, though he often used coarser language to express his thoughts.

In all fairness, and to give the devil his due, it must be admitted that Mussolini did have a point, though the word "duel" might have been an apter choice than "duet" in characterizing the British and French attitudes in the League. It is true that Italy played second fiddle to Britain and France—a fact, however, largely independent of the League itself—and that she had some concrete (though unduly and deliberately magnified) grievances against these powers, especially France. And it is also true that if the League, or any system founded on the ideal of the preservation of peace and law among nations, is considered a priori impossible, then a sound case exists for an overt directorate of the great powers. That is really the crux of the matter: Fascism did *not* believe in peace and law among nations. From this it was a logical step to work *against* the League and all that it stood for.

It was not long after the stillbirth of the Four-Power Pact that Mussolini had occasion to resort to the use of power, and there is not a little irony in the fact that this first use of power was in behalf of the preservation of the *status quo*. Austria was to furnish the occasion for this display of Fascist realism and vigor.

Ever since Austria had appeared on the map of Europe as an independent state, upon the dissolution of the Dual Monarchy, her very existence had hinged upon the possibility of union with Germany. The strength of the Austrian feeling for *Anschluss* is somewhat difficult to evaluate, all the more because it was subject to fluctuations deriving from changing circumstances, those of Austria herself, and those of Germany. But it was inevitable that, under any conditions, the *Anschluss* should be a major, if not *the* major, issue of Austrian politics. The possibility touched upon vital Italian interests. Taking the longer-range view, the eventual restoration of Germany to a position of equality among the powers, Italy could hardly contemplate with indifference the prospect of a powerful Germany, enlarged in addition by Austria, as her next-door neighbor; the millenary record of Germanic interference in the affairs of the peninsula could not be so easily ignored. More narrowly and immediately, the Southern Tyrol or Upper Adige, the annexation of which had brought the Italian frontier to the Brenner, was of the purest Germanic population. Austria, with natural German approval and sympathy, had protested against this annexation. A restored and enlarged Germany might be able to do something about it more effective than mere protestation. The Southern Tyrol, therefore, was for Mussolini one of those settlements covered by the sanctity of treaties rather than by the enlightened need for revision of iniquitous or unviable decisions, and opposition to the *Anschluss* took on increasingly the character of a cardinal principle of Italian foreign policy. It was logical that, in 1931, Italy should on the whole agree with France in viewing the proposed Austro-German customs union as fraught with dangerous political implications and that she should, therefore, like France, oppose it.

The triumph of the Nazis in Germany in 1933, their proclaimed desires, their stress on the unity of Germandom, and the very origin of the *Führer,* made the Austrian question more acute than ever. Passing meanwhile from an attitude of mere negative opposition to the *Anschluss,* Mussolini had turned to the more active policy of turning Austria into an Italian client. The general orientation of the Dollfuss regime in Austria was favorable to the strengthening of the Italian connection. The year 1934 was to witness a series of events centering around Austria which gave full scope to the play of Fascist policy toward that country.

In February of that year, the Dollfuss regime assumed its true and final aspect as the result of the violent suppression of the Socialists in Vienna. Whether or not this was, as has been asserted, the price exacted by Mussolini from Dollfuss for unqualified support (the complete history of our time will be long in the writing), it undoubtedly fitted in to a nicety with Fascist plans and desires. The suppression of the Socialists was almost simultaneous with the issuance of an Anglo-Franco-Italian reassertion of support of Austrian independence, a statement called forth by the activities of German propaganda. A month later were signed the Rome Protocols which drew both Austria and Hungary still closer within the Italian political and economic orbit—or net. Hitler and Mussolini even met in Venice whence they issued the first of a long series of declarations of complete understanding, understanding achieved on this occasion by the simple process of mental reservations, each dictator putting a different meaning into the same words.

Thus the proclaimed agreement did not in any way put a stop to propaganda, agitation, and intrigue directed toward Austria from her northern neighbor. By July, this agitation reached its climax in the attempted seizure of the government by Austrian Nazis. The coup failed, but in the course of the attempt the diminutive Austrian Chancellor was brutally murdered. In the face of failure, Germany assumed a "correct" attitude and disclaimed any responsibility or interest in Austrian affairs. If one overlooks legalistic quibbles in favor of truer reality, German responsibility was inescapable and, in a sense, the Austrian coup had some of the same connotations as the Italian attempt on Corfu eleven years earlier: both episodes were in the last analysis tests of power of a newly established regime, tests which there was no intention of pushing too far in the event that resolute opposition was met. And the most determined opposition came in this case from south of the Brenner. Mussolini, wasting no time over legalistic niceties and discussions of responsibility, promptly mobilized his troops on the frontier and gave it clearly to be understood that the appearance of German troops in Austria would be met by force. Such behavior was far more convincing to the Nazis than delayed declarations of condemnation from French or British sources, and Mussolini unquestionably deserves a large share of credit for preserving the independence of Austria on this occasion. Indirectly, the episode had the effect of placing that country even more tightly in the Italian grip.

The Dollfuss murder was but an incident, however, in a situation fated to steady deterioration. And, in the growingly uncertain conditions of Europe, Mussolini found a congenial atmosphere for the exercise of his gambling propensities. France, though divided and troubled at home, could not help but react strongly to the dangers which these uncertainties presented to her position in Europe, and eventually to her security. Her reaction took the form of an endeavor to tighten the network of alliances that constituted the French security system. That the system needed bolstering is certain, for it depended in the last analysis on the confidence of France's allies in the solidity of her power and her willingness to use that power in case of need. The emergence of the Nazis would by itself tend to strengthen the common bond of interest of these alliances, but if doubts should arise in regard to either the extent of French power or the willingness to use that power, then clearly national interest would indicate the desirability of searching for alternative solutions. The initial French reaction to the Four-Power Pact proposal of the preceding year had not been reassuring to France's allies, and Poland, at the beginning of 1934, had gone the length of making a ten-year agreement with the new Germany. Barthou, the French Foreign Minister, set out on a tour of the capitals of France's various allies in an effort to reknit the ties of the network of connections. In pursuance of the same attempt, it was arranged that King Alexander of Yugoslavia should pay a visit to France.

At this point, the plot begins to thicken. The Little Entente, as we know, was primarily directed against Hungarian revisionism. With the increasingly open espousal of revisionism by Italy, Hungary fell ever more into the Italian wake; the Rome Protocols were the latest manifestation of this trend. All of this could only further estrange Yugoslavia and Italy and throw the former more than ever into the French camp. Hence King Alexander's projected visit to France. The charge in Italy that Yugoslavia had given asylum to some involved in the Dollfus murder was but an additional twig to the fires of enmity. The differences between Alexander's and Mussolini's regimes were after all primarily national rather than ideological and, to Alexander, the Nazi threat was mainly the indirect one of a potential disturbance of the *status quo*.

Whatever one may think of his methods, King Alexander's policy and behavior were dictated by the determination to preserve national unity against internal forces of disruption; for Yugoslavia may still be described as a nation in the making. Alexander's coercive methods, dictated though they may have been by exasperation at what appeared to him Croatian unreasonableness, none the less had the effect, in turn, of exasperating Croatian nationalism, some exponents of which at least were willing to go the length of intriguing with foreign powers. Such a situation is hardly novel in history; it represents a measure of the comparative lag in the degree of national integration between Southeastern Europe and the West. Both Hungary and Italy were willing to encourage those disruptive tendencies in Yugoslavia and provided shelter, assistance, training, and arms to the discontented. Hungary wanted to regain some territory; Italy still talked about "Italian" Dalmatia; a separate Croatian state, inevitably much smaller and weaker than Yugoslavia, would also suit her book very well.

This is the background of the tragedy that unfolded in Marseilles upon the landing of King Alexander in that city in October. In the tradition of 1914 Sarajevo, some Croatian malcontents shot both King Alexander and Barthou while they were driving through the city. To lay the responsibility for the deed directly at the door of either Hungary or Italy would be an oversimplification and an overstatement; it was enough, however, that both countries, in particular Italy which here is our chief concern, were willing to aid and abet such methods of diplomacy in the selfish hope of national advantage. Such things were at once a reflection and a cause of the condition of the international scene in the middle thirties.

The assassination was an international incident of magnitude, and matters were very tense for a time, especially between Yugoslavia and Hungary. The influence of the western powers and of the League was thrown, however, on the side of pacification, and the event might conceivably have been reduced to the proportions of an incident leaving behind it nothing worse than a trail of increased distrust and animosity. But, as it happened, the episode was but one move in the unfolding of a situation which, in retrospect, takes on the appearance of Greek tragedy controlled by blind fate. In some respects, the French reaction was the most interesting and perhaps also the most crucial. Barthou's successor at the Quai d'Orsay was Laval. Laval was able, shrewd, and intelligent, though a man of no convictions. He favored a policy which may be described as plausible from the national point of view, albeit colored by his predilections. Forever dominated by fear for her security, France was now pursuing a policy aimed not only at bolstering the existing alliances but at widening their circle; she was aiming to bring both Russia and Italy in her camp. Laval himself made the connection with Russia, but he personally was rather more interested in Italy. Little concerned as he was with ideologies, Fascism did not arouse any dislike in him; in fact, if a choice were to be made, he could find many virtues in that system, as later events were to prove. We must eschew at this point the temptation to digress into a consideration of the fundamenal weakness that lurks behind the apparent strength derived from having too many friends and allies, some of whom entertain irreconcilable antagonisms among themselves.

At any rate, Laval was set upon a policy of friendship with Italy. For this he had a case to the extent that there was no virtue in a French policy of minor irritations and pinpricks toward Italy. This pro-Italian orientation of French policy served to smooth over what might have been serious differences over the assassination of Alexander and Barthou and the subsequent trial in France of some of the accomplices. We arrive here at a crucial turning point, for it is this new orientation of French policy that helped Italy embark in turn on a policy that was thoroughly irresponsible and reckless. Because of the importance of the conclusion of a Franco-Italian agreement in January, 1935, which initiated a whole train of events, of which the general outbreak of war in 1939 was but the logical end point, and also because this series of events had their beginning in the colonial field, consideration of them must be deferred to the next chapter; and we must pause a while to throw a backward glance at the colonial record of Italy as it was up to 1935, when Mussolini's imperial dreams of grandeur caused him to lose whatever sense of proportion he had so far retained and to embark upon the adventure that was to lead the world to disaster, Italy to her subsequent sorry pass, and himself to a fittingly ignominious end.

THE COLONIAL RECORD OF ITALY (*to 1935*)

The Keys to the Mediterranean are in the Red Sea—(Mancini, 1882)

During the years immediately following the completion of German and Italian unification, most of the major European powers were largely absorbed with the twin problems of internal reorganization and of finding their place in the new system of power relationships which the emergence of Germany and Italy and the events attending this emergence had created. Bismarck's Germany, arbiter of the Continent, was in the eyes of its maker a satiated power; Bismarck, never averse to the use of war as an instrument of national policy, saw nothing to be gained by further adventures and threw the weight of his influence and diplomatic skill on the side of the preservation of peace. He was content to further the moral consolidation of the unit he had welded politically and to let its energies flow into the peaceful channels of industrial progress. Austria-Hungary, excluded from influence in her traditional spheres of primary interest, the Germanic Confederation (outside of Austria proper) and the Italian peninsula, had to reorganize herself into the Dual Monarchy, and it was some time before this exclusion was to reflect itself in a renewed and increased interest toward the southeast, in the Balkans. France, defeated likewise, did not know with assurance for the better part of a decade whether she would be a Republic or a Monarchy; this major internal problem, plus the bad aftertaste of ill-starred Napoleonic adventures, made her foreign policy an essentially timid and negative one.

In this political climate Italy was no exception. It has been indicated earlier how difficult and serious her internal problems were, largely because of historic background and paucity of resources. Unlike Germany, she did not command great power; she was in fact definitely at the bottom of the list of so-called great powers. Unlike Germany also, she did not undergo an enormously large and rapid industrial expansion. And, as a consequence, unlike Germany, she was not a leader and initiator of international policies, but rather a follower of others. She cut her coat to suit her cloth and on the whole with shrewdness and wisdom adhered to certain broad and sound fundamental principles: never to be an enemy of Britain; associating with the dominant group so long as the Bismarckian structure held together; adopting an ambiguous fence-sitting position, when that system passed and was replaced by a more even balance. Simultaneously with the Anglo-French rapprochement we find Italy also flirting with France. Her policy in fact may be described as a sensitive weather vane, accurately reflecting the shifting currents of the power relationships of Europe.

The quiescent period of internal reorganization that followed 1870 came to an end within about ten years. It was to take much longer before the tensions among the powers reached a danger point, but the eighties witnessed the beginning of activity in one of the fields where these tensions were to become most acute, and that is the imperial field. Russian imperialism was the first to clash with British and Austrian in this period, in the late seventies, over that perennial and to this day unresolved issue, the control of the Straits, and the related one of influence in the Balkans. But the Third Republic also, still playing an insignificant role at the Congress of Berlin, soon thereafter embarked upon a new career of empire building. Even Bismarck, initially opposed to colonial adventures, was forced in the middle eighties to yield to the pressure that led Germany to enter the field.

For the sake of historic completeness one may trace the beginnings of Italian imperialism to an earlier period, in fact to a time shortly preceding Cavour's final drive for unification. But these early beginnings are relatively unimportant, save as indications of the locale to which later activity was to be directed. The search for remote penal colonies would hardly furnish the bases of real empire. The economic motivation, always a prime factor in imperial expansion, was relatively weak in Italy, whose industry was progressing in respectable but not sensational fashion. Of greater importance than the search for raw materials and markets was the need of emigration. As early as 1871, a population of 27,000,000 was a strain on the resources of the peninsula, and the consistently high Italian birth rate continued to keep the problem to the fore. The export of human material as labor and the reverse flow of emigrant remittances from abroad were to become increasingly significant items in the balance of Italian economy. There was finally the imponderable of power and prestige, since Italy was now acknowledged a great power. On this level, she would encounter the similar motivation of the other powers.

This is the framework within which Italian imperialism was to operate and which was to condition its activity and the results of this activity. To repeat once again, Italy is first and foremost a Mediterranean power, and if she were to develop colonial interests she might naturally be expected to look first for available sites on the shores of that sea. The chief focus of power rivalry in the Mediterranean was the decaying Ottoman Empire. The fate of the sick man of Europe had for a long time been the concern of four powers: Britain, Russia, the Habsburg monarchy, and France. The new Germany did not consider herself directly involved in this problem at this time and the medieval Italian primacy in Near Eastern trade had long been superseded in that area by other interests, both economic and political. The Balkan region, though European and like Europe at this time deeply affected by the force of nationalism, was also a typical scene of imperial power rivalry. It is an accurate measure of the range of Italian interests and of the degree of Italian power that the important events unfolding in that region which had their climax at the Congress of Berlin left Italy unmoved, or at least unwilling to assert herself. At Berlin it was Disraeli, backed by the Austrians, who blocked Russian progress in the Balkans. Bismarck, though opting for Austria if driven to an unwelcome choice, tried to be no more than the "honest broker." France, still uncertain, was little more than an observer at Berlin whence Italy returned with hands that were clean, but also empty, as was appropriately observed shortly after the Congress.

The Berlin gathering, first meeting of the readjusted European Concert, was a good indication of the relationship of power that the events of 1870 had produced. It is all the more enlightening to contemplate the change that came about within ten years of the gathering. At the first renewal of the Triple Alliance, in 1887, Italy obtained the insertion in the separate treaty with Austria-Hungary of the all-important article which recognized her equal interest in Balkan affairs; good indication of greater assurance on her part and of the greater importance attributed to her by others. But the Balkans, though a prime example of the interplay of imperial rivalry, were too close to the home territory to fall, for Italy, in the realm of what is usually considered colonial. Her activity in this region has been discussed before.

North Africa was a better field for purely colonial expansion. A large sector of it was still, though little more than in name, connected with the Porte. When Italy appeared upon the scene as a political unit, France was already well established in Algeria. But neighboring Tunisia and Tripoli were still functioning under distant Turkish suzerainty and local maladministration, while, on the other side of Algeria, Morocco was a primitive and backward but still independent state. In Tunis, Italy had commercial interests and a population of some size; the country had come to be looked upon by many Italians as a natural extension of the peninsula, under whose sway it was destined some day to fall. And it is again a measure of the negativeness of Italy's policy in the years following Berlin that she let an opportunity slip, thus enabling France to reach Tunis first, in 1881. The reaction of surprise, frustration, and anger was one of the factors (though by no means the only one) that made Italy court the favor of the Austro-German allies and produced the Triple Alliance in the following year.

There was also a flourishing Italian colony in Egypt, but, from the beginning of the century, that other nominal dependency of the Sultan had been mainly the object of French and British interest. The year 1869 had seen the opening of the Suez Canal, an event of capital importance to the Mediterranean world, for it reversed a situation which

went back to the coming of the Ottoman Turks and the great outburst
of expanding European energy of the fifteenth and sixteenth centuries.
Despite early difficulties and the skepticism of many as to the soundness
of the enterprise, the Canal soon proved to be a great economic success,
surpassing the fondest hopes of its builders. The Canal was a French
undertaking, but the country for which it had greatest significance was
Britain. When the successors of the able Mehemet Ali proceeded to go
the way of all despots and Egypt found herself as a result oppressed and
malgoverned by her rulers, and in serious financial difficulties in addition, there came to be established, in the late seventies, a dual control
over that country's finances by the powers most concerned, Britain and
France. It was not long before this arrangement led to further intervention; in 1882 Britain established a virtual protectorate (the name was
not formally used until 1914) over Egypt. Gladstone could see no other
course, though he was reluctant to adopt it, and he sought to associate
France in the enterprise; but he met in that country the same negative
reply as in Italy when she in turn was approached by Britain with the
same end of cooperation in view.

By 1882, then, if Italy was thinking about colonies, her thinking was
still largely in the realm of speculation. But the scramble for Africa was
about to get under way; by 1885 it had made sufficient progress to warrant the holding of a colonial conference in Berlin in that year. Having
let slip the Tunisian and Egyptian possibilities, Italy was to wait another
thirty years before embarking on a colonial program in the Mediterranean proper. In the meantime, however, she was to adopt for a time
the policy which Mancini characterized with his ill-fated phrase, "the
keys to the Mediterranean are in the Red Sea."

Scraps of Empire: Italy in East Africa.—In 1949, East Africa may
truly be described as the grave of Italian imperial hopes and the breed-
ing ground of domestic disaster. But, in view of the activity of other
powers in other sections of Africa and of earlier Italian interests, East
Africa was a logical place for Italy to turn to, if we except the Mediterranean proper. The year 1882 may be said to mark the formal beginning
of Italian colonial enterprise, when the state took over the small region
around Assab on the Red Sea where the Rubattino navigation company
had secured a concession from the local sultan as early as 1869. Mancini's

above-cited phrase was, however, a complete misrepresentation of the situation, for there was in Italy at the time very little interest in matters colonial and nothing comparable to the interests and groups that were pushing Britain, France, and Germany on the path of imperial expansion. In 1885, however, Italy established herself in Massowa, farther up the Red Sea coast from Assab, thereby laying the foundations of what was to become the Eritrean colony.

These small colonial beginnings brought Italy into contact with two local powers and two European ones. Massowa was claimed by Egypt which, during the earlier part of the century, had gradually extended her influence southward in the region of nebulous Ottoman control. But, by 1885, Britain was deeply committed in Egypt and was becoming increasingly involved in the Sudan. From 1885 to the end of the century, when the situation was crystallized in this whole region, there were many dealings between Italy and Britain over the points where their interests came into contact.

Pushing inland from Massowa on the coast, Italian influence touched upon Abyssinia in the Tigrine uplands. The vast region that goes under the name of Abyssinia could scarcely be dignified by the name of state, not at least in the nineteenth century European sense of the term. Although it had an ancient history, it had never progressed beyond a political stage of development which, again by European standards, may be described as medieval. The core of what organization it had lay in the dominance of the Amharic tribes over a congeries of peoples and races, some of them in a still quite primitive stage of development. Its economic development was on a par with the political. Italy soon began to play a part in the local politics of the land, feuds among semi-independent tribal chieftains and between them and the central power. In 1886 she was instrumental in the accession to the throne of Menelik II, from whom, as a consequence, she expected the maintenance of friendly relations and the acceptance of a measure of tutelage.

France was the other European power with East African interests. The small establishment centering around Jibuti, at the entrance to the Red Sea, dating back to the days of the Second Empire, had greater importance than its diminutive size would seem to indicate, and the subsequent construction of a railway connecting it to the Abyssinian capital of Addis Abeba gave France an important stake, economic and political, in the country. French Somaliland was also a base from which French influence, radiating westward, might some day meet the eastward extension of this same influence pushing from the opposite side of Africa. The French dream of an east-to-west African empire was destined to be crushed at Fashoda, in 1898, where it collided with the similar British scheme symbolized by the Cape-to-Cairo project. But the French interest in East Africa, if diminished, remained, and we come to a situation where the fate of Abyssinia was the concern of three European powers: Britain, France, and Italy. In broad and simplified terms, the story of the relations between those three powers in that quarter of the world is one of Anglo-Italian cooperation and of Franco-Italian antagonism.

In 1887, Crispi succeeded Depretis in the Premiership of Italy upon the latter's death. Whatever else may be said of Crispi, a highly controversial figure, no one has ever accused him of lack of vigor, a vigor which he was to manifest in the colonial field as in other aspects of his administration which he unquestionably dominated. Crispi was also given to large dreams—or visions—and may be said to have been the first among Italian statesmen to have held the large conception of a substantial empire. It meant no less than what was realized in 1936, the absorption of Abyssinia and the surrounding coastlands from Ras Casar on the Red Sea to the Juba River debouching in the Indian Ocean. Two important steps toward the realization of this program were taken in 1889. Various treaties with local rulers laid the basis of the colony of Italian Somaliland, fronting on the Indian Ocean between British Somaliland and British Kenya and touching in the hinterland upon the ill-defined limits of Abyssinian control. The other, and more important, step was the signature of the since much-debated Treaty of Uccialli with the Negus Menelik. The crux of this treaty, and the source of the subsequent controversy, was a clause which could be interpreted as giving Italy a supervisory role in the foreign relations of Abyssinia, hence would be tantamount to the acceptance of an Italian protectorate.

Britain at this time was involved in the Sudan and concerned with the French rivalry. She had looked with a kindly eye upon the extension of Italian influence in the Red Sea and had encouraged the expedition to

Massowa in 1885, when she was suffering setbacks at the hands of the Mahdi. In March and April, 1891, there were concluded between Britain and Italy agreements which delimited the boundaries of Abyssinia and of their own possessions in the territory surrounding that country. Crispi was out of office for the next two years, as the result of some of the less savory manifestations of Italian domestic politics, but resumed the Premiership again in 1893. Further agreements with Britain in the following year completed those of 1891. These agreements, together with the Treaty of Uccialli, form part of a consistent whole, a policy whose outcome would have been, with British acquiescence, the creation of Crispi's African empire. But Abyssinia, instead of being amenable, proved recalcitrant to the Italian interpretation of the Treaty of Uccialli, and the consequent dispute led to an open clash, as the result of which Italy conquered and annexed the whole province of Tigre. The campaign of 1894–95 proved to be but a preliminary skirmish, however, and things went very differently in 1896. In March of that year the Italian forces met complete disaster at the hands of the Abyssinians at Adowa. In Italy, humiliation and anger turned upon Crispi, whose political career came to an end as the result of Adowa; instead of seeking revenge, Crispi's successor came to terms with Menelik. The Treaty of Addis Abeba, in October, 1896, superseded that of Uccialli and Italy emerged from the episode embittered but on the whole resigned to the vanishing of a temporary dream. It was another forty years before the project of an East African empire was to be taken up again in earnest and for a brief moment realized. After 1896, Italy did not abandon East Africa but was content to maintain herself in the two colonies of Eritrea and Somaliland. By themselves, these two discrete pieces of territory were of little interest or value. Largely desert, situated in some of the earth's least attractive regions, devoid of resources of any consequence, certainly of no use for purposes of emigration, they served to justify the quip which has described Italian colonial activity as the collecting of deserts.

The true reasons for the failure of 1896 must be sought at home rather than in the local military situation. There is little doubt that Italy had the physical power to overwhelm Abyssinia in the end, had she been determined to do so. But, unlike Britain who, just a few years later, found that she had miscalculated the difficulty of defeating the Boers but reacted with the determination to see the thing through to a successful conclusion—and in the end did so—Italy lacked the will to make the necessary effort. And this lack of will was in itself a measure of Italy's standing among the powers, for it was in the last analysis merely a reflection of the fact that the Italian nation, still largely wrapped up in the problems of internal existence and organization, lacked the reserves of resources and energy which would have been necessary for the pursuit of a successful colonial policy. Crispi's large vision of empire was too personal a policy, lacking any substantial basis of support at home, where it did not command any great degree of interest. There was no adequate support, financial or otherwise, coming from the Italian Parliament, with the result that the whole enterprise was undertaken without understanding or resources commensurate with the risks. Crispi could be a rash man. The first real setback produced a belated awakening to what had been going on, some rather undignified recriminations, the fall of Crispi, and abandonment of the attempt.

The events of 1896 inevitably superseded in large part the Anglo-Italian agreements of 1891 and 1894, which retained little value other than that of historic record of one-time Italian interest which might or might not be resumed; and the following year saw, as mentioned before, a crystallization of the status of Abyssinia and the surrounding territories. Thus, Kassala, occupied by Italy in 1894 upon British urging, was evacuated in 1897 and formally joined to the Sudan in 1901. From 1900 to 1904 Britain, France, and Italy came to far-reaching understandings covering the whole of North Africa from the Nile to the Atlantic. Abyssinia had survived the Italian effort at subjection; neither France nor Britain had any desire to establish political control over her. The result of this interplay of forces was the conclusion among those three powers of the tripartite agreement of 1906 which defined the status of Abyssinia. The agreement professed a desire to maintain Abyssinian integrity, but went on to enumerate and specify the respective interests of the three powers in the event that this should prove impossible. Britain was mainly interested in the water supply of the Nile, one of whose branches, the Blue Nile, rises in Lake Tsana; France's main concern was in the Jibuti–Addis Abeba railway. Of chief interest here is the definition of the Italian stake which took the form of establishing a territorial connection between the two existing Italian possessions of Eritrea and Somaliland. In order to accomplish this, three zones were delimited: a hinterland of Eritrea centering around Lake Tsana, between the Blue Nile and the Eritrean border; a hinterland of Italian Somaliland between that colony, British Somaliland, and the French Jibuti–Addis Abeba railway; a connecting zone, joining the other two but excluding the capital.

Up to a point, therefore, Italy did manage to safeguard her future interests and we shall see what the significance of this precedent was to be during the First World War and later. But, before that, we must return to the Mediterranean where the next manifestation of her colonial activity was to take place.

Italy in North Africa: More Deserts Acquired.—Just as in 1906 Italy safeguarded the future in East Africa, so likewise, after the Tunisian disappointment, she had safeguarded the future in North Africa. Tripoli and Morocco were, after 1882, the two non-preempted Mediterranean areas of the African continent. The Triple Alliance was a source of some disappointment to Italy, who had thought of deriving from it support for her colonial ambitions. But this was precisely what Bismarck did not want the alliance to be used for; he, unlike Britain, had not seen with satisfaction the Italian occupation of Massowa, and when the treaty came up for renewal in 1887 he was at first very cool to the prospect. But the general state of the European situation enhanced the value of Italy and caused him to change his mind. The advantages which Italy obtained in 1887, particularly in the Balkan clauses of the Austrian treaty have been discussed. The separate treaty of 1887 with Germany also gained for Italy German acquiescence and support for her eventual acquisition of Tripoli. Crispi took office shortly after the renewal of the alliance, and it fell to him to renew it once more in 1891. His subsequent failure in East Africa was followed by a period of retrenchment, but it had also the effect of making possible better relations with France. These relations had been very bad so long as Crispi's suspicions of that country, fully reciprocated as they were, had presided over Italian foreign policy. The standing quarrel over Tunis was largely composed in 1896, after Crispi's fall, and, with the changing position of Germany after Bismarck's dismissal, Italian policy under Crispi's successors began to take on a very different orientation. Relations with France continued to improve and, following the pattern laid down between France and Britain, as early as 1900 Italy and France achieved a *quid pro quo* whose terms were Tripoli and Morocco.

We have spoken in an earlier chapter of the revived nationalism which made its appearance in Italy during the first decade of the century. Nationalism and imperialism were everywhere closely allied in this period and it was inevitable that Italy's nationalists, impressed with the greatness of their country's past and desirous to revive in some measure this greatness, should want her to play a more important and assertive role, not only in the councils of Europe, but in the imperial domain as well. These nationalists were not very numerous, but there were among them able men, so that the degree of their influence far exceeded the proportion of their numbers, affecting the intellectual and middle classes in the main and thus creating a new climate of opinion in the country.

During this same period, the government was presided over, either overtly or from behind the scenes, by Giolitti. Giolitti, all sanity and coolness, was in this respect the very antithesis of the mercurial Crispi, anything but a rash and bellicose imperialist. His chief concern was the domestic scene, but he owed his retention of power in large measure to his keen sensitivity to political trends. He was well aware of the new temper of the times and felt fully able to keep under control the new nationalism as well as the growing power of the Socialists. By 1909, the Racconigi agreement which secured Russian support for Italian ambitions in Tripoli in exchange for a corresponding promise of Italian support for Russian designs on the Straits—should suitable circumstances arise —was for Italy the culmination of a slow and careful policy, which consisted in obtaining from all the major powers the endorsement of a blank cheque for Tripoli. Russia's endorsement completed the list and, with his usual deliberateness, Giolitti, always with an eye on the home situation, shortly thereafter decided that the time had come to collect on the cheque.

The vilayets of Tripoli and Cyrenaica did not present a very attractive temptation from the economic point of view. If, like other territories under the suzerainty of the Porte, they had declined as a consequence of unprogressive Ottoman rule, they could not, under the best of administrations, provide the basis for important development. For, with the exception of some sections on the coastal fringe, they were nothing but a vast desert stretching indefinitely into the heart of Africa. The population, only about one million, was a fair indication of the possibilities of the region. It has somewhat greater significance, however, in terms of prestige and strategy. Situated as Tripoli is directly to the south of Italy across the Mediterranean, between British Egypt and French Tunisia, it unquestionably would have been a blow to Italian prestige had either of these neighboring powers established itself there; had this happened, it would also have been a severe setback to Italy's standing as a Mediterranean power. The reasons for going to Tripoli were, to a considerable degree, negative, but none the less compelling. Italy's diplomatic preparations in the form of securing the consent of all the powers with possible interests in Tripoli had been slow, careful, and thorough.

Reasons for going to war with Turkey in 1911 there were really none, but such a consideration must be acknowledged essentially extraneous —certainly at the time—and pretexts could always be found. Italian imperialism merely followed in this respect the well-established pattern of the British, French, and German, that of any major power in fact. So Italy went to war with Turkey in 1911 and proceeded to land an expedition in Tripoli and at various points along the coast. The course of military operations need not detain us. Like many another colonial adventure, Italy's own in Abyssinia for example, this one proved to have been based on an underestimate of the difficulties to be overcome. But there was no Adowa in this case; Giolitti was a more careful and tenacious man than Crispi, and the adventure also commanded far greater support and interest at home than had earlier colonial attempts. It could therefore be seen through to a successful conclusion. Annexation of the territory was proclaimed by Royal Italian decree in 1912 and Turkey eventually bowed to the inevitable. Libya, as it came to be known, was another desert in the Italian collection, certainly no source of wealth for its new rulers, and the source of sad disappointment to those rash enthusiasts in Italy who had thought of it in terms of setting up there a flourishing establishment whither Italian settlers would flock.

It should be mentioned that, despite the fact that all the powers had acquiesced in advance in the Italian taking of possession, the Italo-Turkish war was not popular with any of them, least of all with Italy's formal allies, Germany and Austria-Hungary. In this respect the Italian undertaking, small as it was, had far greater repercussions than did the much larger adventure of Britain's Boer war some ten years earlier. This was due to the deterioration of the international situation which had occurred during the interval. By 1911 Europe was an armed camp precariously poised on the rim of a powder barrel; in the pervading atmosphere of suspicion, the powers, for the most part disinclined to war, were fearful of any additional disturbance. The whole affair was particularly unwelcome to Italy's allies, intent at the time upon an effort to establish their influence in Turkey. Austria-Hungary in fact exerted her influence and appealed to the clauses of the alliance to restrain Italian action toward the Straits, a gesture hardly calculated to cement the already loosening bonds of the alliance. And Italy in turn, while willing to confine her operations to Libya, made use of this very anxiety of the powers lest she should carry hostilities to the Straits, to induce them to exert pressure on the Porte to accept Italy's terms as the easiest and quickest way to liquidate the disturbing episode. If this was skillful use of diplomatic weapons on Italy's part, it was also willingness to play with fire. One should not overstate Italy's share of responsibility in the immediate chain of events that led to Sarajevo, for there were other and more important factors; but there is no denying that a connection exists between the Tripolitan War, the difficulties it brought to Turkey, and the decision of the Balkan allies that 1912 was an opportune time to drive the Turks out of their peninsula. The powers succeeded in circumscribing the Balkan conflagration of 1912-13, but the successes of the Balkan countries were unquestionably a fillip to their aggressive nationalisms.

Also, as a by-product of the Italo-Turkish conflict, Italy found herself in occupation of the Dodecanese islands off the coast of Asia Minor. The occupation was supposed to be temporary, a mere token of fulfillment of the terms of the Treaty of Lausanne which put an end to the war. Ethnically the Dodecanese islands are Greek—the Italian occupation, as a relief from Turkish rule was, at first, not unwelcome—economically they are of no particular consequence. The move was nevertheless significant for two reasons: the whole importance of the islands is strategic, and the occupation of this base coincided with the adoption of a policy of economic penetration in Asia Minor, the fruits of which were soon to appear. Following in this respect also the example of other powers, Italy obtained from Turkey concessions for the building of railways in southern Anatolia.

On the eve of the First World War Italy therefore stood in possession of three colonies: Eritrea, Somaliland, and Libya, the last still in process of definition and organization. None of them was of any economic importance and Italy ranked low on the list of colonial powers. Was her last effort in the colonial field the starting point of a new and vigorous policy of expansion, or the picking up of a crumb, or an essentially negative gesture dictated by the necessity of avoiding the loss of standing which the presence of anyone else in Libya would have meant?

Italian Colonial Policy during the First World War.—When general war broke out in the summer of 1914 discussions had been going on between Rome and London in regard to the interpretation of the agreements dealing with East Africa. The explosion in Europe was bound to supersede and push into the background such relatively secondary matters. Italy remained neutral in 1914, thereby gaining time to appraise the situation with coolness and deliberation until she threw in her lot with the Allies in May, 1915. The Marquis di san Giuliano, who presided at the Foreign Office in 1914, died in the autumn of that year; he was succeeded, after a brief interim, by Baron Sonnino. Sonnino remained continuously in charge of foreign affairs from November, 1914, to June, 1919. This long tenure served to give Italian foreign policy a considerable degree of continuity and consistency during the war years and at the peacemaking that followed. This policy, in so far as it affected Italy's position in Europe, has already been discussed and we merely wish to consider here its purely colonial aspects.

Colonial policy in Italy had long been a mere subsidiary of the Foreign Office, a fact which in itself was a measure of its relative importance, and it was not until the Tripolitan War that a separate Ministry of Colonies was created. It is therefore perhaps not very surprising that the colonial ministry should play a wholly subordinate role to the *Consulta* during the war, and it is one of the most interesting aspects of the situation that the colonial program formulated by Martini and Colosimo, the successive holders of the colonial office during Sonnino's tenure, should have been totally ignored by the latter. For Sonnino had his own colonial policy—such as it was.

The Treaty of London of April, 1915, which set down the conditions of Italy's intervention and the advantages that were to accrue to her in the hoped-for event of Allied victory was Sonnino's own masterwork. That instrument, as indicated earlier, was very clear and precise in defining the new frontiers of Italy, but its colonial provisions were of an entirely different character. Italy had colonial interests in two sectors, Asia Minor and Africa. Article 9 of the treaty, which covered the first of these, stated in part:

> Generally speaking, France, Great Britain and Russia recognize that Italy is interested in the maintenance of the balance of power in the Mediterranean and that, in the event of the total or partial partition of Turkey in Asia, she ought to obtain *a just share of the Mediterranean region adjacent to the province of Adalia.* . . . The zone which shall eventually be allotted to Italy shall be delimited, at the proper time, due account being taken of the existing interests of France and Great Britain. (Italics added.)

As a complement to this, Article 8 provided that the temporarily occupied Dodecanese islands should pass under full Italian sovereignty. African interests were dealt with in Article 13, the tenor of which is even more imprecise than that of Article 9. It read as follows:

> In the event of France and Great Britain increasing their colonial territories in Africa at the expense of Germany, these two Powers agree *in principle* that Italy *may claim some equitable compensation,* particularly as regards the settlement in her favor of *the question relative to the frontier* of the Italian colonies of Eritrea, Somaliland and Libya and the neighboring colonies belonging to France and Great Britain. (Italics added.)

From these provisions one can only draw the conclusion that Sonnino attached but secondary importance to colonial questions in general and that in that field his interest was primarily directed toward Asia Minor rather than Africa. It was inevitable and proper that Europe should have primacy in his outlook and, especially in view of his reputation as a hard bargainer; the vague statement of colonial claims may be judged the best that he could obtain in the circumstances, favorable as these were to Italy at the time. Sonnino had a very sane and conservative estimate of the relationship of power. It should be added that, apparently, during the negotiation of the Treaty of London, the question of French Somaliland was mentioned—whether on Italian or French initiative is not quite certain—but France made it clear that she would not entertain any discussion of that particular subject.

If Sonnino concentrated his attention on the European aspects of the settlement, he was not wholly oblivious to the possibilities of colonial expansion. Apparently little interested in Africa, he put his entire effort into obtaining a clearer definition of the promises contained in Article 9. His task was not easy, for his allies felt that, even as things stood in the Treaty of London, Italy had driven a hard bargain and taken advantage of their plight. Unknown to Italy, they proceeded to define their respective zones of interest (British, French, and Russian) in Asia Minor, and it was not until 1917, after much insistence and pressure, that Sonnino managed to extract from them, first, information about the nature of these agreements, and secondly, a clear definition of the Italian share. His persistent efforts were well rewarded, for in the St. Jean de Maurienne agreement of April, 1917, Italy's portion was delimited to cover roughly the southern half of Anatolia including its most important port, Smyrna.

From the two instruments discussed, the Treaty of London and the agreement of St. Jean de Maurienne, it appears that Sonnino had a perfectly definite colonial policy which he held, however, wholly subordinate to the defense of Italian interests in Europe. In the context of the time, his policy was sound and, considering the difficulties with which he had to deal, he may be said to have made a definitely favorable bargain for his country. The degree to which the policy he pursued was his own is all the more apparent when we consider that there was in Italy another and quite different colonial policy, the policy of what may be called the colonial party represented by the holders of the colonial ministry and their followers in the country. And even though that policy had little influence in the days of Sonnino, it is worth indicating briefly its main outlines because it represents a continuity of development in Italian colonial thought—especially when taken in conjunction with the events of the Crispine period—and because Fascism was to make that policy its own in 1935.

As early as November, 1914, before Italy had entered the war but with an eye on the possibility that she might do so, the Colonial Minister, Martini, had had drawn up a thoroughgoing survey of Italian colonial interests. The documentation was passed on to Sonnino, leaving him "to decide what use may or should be made" of it at the time. The survey took the form of eight separate memoranda, the mere enumeration of which is enlightening, for their titles were: Jibuti, Kismayu, Lake Tsana, Arabia (Yemen), Kassala, Jarabub, Portuguese colonies, and Ethiopia. Taken together, these memoranda were evidence of a well thought-out and coordinated plan of action. The last memorandum, which incidentally had been drawn up as early as August, 1913, was by far the longest and most important, and we observe that five of the remaining seven dealt with related phases of the same central subject. The policy advocated consisted first in eliminating French influence through the acquisition of Jibuti, then in dealing with Britain alone. The prospect of Anglo-Italian agreement *to the exclusion of third parties* is stressed repeatedly, and the central idea of the scheme was to go back to the situation of 1891 and 1894 and from that basis proceed to the implementation of the possibilities outlined in the tripartite agreement of 1906; in brief, to establish a predominant and exclusively Italian influence as a stepping stone to the creation of an East African empire. Though well conceived in detail and organization, the plan had many weaknesses from the political and juridical points of view, and it is not surprising that it was merely pigeonholed at the time and that no trace of its influence appeared in the Treaty of London—save in the possible mention of Jibuti in 1915 previously referred to.

There seems to have been remarkably little coordination between the Foreign and Colonial Offices for, while Sonnino was pursuing the policy which has been described, the Colonial Minister proceeded along wholly divergent lines. In 1916, the Minister of Colonies, Colosimo, returned to the charge with a scheme consisting of two alternatives which he described as maximum and minimum programs respectively. The maximum program was an ambitious one. It embodied the same features of the program of 1914 for East Africa and, somewhat casuistically, sought to present the Italian case as a claim for mere restoration rather than a plea for expansion. In addition, Libya was to be vastly enlarged to reach Lake Chad in the south, thereby severing the French possessions in North and West Africa from those in Equatorial Africa. But Colosimo was evidently not very sanguine about the likelihood of realizing the dream of the more extravagant Italian colonialists, and his alternative minimum program was far more moderate. It was content with some substantial frontier rectifications for Libya—interestingly enough, the boundaries of 1935 for that colony—and some likewise minor extensions of the existing Italian holdings in East Africa. The most significant feature was the renewed attempt to eliminate French influence through the demand for French Somaliland. Some rather fanciful statistics accompanied Colosimo's brief.

But Sonnino's mind was made up; despite repeated urgings and even attempts to interest Prime Minister Orlando directly, in these projects, the only use Sonnino saw fit to make of the data and pleas sent him by his colonial colleague was to ignore them. Sonnino had a deserved reputation for rectitude and set great store by his signature—and that of others. The narrowness of his outlook completely blinded him to the different character which the war had assumed by the time it drew to a close. The disastrous consequences for Italy of his unbending legalistic approach in combination with Orlando's weakness (that made the latter resort to opportunistic expediency) have been described in a previous chapter. The threat to the Italian position in Europe in 1919 served to emphasize how secondary her colonial interests were, for, at the peacemaking, she gave virtually no sign of having any colonial policy at all, despite the loud outcries of some individual enthusiasts at home.

In 1919, Orlando having once made the very proper statement that Italy had an equal claim with others to the benefits—or burdens—of mandates, the virtual disposition of these mandates during her absence from Paris over the Fiume crisis was allowed by her to pass unprotested. More serious than the failure to share in the distribution of mandates, Asia Minor—the very keystone of Sonnino's colonial policy—was also threatened. For the Allies impugned the validity of the St. Jean de Maurienne agreement on the rather specious plea that it was subject to Russian ratification, a ratification which had never been given, as a

Essays in Power

result of the Russian Revolution. In the end Italy did secure a zone in Asia Minor roughly similar to what Sonnino had originally obtained, but with the important qualification that Smyrna was detached from it. The wily Venizelos—who proved to have overreached himself in the end—secured the city for Greece instead.

But if one could quibble about the validity of the St. Jean de Maurienne agreement, the same argument could certainly not apply to the Treaty of London. A special committee of Great Britain, France, and Italy was therefore set up to examine the implementation of Article 13 of that treaty. The committee held a few meetings in May and June, at a time and in circumstances which could hardly have been less auspicious for the Italian case. Personal feelings were such among the Allied representatives that Sonnino preferred not to sit on the committee and delegated Crespi to take his place. Crespi was a convinced imperialist. He presented two demands on behalf of his country: 1) a rectification of the frontiers of Libya to the west and to the east; 2) the acquisition of British and French Somaliland and of the railway to Addis Abeba. As an alternative to the second request, Italy would accept a mandate for Togoland. The committee was unable to provide a solution satisfactory to all parties and adjourned after drawing up a statement of the respective positions of its members. This statement is of interest as an indication of the continuity of Italian imperial policy, however weak that policy may have been at the time and however poorly integrated in the general scheme of her whole foreign policy.

For the final report of the Committee on Article 13 stated that Italy accepted the British offer of frontier rectification for Libya and of the cession of Jubaland with Kismayu. This was the only point of agreement. Britain and France declined to consider the cession of their respective Somalilands and argued that the issue of mandates was closed and was not within the competence of the committee. France maintained the offer she had made of frontier rectifications for Libya; but Italy, considering the French offer inadequate, preferred not to accept it and to leave the issue unresolved. It was destined to remain so until 1935, despite the fact that an agreement of September, 1919, gave Italy the territory that she had demanded for Libya in the west.

This niggardly policy of Italy's allies has often been criticized, both in and outside Italy, and it has been argued that Italy should have received a mandate, such as Togoland, for example. The criticism is warranted, but it would be illusory to believe that the granting of a mandate to Italy would have made any essential difference in her position. The Italian grievance over colonies was but one, and a relatively small one at that. The cavalier treatment of Italy at the hands of her allies and associates in 1919 was no doubt a useful talking point at home and a convenient focus of recriminations; but the fundamental difficulty and the most real (though not avowed) source of Italy's disgruntlement was the fact that the outcome of the war had destroyed the European balance which her diplomacy had exploited hitherto with skill. It was not within the power of the Allies to alter this condition and, even had they been generous to Italy, it is difficult to see how she could have been really satisfied with the new relationship of power that the war had established—not unless she should radically alter the traditional direction of her foreign policy, or unless the new League of Nations had commanded such genuine and wholehearted acceptance by all as to supersede the need for power politics in the future.

At the same time there is no denying that Italy felt genuinely aggrieved at her treatment in 1919. The settlement of 1919 as between the Allies represented fairly accurately the relative measure of their power, in the colonial as well as in the European field. The most remarkable aspect of Italian colonial policy at the time was its negativeness, one might almost say the apparent absence of such a policy, in the obsession over such a relatively small trifle as Fiume. That such a thing should happen was not only an indication of poor statesmanship on the Italian side, but a good criterion in itself of the relative degree of Italian power.

As between the two dominant powers of Europe after the war, Britain and France, we find Italy chiefly at odds with the latter. Franco-Italian differences were no novelty, and they were destined to grow deeper with the passage of time. For these differences there are many reasons, but certainly one of them is to be found in power. The cardinal principle of Italian policy that there must never be open conflict with Britain was, in the last analysis, based on respect and fear of British power. But French power, if considerable, was less solid, especially in view of the deep injury which the war had caused to France. It might be more promising to seek concessions from that power, especially if it could be isolated from the British connection, and even better if British sympathy could be enlisted on the Italian side. In the colonial sector, Italy accepted the British offer but preferred to keep the question open with France; and in general if Italy was friendless in 1919, the Latin sister was the particular butt of recriminations. And conversely, on the French side, the deep-rooted feeling of insecurity and weakness which victory did not dissipate, made France all the more sensitive to Italian attack and accounts in large measure for the ungenerous aspects of France's policy toward Italy.

For the sake of completeness, it may be added that, for a brief moment in 1919, there was discussion of the possibility that Italy might take Britain's place in the Caucasus. The prospect had considerable appeal in some Italian circles and things got so far as a discussion of the details and size of the necessary expeditionary force. Finally, nothing came of the scheme and Italy may be thankful that she never became involved in such a potential hornet's nest.

Liquidation and Consolidation: 1919 to 1935.—The years following the First World War may be compared in some ways, as far as Italian colonial policy is concerned, to the period from 1896 to 1911. In both cases, foreign policy in general and its colonial aspects in particular followed a rhythm parallel to that of the domestic scene: division and uncertainty at home were accompanied by retrenchment in the imperial domain, to be followed by a period of unobtrusive but steady preparation while the country, guided by surer hands—Giolitti's or Mussolini's—was, in appearance at least, given a stronger sense of direction and purpose.

As we have seen, the entire effort of Sonnino's colonial policy had been directed toward the eastern Mediterranean and had suffered a severe setback, though not total defeat, in that quarter. The story of Allied dealings with the Turks immediately after the war is neither an inspiring nor a creditable tale. Resuming an age-old, but now out of date, rivalry, the British and the French fought it out in the Near and Middle East: the result may be set down in brief as a British victory in the Arab world through a further relative diminution of French influence; but in Turkey proper British policy suffered a setback through the defeat of its Greek client, while the French after some fighting in Cilicia decided to come to terms and even to espouse the cause of resurgent Turkish nationalism. Italy took little part in these quarrels, and her behavior in the Near East, even though born of weakness, was the sanest of any of the three allies. Early in 1920 these were busy discussing the futile implementation of what was left of the wartime accords. At London and San Remo the partition of Turkey was finally agreed upon; it was written into the Treaty of Sèvres which the representatives of the impotent Sultan signed in August. The instrument represented for Italy the salvage from the wreck of the Sonninian ambitions in Asia Minor, but Nitti's government does not seem to have been seriously concerned over the diminution of his country's share, perhaps because of the belief which he voiced at San Remo that he did not see much point in discussing arrangements which could neither be executed nor enforced. This was a correct appraisal of the forces stirring in the new Turkey; the Turkish National Pact had been issued in Angora in January, 1920. When the Italians had been driven out of Konia, in May, they did not attempt to recover the position, and Kemalist Turkey eventually proceeded to throw its full weight against the Greeks established in Smyrna since May, 1919—amid scenes of disorder that earned them a rebuke from their allies. By the time the armistice of Mudania, in October, 1922, sanctioned the triumph of Nationalist Turkey through the complete rout of the Greeks and their eviction from Anatolia, the Italians had long since evacuated the zone assigned to them in the Treaty of Sèvres.

These events had occurred not long before the advent of the new regime in Rome, and the year 1922 may be said to coincide with the end of the period of liquidation. Wisely, the Fascists did not consider restoring the lost position in Asia Minor; the signature of the Treaty of Lausanne, which superseded the stillborn instrument of Sèvres, was one of the first international acts in which Fascist Italy participated. Her attitude in this connection is comparable with that of Mussolini with regard to the Adriatic, when he decided to let stand the arrangements of the Treaty of Rapallo concerning the Yugoslav frontier.

It should be emphasized, however, that this policy of retrenchment and reasonableness did not serve to establish relations of confidence between Fascist Italy and Kemalist Turkey. There was, for one thing, a general uncertainty in all quarters as to the real aims of Fascism; in the particular case of Turkey, an inevitable suspicion of all the powers derived from the circumstances of the birth and hard-won recognition of the new regime. But there was, more specifically, the matter of the Dodecanese. These Greek islands were supposed to pass under permanent Italian sovereignty at the end of the war, but the Italian policy of abandonment had gone so far that in 1919 one of the first acts of Tittoni, upon succeding Sonnino at the Foreign Office, was to make with Venizelos an agreement looking to the cession of the islands to Greece. The agreement was virtually confirmed a year later by an instrument simultaneous with the Treaty of Sèvres, this latter treaty providing for the formal transfer of the islands from Turkey to Italy. Rhodes was excepted from the arrangement: Italy would recognize its right of self-determination—tantamount to union with Greece—when Britain would do likewise for Cyprus, but in any event not before fifteen years, and the islet of Castellorizzo was retained without qualification.

These provisions for Rhodes and Castellorizzo were an indication of the unforeseeable course of Italian policy. If the arrangements embodied in the Treaty of Sèvres proved unviable, the mere retention of Rhodes and Castellorizzo would be little more than an irritant to both Greece and Turkey and would serve to cast suspicions upon future Italian intentions; in the opposite case, the action was but logical. Again, this may be compared with the evacuation of Albania while Saseno was retained. However, the Italo-Greek treaty never came into force any more than did the Treaty of Sèvres; it was denounced during Giolitti's last tenure of the Premiership while the whole Anatolian question was being thrown into confusion by the actions of Mustapha Kemal. When the situation was finally disposed of and normalized at Lausanne in 1923, the Turks were firmly in control of all Turkish territory proper and the Dodecanese islands passed definitely under Italy's unobstructed title. The policy of liquidation and cutting losses was definitely at an end for Italy. Once again we may emphasize the results of the war for Italy in the colonial field. That she acted wisely in withdrawing from Anatolia is beyond debate; nor could she blame her allies for her own decision in this regard. But the fact remains that since her imperial efforts had been concentrated in that sector the result was a disastrous setback.

Little remained, then, of Sonnino's hopes save the small matter of frontier rectifications in Africa. The short-lived activity of the Committee on Article 13 in May–June, 1919, has been mentioned. Although the divergence was greatest between the French and the Italian views on how to give effect to the provisions of this article, it was with France that a limited agreement had first been reached in September, 1919. This agreement established the western frontier of Libya but, it must be stressed, did not supersede Article 13 of the Treaty of London.

For that matter the Italian position in Libya at the end of the war was not a brilliant one. Actually, the possession was Italian in little more than name, for effective control by Italian arms and administration was confined to a narrow strip of the coastal region, and not even the whole stretch of coast. It was hardly conceivable that even the most radical policy of retrenchment would lead to an abandonment of the Libyan colony; the prospect of military reconquest, on the other hand, had little attraction for governments beset by the difficulties described earlier in this book. The result was a compromise, an attempted policy of peaceful reconquest, combined with a halfhearted effort to exploit the differences among the native population. Such a policy might have succeeded had there been knowledge that the Italian government was strong, and capable and willing to resort to vigorous measures in the event of failure of the policy of conciliation. But the unreconciled Arab elements were not insensitive to the difficulties of the Italian government; to them the attempted conciliation was a sign of weakness and an invitation to exploit the home difficulties. It is all the more significant that the year 1922, when Italy had her weakest government and Amendola, anything but an imperialist, held the Colonial Office, witnessed a change in policy and the decision that there was no alternative to sustained military action. The reconquest of Libya, begun at that time in still hesitant fashion and with parsimonious means, was to be pushed more vigorously after Fascism took over. Even so, it was not fully completed until the opening of the following decade, after the rebellious Senussi had been thoroughly, and even brutally, crushed. The two component parts of Tripoli and Cyrenaica were formally merged in 1934, but it was not until the beginning of 1939 that, following the model of French Algeria, the four coastal provinces of Tripoli, Misurata, Bengasi, and Derna were assimilated to the metropolitan territory, leaving the more extensive but almost uninhabited Libyan Sahara under military rule. Even then, the four provinces continued under the Ministry of Italian Africa.

The eastern frontier of Libya was also settled in consequence of the application of Article 13 of the Treaty of London. In this case, however, the settlement involved Egypt as well as Britain. In 1925 an Italo-Egyptian treaty established the frontier from the Bay of Sollum along the meridian of longitude 25 and definitely placed the Oasis of Kufra in the Italian colony. Finally, in 1934, a tripartite Anglo-Italo-Egyptian agreement extended this line to form the boundary between Libya and the Anglo-Egyptian Sudan. Pending eventual liquidation of the issue with France, the southern boundary of Libya from Tummo to the above-mentioned meridian remained the line of the Anglo-French Convention of 1899.

Of the policies pursued by Fascist Italy in the newly reconquered colony little need be said for the simple reason that, whatever the regime, the economic possibilities of Libya remain so limited as to be virtually nonexistent. Native policy did little to earn the acquiescence of the local population; for the rest, there was a considerable expenditure of sweat and treasure resulting in some noteworthy, if largely futile, achievements. The frugal Italian peasant could settle and prosper in Libya but, however great the efforts of the government, the fact is that there is no room on Libyan soil for immigration to a degree that could make any dent on the problem of Italian surplus population. This will appear obvious from the observation that while the yearly increase of Italy's population exceeded 300,000 at the time of the outbreak of the Second World War there were altogether in Libya some 150,000 Italians, less than a quarter of whom were settled on the land. As to the economic picture, some idea of it may be gathered from the figures for the year 1935—the last "normal" year for Italian economy. Libyan exports in that year amount to some 60,000,000 lire, just over two thirds of which were taken by Italy; imports were around 400,000,000 lire, over three fourths from Italy. But this did not mean that Libya was a profitable market for the mother country; a large part of the imports were in the nature of capital investment connected with land settlement (an investment of doubtful value) and with the even less profitable, if outwardly more spectacular, manifestations of Fascist display. The Libyan colony was a steady drain on the Italian exchequer and better returns could have been had for the same effort by concentrating it in Italy herself. For Fascism, even more than for the preceding Italian regimes, the chief significance of Libya must be seen in terms of prestige and even more of strategy.

The "frontier rectifications" of Article 13 of the Treaty of London resulted also in the British cession of Jubaland with Kismayu (Chisimaio) which, after some delays, finally became effective in 1926. In that territory, an adjunct to Italian Somaliland, as well as in Eritrea, Fascist Italy did little more than reorganize and consolidate. Although Abyssinia was a somewhat troublesome neighbor, unable to prevent raids by her constituent tribes upon the adjacent possessions of European powers, she was admitted to membership in the League of Nations in 1923—ironically enough in retrospect, with Italian support and despite British reluctance. Nevertheless, the traditional Anglo-Italian tendency to cooperate in East Africa appeared again in 1925 in the form of an agreement between these two countries defining spheres of economic interest in Abyssinia. The agreement was frustrated by an Abyssinian appeal to the League, and three years later Italy and Abyssinia concluded a pact of conciliation and arbitration. Certainly, until the advent of the Nazi regime in Germany there were no outward signs of aggressive Italian intentions, a fact which served to bolster the widespread belief in the essential reasonableness of Fascist policy and led many to dismiss its occasional bellicose utterances as designed for home consumption rather than as indications of serious intent.

Of greater importance, and sounder, was the steady progress in fostering Italian commercial interests throughout the Levant. Italian banking, for example, pursued an aggressive and on the whole successful policy of expansion throughout this region, and this fact, together with the firm hold maintained on the Aegean islands of the Dodecanese, prevented Turkey from shedding the suspicion with which she continued to regard Italian policy.

The opening years of the third decade of our century were dominated by two facts, distinct yet closely related, the impact of which was felt by Italy as by the rest of the world: the economic crisis and the advent of the Nazis to power in Germany. On the political level, as far as Europe was concerned, Mussolini offered a solution of the German problem in the form of the Four-Power Pact of 1933. As has been noted, Mussolini was not blind to the essential failure of this attempt. How to retrieve the situation or take advantage of it, from the Italian and the Fascist point of view, by picking up the threads of colonial aspirations in combination with the situation in Europe we must now proceed to examine.

Chapter VIII · *THE FABLE OF THE BULL AND THE FROG*

We shall be in a position then—tomorrow—when, between 1935 and 1940, we shall find ourselves at a point which I should call a crucial point in European history— we shall be in a position to make our will felt, and to see, at last, our rights recognized. (Speech by Mussolini, May 26, 1927)

The most unfortunate situation into which a state can fall is that when neither peace can be accepted nor war can be continued. . . . But into such a situation the state can only fall if it has followed a clumsy and mistaken policy, and if it has overrated its own forces. (Machiavelli, DISCOURSES)

COMBINAZIONE: THE LAVAL–MUSSOLINI AGREEMENT OF 1935

In the unique situation that led to an unprecedented opening of archives at the end of the First World War, Italy was the only exception among the major powers. A little later, Fascism was in the saddle, and it had little respect for the purported virtues of that democratic illusion, open convenants openly arrived at. Defeat in the Second World War and the overthrow of the Fascist regime have opened the floodgates to a torrent of personal accounts, many of them self-justificatory. These throw much valuable light on the activities of Fascism, but it will take more than a number of *Ciano Diaries* before the historian is in a position to perform his task with adequacy.[1] Certain phases of the evolution of Fascist policy may long remain in the dark. But if immediate motivation, the cause and timing of particular decisions, must at times remain obscure, the known course of events plus our knowledge from other sources provide sufficient material for interpretation.

This particular story begins with the opening of the year 1935 when M. Laval was visiting Sig. Mussolini in Rome, at which time it was announced that they had reached an understanding for their respective countries, an understanding which "assured the settlement of the principal questions which previous agreements left outstanding between

---

[1] The purely documentary record is still greatly incomplete, although a number of publications have either recently appeared or are about to appear which will make a fuller tale possible. It is to be hoped, in particular, that the State Department will see its way to an early release of the important collection of material in its possession.

them, and especially of all questions concerning the application of Article 13 of the London Agreement of April 26, 1915." The known terms of the Laval-Mussolini agreement may be stated briefly; they dealt with two main categories: Europe and colonies. In Europe the two countries asserted a common policy, particularly in regard to the preservation of the independence of Austria. In view of the consistent position of both France and Italy on the score of that independence, and especially of the attempt of 1934 dramatized by the assassination of Dollfuss and the prompt Italian reaction to that event, there is no need to comment on this particular declaration of policy. For the rest, in liquidation of all outstanding differences, France made certain concessions to Italy. A strip of territory to the south of Libya was to add some 44,000 square miles to that possession by redrawing the boundary from Tummo to the Sudan along a line parallel to the existing line of the Anglo-French Convention of 1899. A small section, some 300 square miles, of French Somaliland was likewise to be added to Eritrea, together with the strategically situated island of Doumeirah and a block of 2,500 shares in the Jibuti-Addis Abeba railway. The vexed question of the status of Italians in Tunisia was also disposed of, and in a manner satisfactory to France.

These French concessions can only be described as trifling; far more important was the fact that an understanding had been reached, and this could hardly be due to the openly specified price. Either there must have occurred a change in Italian policy, or else the price must have been other than that publicly avowed. A change in the orientation of Italian policy would have been understandable in view of the German situation, but even had Mussolini been more impressed with the German danger, still more potential than actual at this time, it would not have been in character for him personally, nor in keeping with traditional Italian policy, to surrender so cheaply the enhanced value of a bargaining position. The root of the agreement is to be found rather in the fact that France, in her alarm at the reappearing German danger, was willing to pay a higher price for the sake of bringing Italy within her security system. The personality of Laval who, unlike many French political leaders, had no dislike for the Fascist system made it of course easier to come to an understanding; but, allowing for the personal element, considerations of national policy are sufficient to explain the

French behavior in this instance. On the Italian side, the agreement represented cold calculation, the exploitation of a European situation for a price which could not otherwise have been commanded. The price lay, not in the public terms of the understanding, but in the letter, hitherto unpublished, wherein Laval agreed to give Italy a free hand in Abyssinia.

Certain obscurities continue to surround this point—which may never be cleared up for that matter, for much may hinge upon unrecorded verbal statements—and differences arose subsequently over the meaning of free hand, or *désistement,* the Italians claiming to attach a political, Laval merely an economic, significance to it. Such a bargain was not dissimilar from the one which had been made in 1900 between the two countries regarding Morocco and Tripoli; but the circumstances of 1935 were different from those of 1900 and what was proper and legitimate at the earlier date must inevitably take on a different color in the context of the existence of the League of Nations of which Abyssinia was a member. The simple truth is that Mussolini did not believe in such an institution as the League—a fact of which he had never made any secret—and that Laval fundamentally shared the same attitude. Now, from the French point of view, a strong case could be made for distrusting the ability of the League to provide security, from which it would logically and reasonably follow that substitute ways must be found to obtain this security; but one thing could not be done, namely, pursue a policy fated to impair the League while at the same time pretending to support that institution. This is the fundamental vice of ambiguity which magnified the whole Abyssinian affair into something vastly different from a pre-1914 colonial bargain.

To be sure, it would be incorrect to say that France, or even Laval, was primarily responsible, for Mussolini's decision to have his way with Abyssinia antedates the agreement with France, as the frank revelations of Marshal de Bono have made clear beyond a doubt. But the fact remains that, once the decision had been made, there remained the important task of diplomatic preparation, and it is in this that the Laval-Mussolini agreement is of capital importance, may be described indeed as the green light for Italy to act. Both Mussolini and Laval may also have felt that, in view of the Manchurian precedent, a similar situation might develop over Abyssinia without complications that would be more far-reaching than had been the case with Manchuria. If the League were further weakened in the process, neither would shed any tears over that result. In fairness, it should also be pointed out that the admission of Abyssinia to membership in the League had perhaps been less than wise, for it involved an element of false pretense. It simply was not true that Abyssinia was a state with an effective and responsible government in control.

The decision to settle scores with Abyssinia apparently dates from the autumn of 1933, when 1936 was set as a deadline. Precisely what the nature of the Italian plan was, may be open to question, and the nature of the settlement might, for that matter, have to depend upon circumstances, but the date of the decision makes it clear that it was taken with an eye on the development of the German situation: assuming—which turned out to be correct—that France and Britain would not nip the German danger in the bud, three years would provide a period of uncertainty and confusion which could be exploited with safety and skill: it might not be prudent, on the other hand, to allow so much time to pass that Italy might find herself embroiled in a colonial adventure when it would be desirable to be free to move on the European scene. If this be a correct reading of Fascist calculations, the first part of the program was carried out with outstanding success—considering results by 1936—but after that the situation got out of hand.

THE CONQUEST OF ABYSSINIA

The events which led to the proclamation of the Italian empire in 1936 have often been rehearsed and can be recalled very briefly. Of greater interest and importance in this treatment are the manifestations of Fascist policy and method which they illustrated and their wider impact on the general situation. Given the condition of Abyssinia, pretexts for a dispute would be no more difficult to find than, for example, French reasons of Algerian security which had been used to justify the march into Tunis in 1881. The specific incident that started the machinery of aggression in motion in this case occurred at Walwal in December, 1934, when an Italian outpost was attacked. The Italians had been in occupation of the region for some years; whether they were within their own territory or a good distance beyond the borders of Somaliland was open to debate. Here, then, was a dispute with two sides to it; legally, or legalistically, Italy had a case in court. But, in actual fact, the handling of the incident itself, like the course of the whole Abyssinian affair, provides a prime object lesson in the difficulty of instituting a rule of law among nations, and of the meaninglessness of covenants among them in default of honesty of intent. From beginning to end Italian bad faith was manifest. From the very start Italy refused either to discuss the issue of the sovereignty of the region or to consider the very proper Abyssinian offer of arbitration under the 1928 treaty. From the Italian point of view Abyssinia made things more difficult by consistently playing the part of Aesop's lamb—this was indeed her best and only hope—forcing ever more clearly her antagonist to assume the role of the wolf. The results were the same as in the fable.

It was perhaps awkward that the date of January 3, 1935, should be chosen by Abyssinia for an appeal to the League under Article XI of the Covenant; the Laval-Mussolini agreement bore the date of January 7. But even the Abyssinian move could be turned to advantage, for an Italian change of position, whereby the proposal of arbitration under the treaty of 1928 was accepted, served to induce a withdrawal of the appeal to the League—a withdrawal which the members were only too glad to encourage. There was little difficulty in producing a deadlock when it came to implementing the arbitration, and the time was not wasted by Italy but used instead to make the necessary military preparations, which went on at an undiminished tempo.

What could Abyssinia do but again appeal to the League, under the terms of Article XV this time, indicating the growing seriousness of the situation? The date of this second appeal coincided with the German unilateral denunciation of the disarmament clauses of the treaties of peace, an announcement of far greater consequence in European, particularly in French, eyes than the Abyssinian imbroglio. If we bear in mind the internal weakness of the French position at this time, a weakness which was a factor in the pro-Italian orientation of French policy, it is easy to appreciate the effectiveness of the Italian advantage in exploiting the situation. Mussolini could indeed feel scorn for impotent democracies meeting resolute Nazi action with pious and ineffectual verbal condemnation. There was no need of the later close and formal cooperation between Nazism and Fascism for their mutual help to be effective. In the circumstances, it was perhaps appropriate, if peculiar, that the Stresa meeting held in April for the purpose of considering the effects of the unilateral German declaration of rearmament should take no cognizance of the accelerating Italian preparations for war in the Red Sea.

This French and British impotence was reflected in the League, of which these countries were the remaining core; its—and their—greatest wish was to avoid the issue raised by Abyssinia. In May, the Council put it off for three months, leaving the disputants further to explore the possibilities of compromise. If, by that time, the issue had not been resolved, the Council would then take cognizance of it. When this could no longer be avoided, a commission of inquiry into the facts and responsibilities of the Walwal incident was finally appointed at the end of July, and the task of finding a compromise was delegated to the three European powers concerned, Britain, France, and Italy. This was merely playing into Mussolini's hands and an invitation to him to raise his bid. There could be no better indication of Italian bad faith and disingenuousness—based though it was on a correct reading of the situation—than the rejection in June of the British plan to give Abyssinia an outlet to the sea at the British Somaliland port of Zeila in exchange for the cession by Abyssinia of a part of Ogaden to Italy, and the further rejection of the proposals of the Committee of Three in August.

Finally prodded into action, the commission of inquiry returned a finding over the Walwal incident; characteristically enough both disputants were exonerated. But the time was past for such compromise and, in the face of Geneva's impotence, Italy proceeded on her set course; formal hostilities against Abyssinia were opened with the crossing of the Eritrean frontier on October 3. Aggression was too clear to be denied or even talked away behind the screen of diplomatic verbiage, and the Council could do no other than acknowledge the blatant fact. A few days later its action was upheld by the Assembly of the League, where unanimity was only qualified by a Swiss reservation and the dissent of Italy's three satellites, Austria, Hungary, and Albania. Driven by the inescapable logic of the situation, the League went on to impose sanctions against the aggressor, but, hedging to the last, sanctions of a limited nature, the most significant qualification being the fact that certain imports only were denied Italy.

From this point on, two distinct aspects of the situation were clearly marked: the more limited issue of military operations against Abyssinia, and the broader and in the last analysis more important aspect of the challenge to the League. Italy, at the center of both situations, from engaging in a perhaps relatively minor colonial adventure was put into the position of the proud challenger of fifty nations. That Mussolini had foreseen this particular turn of events may be doubted, but that, in a general way, he was willing to gamble on the impotence of the League is probable. From the standpoint of his position at home, he had been presented with a marvelous instrument of propaganda which he knew well how to exploit. Very naturally, the controlled press and public opinion of Italy were encouraged to magnify the comparison between the current dispute with Abyssinia and countless British, French, and other colonial disputes of the past. On that level, there was little to choose, and it is not surprising that the episode should have witnessed what may have been the high watermark of the hold of the regime on the country. The fact must be acknowledged that national pride and a sense of unfair discrimination made the Abyssinian war a popular undertaking in Italy.

There were risks nevertheless. There was no question of the potential ability of fifty nations to coerce Italy into submission, and the war itself, however well prepared, might offer surprises; Adowa, which had not been forgotten, was after all in Abyssinia. These risks Fascism, spurred on for one thing by the economic difficulties of the domestic scene, was willing to take. We may dispose briefly of the military course of events. There were many who foresaw at best a difficult and long war ahead for Italy, in which event even limited sanctions might become an effective instrument of pressure. This view proved to be mistaken. To be sure, military operations under the leadership of De Bono did not make too promising a start, but once the abler Badoglio had been put in charge the campaign was brought to a successful and surprisingly speedy conclusion, culminating in the entry of the Italian forces into

Addis Abeba at the beginning of May, 1936. As an exercise in civil engineering the Abyssinian campaign redounded to Italy's credit; the Italians have never lost the Roman heritage of excellent road building. In purely military terms there was little cause for pride in the unequal contest between rifles of Adowa vintage and airplanes equipped with modern explosives and mustard gas. The aesthetic exhilaration which was described by Mussolini's own son in observing the effects of dropping bombs from the safe distance of an aircraft on bewildered and helpless natives was an adequate expression of the contribution of Fascism to our civilization. The battered crown of the Lion of Judah was placed on the head of docile Victor Emmanuel and, with suitable and self-conscious fanfare, the birth of an Italian empire was announced to the world. Defeated in the halfhearted attempt at coercion, the League could do little else than acknowledge the fact; in July it recommended the dropping of sanctions and its members gradually came to accept the Italian title based on the right of conquest.

What Italy might have made of Abyssinia had she been able to develop it undisturbed must forever remain a hypothetical question. The resources of the country, often exaggerated and in great part uncertain, were nevertheless such as to make this the first respectable acquisition that Italy had made in the colonial field. Far more important were, however, the consequences of the episode on the international scene. Even after the Manchurian affair and the failure of the League to prevent Japan from securing the fruits of aggression on that occasion, there were many who, though not approving, consoled themselves with the thought that Manchuria presented a special case, one in which the vast majority of League members felt no direct concern; that the League was primarily a European institution and that it might yet prove effective in the event that an issue involving a European power should arise. After 1936 these views were no longer tenable and the Abyssinian affair may be said to have marked the real death of the League.

But the League after all was but an instrument, the main purpose of which was to insure the maintenance of peace—though not at the expense of justice to be sure. The League, in the last resort, was but the sum total of its members, and, in 1935, its core was reduced to two nations, Great Britain and France. Upon these two must depend the answer to its fate. It would take us too far afield to enter into a detailed discussion of the policies of these two countries about which sufficient has been said in other connections. The handling of the Abyssinian issue may be cited as one more illustration of the tragedy which lay in the divergence between Britain and France. Over a period of years, the generalization holds that France had been the protagonist of a strong League endowed with real powers of enforcement, while Britain, conditioned by her past tradition, had been reluctant to extend the range of her commitments. There is not a little irony in the fact that, precisely at this moment, the roles of the two countries were reversed. The so-called Peace Ballot whose results were announced in England in June, 1935, had shown a strong current of opinion in favor of a foreign policy based on support of the League, and the results of this poll had considerably influenced the election which took place in the autumn. The events following 1933 had produced the opposite result in France, where foreign policy more than ever had come to stress alliances. The fact that the latest associate, Italy, chose to raise an issue that the League could not ignore put France in an awkward dilemma. To many in that country, the newly found British fervor which elected to manifest itself over the case of Abyssinia was odd, not to say suspicious, when Britain had been unable to see the (to France) much greater importance of commitments in Eastern Europe. However understandable this French reaction, the result was an impossible policy of half measures designed to retain the Italian connection while saving face where the League was concerned. Such a policy could not but have elements of duplicity in it, and it had the curious effect of putting Britain in a position of isolation as defender of the League. It looked at times, in the autumn of 1935, as if the policy of upholding the League might lead to no more than an Anglo-Italian armed clash. While Britain could doubtless defeat Italy, such a possibility could have no attraction for any British government, especially in view of the likelihood of broader European complications. The outcome of all this was the famous Hoare-Laval scheme of the beginning of December, 1935. The proposal was unquestionably a betrayal of Abyssinia, a shameful bargain by any standards of decency and justice, yet an understandable one by the standards of power politics.

At this point there appeared a further weakness of democratic gov-ernment. Very understandably, British popular opinion was aroused at what it rightly considered a break of the pledges of the government just installed in office. The Hoare-Laval proposal, which Mussolini would not entertain for that matter, caused the British Foreign Minister to resign, while his French counterpart survived him only until the begin-ning of the following year. This tragedy of errors played into the hands of Mussolini, who could look upon these developments as evidence of his oft-repeated assertion of the impotence of decadent democracies. From the short-term point of view he may be said to have exploited the situation with skill—and with luck. There is no denying the weaknesses, hesitations, unsavory compromises which can be laid at the door of democratic regimes and the responsibilities which fall to them as a consequence for the state of the world in our time. Had Britain fought Italy in 1936, had the French marched into Germany when that coun-try denounced the disarmament clauses of Versailles or again when she remilitarized the Rhineland a year later, to cite but random illustra-tions, our present plight might have been avoided. But this must be remembered: that these weaknesses, hesitations, and divided counsels are inevitable concomitants of institutions that stress the value of the in-dividual and encourage his right to dissent, even in the mistaken belief that conflict must be avoided at any price.

Fascism, like any totalitarian system, is untroubled by such niceties and weaknesses. It need not show concern for a public opinion which it is most careful to corrupt and control. It can indeed, as in the case of the Abyssinian episode, secure the well-nigh unanimous consent of the nation. It can even expatiate about justice, rightly point to certain dis-abilities under which a "have-not" nation like Italy labors, and make a case of sorts for its aggression. But this talk is fundamentally insincere, for its concept of justice rests in the last analysis upon the callous and brutal denial of all rights but its own. Nor should it be forgotten that the apparent strength and unanimity of action, the certainty of decision that a totalitarian system can boast, conceal deep-seated flaws. No better object lesson of this could be found than the case of Italy herself as the subsequent story will show.

THE SPANISH CIVIL WAR

As it appeared in 1936, Mussolini had scored a brilliant success for himself, for Fascism, and for Italy. The newly created empire, over-advertised in a way that reminds one of some of the less attractive traits exhibited by the *nouveau riche,* was after all substantial. To put it more grandiloquently, as was often done in Italy, that country had not only acquired an empire, she had successfully withstood the pressure of, and in the end defeated, some fifty nations. The success of the gamble had exceeded what must have been the wildest hopes of the player.

It should not be very surprising, therefore, that the extent of this success should have resulted in the loss of a sense of proportion in the direction of Italian policy. It has been pointed out before that this policy had been characterized by a sure sense of the possible, an accurate and sound appraisal of the relationship of power, and therefore on the whole had been moderate, sane, and successful. Even Fascism despite its bombast, had seemed to pursue the same traditional course, until it succeeded in convincing many of the essential reasonableness of its aims. The Abyssinian adventure unquestionably abandoned these criteria. But once it was successfully liquidated—and Italy a satisfied nation, by her Duce's own avowal—it would have been possible, in fact easy, to return to a policy of moderation and to cooperate with the western powers, willing enough to let bygones be bygones and to forget the victim of aggression, toward the maintenance of general peace. Germany, to be sure, had profited handsomely from the Abyssinian disturbance and her ultimate ambitions were unknown; like much of Fascism's talk, *Mein Kampf* was not taken very seriously in 1936. On the other hand, Russia, disturbed by the success of Nazism, had joined the League of Nations, where she was strenuously advocating the doctrine of collective security. The smaller nations, torn by doubts and concern for their own safety, had not yet irrevocably committed themselves; they would gladly support such collective security should it show any prospects of becoming seriously defended by the greater powers. Clearly, Italy's position was crucial and the choice was hers of two entirely divergent courses: she could either throw the weight of her enhanced influence on the side of stability, or she could endeavor further to exploit a state

of affairs to the uncertainty of which she herself had made a major contribution and that she could render more uncertain still, in the hope of
yet further advantage to herself. The juxtaposition of three dates tells
by itself a tale: on May 9, 1936, the annexation of Abyssinia was decreed
and the imperial title assumed by the Italian King; on July 17 civil war
broke out in Spain; on October 25 the Rome-Berlin Axis came into
existence.

Coups d'état and the intervention of the military in the politics of
Spain were, by 1936, more in the nature of a tradition than a novelty.
Ordinarily, there would have been little cause for the rest of Europe
to concern itself with this upheaval on its fringes, and the words of
Lord Castlereagh, written in 1820, might well have been allowed to
apply at this time: "There is no portion of Europe of equal magnitude
in which such a revolution could have happened less likely to menace
other states with that direct and imminent danger which has always been
regarded—at least in this country [Britain]—as alone constituting the
case which would justify external interference." If, in the broader sense
it is true that the Spanish Civil War was the first phase of the Second
World War in Europe and that the ideological aspects were for that
reason important, what gave that episode its real significance in the
more immediate context of the time were the facts of the international
situation—more narrowly, considerations of short-range political advantage and military strategy. In that story, Italy chose to cast herself
in the role of chief protagonist.

As the result of an election in Spain in 1936, the infant republic was
ruled by the somewhat precarious coalition of Left parties known as
the Popular Front. In view of the historic tradition of Spain, the backwardness of her economy (at once cause and effect of an outmoded
social structure, a state of affairs in turn reflected in the quality and
nature of her politics), conditions were ripe for an outbreak of violence.
What brought Spain into the broader picture were the international
possibilities of her position. And while here also the completely docu-
mented story may be long in the telling, the promptness of Italian assistance to the rebelling General Franco is clear indication that Italy had
been a party to the preparation of the revolt. To Mussolini the prospect
may have seemed attractive, the lure of gain at little cost. There is no

reason to believe that, at this time, he was contemplating the unleashing of a major conflagration; but, if the coup were managed properly, the Spanish government could be easily and speedily upset and a sympathetic regime instituted in its place. In view of the behavior of Britain and France during the Abyssinian controversy, it seemed unlikely that they would fail to accept the *fait accompli,* and thereafter there might be enhanced possibilities for the skillful exercise of the gentle art of blackmail, which could be indulged in as occasion might offer.

The Spanish Civil War unfolded in some respects in a manner resembling the Abyssinian affair. The original calculations of Franco and his foreign supporters proved incorrect, destroying their fundamental premise of quick action. As a consequence the war, which it took the better part of three years to liquidate, developed far-reaching implications and, as in the Abyssinian case, served in the end to procure greater gain and prestige for Italy than was initially contemplated. Looked at in another way, it may also be said to have led her further along the road to ultimate self-destruction, an illustration of the adage that whom the gods would destroy they first make mad.

The initial attempt of July 17 in Spain was a failure, though not a complete one. Very shortly, it appeared that neither could the existing government of Spain be overthrown nor was the government able on its side to crush the rebellion out of existence. The stalemate put a wholly new color on the matter, and the attempted coup degenerated into civil war, the duration, outcome, and consequences of which could not, in the closing days of July, 1936, be foretold. Across the border from the Pyrenees, France was also under the rule of a Popular Front government, somewhat similar to that of Spain, toward which it would naturally be sympathetic. The triumph of the Popular Front in France had not led to the same result of attempted reactionary violence as in Spain, but feeling between Right and Left ran very high in France, with the result that, despite its sympathies and in an effort to avoid a widening of the rift, the government of the day, led by Premier Blum, as early as August 1 made an appeal to the powers for non-intervention in the Spanish trouble. Coming from such a source the gesture was one of extreme moderation. The appeal elicited an eager response from Britain, where for that matter there was much less sympathy than in

France for the existing government of Spain. There was the further consideration that, in the steadily deteriorating international situation, the French government, beset as it was by internal difficulties, made it the first axiom of its foreign policy not to become separated from Britain. This was sound calculation, save that, by failing to stress that France was as important to Britain as Britain was to France, it tended to surrender to an unnecessary degree the guidance of French policy into British hands.

In this atmosphere, Mussolini proceeded to unfold, and improvise, his policy. From the beginning of September, 1936, a non-intervention committee began to function in London, but it soon appeared that the totalitarian states, Italy, Germany, and Russia, were not to be hampered by such niceties as respect for the pledged word. Of the three, Italy was to prove by far the greatest offender, and in fact the pretense of international collaboration could, as in the instance of the first Abyssinian appeal to the League, be used for the very end of defeating its proclaimed purpose. Ambassador Grandi in London was never at a loss for suggestions and resolutions that, within the formal scope of non-intervention, were designed to block or delay action and gain time for intervention to achieve its ends. It was a long battle, for the war was prolonged, and the pretense at times wore very thin. Intervention was naturally at first denied, and one can but wonder at the time and effort consumed in the pretentious fraud of haggling over the existence, the nature, and the numbers of volunteers—some genuine, but most of them regular formations of the Italian army with no choice in the matter—and the mode of instituting their withdrawal. A year had elapsed when the British were still suggesting the institution of commissions to supervise the withdrawal of foreign nationals in the Spanish war. With fine irony, Mussolini could even for a time, as in the beginning of 1937, forbid volunteers from Italy; he thought that there were enough by then, but, when proved mistaken, more volunteers found their way to Spain.

The details and vicissitudes of the Spanish war will not be rehearsed here. But its effects on the course of Italian policy must be examined. Italy took an important—and, as it eventually turned out, fatal—step.

From tacit and unplanned coordination, the fruitful collaboration between German and Italian policy was brought into the open and even advertised. In October, 1936, the formation of the Rome-Berlin Axis, the name itself a symbol of intentions, was proclaimed to the world. And shortly thereafter, in November, the two countries nailed their flags to the mast by giving Franco their formal recognition. Spain served as a convenient proving ground for Italian, and even more for newer German, weapons. The name of Guernica—though overshadowed by subsequent countless repetition of similar performance—will live long as a symbol in the annals of efficient brutality.

But Spain was even more important as a proving ground of the methods and aims of Fascist diplomacy. It was essential for Italy to know how far Britain and France would go along the road of renunciation or, as it came to be known in those days, appeasement. Of the two western powers, Britain, as mentioned before, had now the leadership, and the British government under the guidance of Neville Chamberlain was firmly committed to the policy of appeasement. The word has fallen into disrepute and is now often used with a connotation of opprobrium; by itself, however, appeasement is preferable to conflict, provided only that it is not based on false premises; appeasement, in brief, should only be directed toward the appeasable; it becomes indefensible if it merely serves to create a further appetite for demands and eventually to precipitate conflict under less favorable conditions for the appeaser. Unwisely used, appeasement may serve to make more likely the very results it is intended to avoid. Therein lay Britain's unpardonable blunder. Willfully blind to the inner nature of Fascism and to the course of Italian policy under its guidance, the British government was determined to win Italian friendship at any price. Its efforts to that end were untiring. At the beginning of 1937 there occurred another pious fraud, the so-called Gentleman's Agreement between the two countries proclaiming their intention not to disturb the Mediterranean *status quo*. Whereupon Italy proceeded to announce that she would consider the existence of a Bolshevist government in Spain— meaning, by that, a government other than Franco's—a change in the *status quo* within the meaning of the agreement just made. Britain failed to react; in the last analysis, she was willing to pay the price of Spain for the sake of Italian amity.

It was difficult for Mussolini to believe this; judging others by himself, the acceptance of humiliation on the part of proud and powerful imperial Britain (that was still the image of her in Italian eyes) must be due to some subtle Machiavellian revenge in preparation, unless the customary Fascist scorn of decadent pluto-democracy were an accurate assessment of reality. Chamberlain was not to be deterred by such minor rebuffs. When, a year after the conclusion of the stillborn Gentleman's Agreement, Anthony Eden came to differ with him on the wisdom of the course upon which Britain had been set, even Eden must be allowed to go, to make way for the more amenable Lord Halifax. It is true that Eden was the first to agree that if the policy of appeasement were to be pursued *à outrance* he would be an unconvincing candidate for the task; but in the circumstances the effect could not but go to the head of the Italian Duce. If Bülow could congratulate himself and arrogate to himself the credit for Delcassé's fall in 1905, what measure of the relationship of power could this be when Italy could bring about the resignation of the British Foreign Minister? Little wonder that the sacrifice of Eden served no purpose other than to convince Mussolini that a reckless policy of force was paying handsome dividends.

By the time Eden resigned his office, Mussolini had already taken to boasting about the role of Italian arms in Spain and publicly bestowed medals on the unwitting heroes which his policy produced. Yet how flimsy Italian self-assurance was may be judged by the episode of piratical submarines. During 1937 there occurred in the Mediterranean a number of attacks on ships bound for Loyalist Spain. The mystery was only official, however, and few had real doubts about the nationality of the mysterious "pirates." Actually, this was only a further way of testing how far Italy could go. Some useful conclusions might have been drawn from the prompt disappearance of the pirates as soon as the British Admiralty showed a determination to act and the Nyon Conference (which Italy declined to attend) in September had instituted a system of patrolling.

UNLIMITED PROSPECTS: THE END OF THE VERSAILLES SYSTEM

The year 1938 which opened with the resignation of Eden did not see the end of the civil war in Spain. Deeply committed as she was by now in this adventure, Italy had no choice but to see it through, even if that meant a far greater investment than was originally intended and a consequent limitation of her freedom of action in other directions. By the closing days of the year the end in Spain was in sight, but meanwhile the effects of Italy's involvement had been far-reaching and perhaps unexpected. The two outstanding events of the year 1938 on the international checkerboard were happenings in which Italy, though deeply concerned, played only a secondary role. They affected her no less than they did other powers, however, and caused her to pursue thereafter a path which she had been largely instrumental in opening, but the direction of which had passed out of her hands.

There never was overabundance of either mutual love or confidence between the kindred regimes of Germany and Italy; each knew itself too well to entertain illusions about the other, and from the beginning to the end of their association each thought primarily of the use it could make of the other. There was not even a true and deep-rooted community of interest between them (as there was between Britain and France for example) on which a genuine understanding could be established. In the long run, German desires could not but be a far more serious threat to Italy than any real or pretended French hegemony on the Continent, however irksome in detail the latter. To a degree, of course, it may be said that the confused supineness of Britain and France was responsible for the Axis, to which the course of the Spanish war gave an unexpected, or at least premature, turn.

Accurately assessing the situation, the reluctance to action of the western powers and the involvement of its partner, the Nazi regime in Germany came to the conclusion that the time had come to initiate the process of expansion. Logically, Austria was its first victim. Austria, it will be remembered, had become, especially since 1934, a thoroughgoing dependent of Italy. Making use of the internal situation in Austria, where the Nazis commanded a substantial following on both ideological and nationalistic grounds, plus her own enhanced military strength, Germany at last forced the issue of the *Anschluss,* which was finally effected in March. There had been no consultation between the Axis partners prior to the annexation of Austria and, especially in view of Mussolini's determined behavior in 1934, there seems to have been some nervousness in Berlin. There was corresponding relief when Mussolini decided to *faire bonne figure au mauvais jeu,* and Hitler was profuse in his expression of gratitude: "Mussolini, I will never forget you for this," ran a telegram from Berlin to Rome. Reassurances were also forthcoming in abundance—they cost little—though there was perhaps unintended irony in the German promise that the Italian frontier would henceforth be as safe from encroachment as that of France. The absorption of Austria was naturally a sensation of the first magnitude in Italy; but what could Italy do? She was deeply committed in Spain, unfriendly to France, which country, like Britain, was unwilling to take action against Germany; opposition to the *Anschluss* on Italy's part would have placed her in a position of ludicrous and dangerous isolation. Empty words and pious condemnation of unilateral action *à la* British and French could serve no useful purpose; but the pretense of cheerful acquiescence was notice to the world that the leadership of the Axis association had definitely passed to its northern end.

The more one looked at the significance of the *Anschluss* from the Italian point of view, the gloomier the prospects. Whatever the ultimate aims of Germany may have been—a matter still not clear to most people at the time—certain consequences were obvious and inevitable. From the limited standpoint of military strategy, the German position in Central Europe had been greatly strengthened with the surrounding of Bohemia. The political implications were even more significant. Germany had now direct frontiers with Italy, Hungary, and Yugoslavia. The Brenner frontier might well be proclaimed sacred and everlasting, the fact that German arms were on it could not be blinked; disgruntled Hungary would see better prospects of achieving some satisfaction of her revisionist ambitions through a connection with the stronger German power than with the Italian. Yugoslavia could not fail to take to heart the lesson of French timidity and weakness that was content to follow docilely the lead of British appeasement. The spread of Italian influence in Central Europe had been blocked by the French system of alliances; it was now to be confronted by a far more determined and ruthless competitor, in the form of a nominal ally. Likewise the technique of economic penetration evolved by the Nazi regime was far more ruthless and effective than the comparatively benign influence of French loans. But all this must be denied or at least soft-pedaled by Fascism in the pretense that the *Anschluss* was wholly satisfactory to Italy. The simple fact was that Italy had, to a large extent, lost her freedom of action and exchanged her position in the Axis from partnership to dependence. The Spanish war and its consequences did not elicit the same enthusiastic support for the regime as had been the case with the Abyssinian adventure.

The incorrigible optimism—or the blind stubbornness—of Chamberlain caused him to see in the consequences of the Austrian coup an opportunity to retrieve the poor success of his Italian policy. Mussolini seemed to be willing, and, in April, 1938, an Anglo-Italian agreement was signed which looked to the liquidation of outstanding issues and a stabilization of the situation in the eastern Mediterranean and around the Red Sea. To be sure, the agreement was not to be effective until the Spanish situation had been stabilized. This meant a solution satisfactory to Italy, but that, in view of the successes of the Franco forces aided by an ever-growing volume of Italian assistance, seemed a near prospect at the time. As mentioned before, Britain was willing to pay the price of Spain; she was even willing to put the seal of formal recognition on the Abyssinian conquest. In the uncertainty of the time, why not seize what was offered? *Carpe diem* might not be an ill-fitting description of Fascist policy. Moreover, lest the world should be led to think that Italy was taking a definite and different position, within a month of the signature of the agreement with Britain, a triumphal, if rather synthetic, welcome was arranged for Hitler in Italy.

The surmise that the Spanish war was about to be liquidated again proved a miscalculation; the Anglo-Italian agreement had the same success as the Gentleman's Agreement of the preceding year. In the summer, the Fascist government indulged in the undignified gesture of instituting in Italy racial laws modeled on the German, and in more petty ways—the absurd institution of the *passo romano,* the Italian goose step, for instance—Fascism seemed to revel in a show of abject aping subservience to its more virile and efficient counterpart of the north. Time seemed to be pressing for the now dominant partner of the Axis, and the March crisis was followed within six months by the more critical events culminating in the Munich settlement.

There was no need of the information about German aims and plans which has recently become available with the defeat of Germany and the Nuremberg trials in order to realize that a move against Czechoslovakia was a logical extension of the absorption of Austria. The pattern of aggression so often repeated since had already taken shape, and the reassurances profusely given by Berlin to Prague at the time of the *Anschluss* were but a prelude to the raising of the Sudeten issue in the summer of 1938. Officially and in its early stages, the Sudeten problem was a domestic issue of Czech politics of no concern to Germany, though naturally the German people could not remain insensitive to the plight of their persecuted brethren; at least a controlled press would see to it that they did not.

The case of Czechoslovakia was of more immediate interest to France than to Britain. For one thing, France had a formal alliance involving specific commitments with Czechoslovakia; she could not take shelter behind Chamberlain's unforgettable statement about "far away countries of which we know little." Her recent alliance with the Soviet Union, reinforced by a Russo-Czech treaty, was in line with the security system which she had striven to build up since 1919. In view of the doubts to which her behavior toward Germany, Spain, and Austria had given rise among her Central European allies, Czechoslovakia was the last possible test case of the validity of her intentions. The time had come to think in purely military terms about the significance of the Czech bastion—as of the Pyrenees frontier. The motivation and confusion of French policy constitute an important, complex, and interesting, if rather sorry, tale, which this is not the place to tell. We need only retain the fact that, despite the primacy of French interest and the urgency of the matter, France continued to leave the leadership in British hands. This leadership Chamberlain was willing enough to exercise. His devotion to the preservation of peace may not be doubted;

its strength may rather be admired and its blindness wondered at. To a considerable degree he had the support of British opinion, which found in the moral aspect of the claim to self-determination a convenient shield from the real significance of the German regime, its intentions and policies. The dramatic manner in which Chamberlain did manage to save the peace when the crisis manufactured in Germany threatened to get out of hand, the pusillanimous behavior of the French government, and Chamberlain's triumphant, if in retrospect pathetic, return to London from Munich waving the scrap-of-paper-promise of peace in our time are recorded history.

At the height of the crisis, during the closing days of September, Mussolini preserved an appearance of coolness, self-control, and satisfaction with the course of events. He proclaimed the solidarity of the Axis, joined in the campaign of vilification against the "mosaic" state of Czechoslovakia, and, at the eleventh hour, when Germany had virtually secured all the concessions, he threw his influence on the side of peace, which blazing posters proclaimed in Italy he was responsible for having saved. Much of this may be written off as play-acting in the bombastic Mussolinian manner. But the Munich settlement was no humourous play. There is an apocryphal tale connected with Daladier's return from the Munich meeting. The story has it that upon reaching the airfield near Paris he saw that a large crowd had gathered to await his arrival; whereupon he was seized with apprehension for, in view of what he had just done, such a mob he thought must surely be animated with murderous intent toward him. It was a welcoming crowd, as it turned out, like Chamberlain's at Croydon, for the French people, too, yielded to the immediate relief at having avoided war. But Daladier had no illusions about peace in our time or the true significance of Munich. The real meaning of that event was not the destruction of Czechoslovakia, important as that was, but rather the fact that it was tantamount to public notice that the system which had held the European community together since 1919 was definitely at an end, and that leadership in the organization of whatever new order would take the place of the old had passed into German hands.

Whatever doubts France's allies may have entertained before Munich were now definitely set at rest. France had renounced her leadership (whether the world was a gainer thereby, her critics may well ponder); she had consented to the exclusion of Russia from Munich and, whatever justification there may have been for this decision in the light of the strange course of Russia's internal affairs at the time, that country could not but lose faith in the value of her recently made western connection. Czechoslovakia herself, bulwark and cornerstone of the post-war system in Central Europe, lay now defenseless. She had been the strongest member of the Little Entente; what was left of her had no choice but to accept docilely German dictation, and her two Little Entente allies, not surprisingly, endeavored to protect themselves as best they could by hitching their wagon to the rising Nazi star. Nor did they entertain illusions about the possibility that Italy could protect them against her Axis partner. To Italy herself, like the *Anschluss* of March, the Munich settlement, though loudly and officially endorsed, was a serious setback; it was no longer so much a question of protecting her interests in Central Europe as of seeking to safeguard the Mediterranean from German control.

The Munich settlement was in effect the application of the policy advocated in Mussolini's Four-Power Pact of 1933; it was indeed the application of this policy with a vengeance. The Little Entente members had shown a sound instinct in raising the loudest outcry against Mussolini's proposal in 1933: Munich was the confirmation of their worst premonitions, preserving the peace among the great powers through the device of agreement among them at the expense of a small nation.

Much has been said in defense of Munich, on the basis of the British and French military unpreparedness, as a useful time-gaining device. A case can be made for this, especially in the light of military developments during the summer and autumn of 1940; but it remains difficult to assess the balance of time gained and consequent better preparations against the obvious immediate losses. At the time also, it must be remembered, in view of the background of British and French policy in the years immediately preceding the Munich pact, that agreement could not but appear as a continuation of the policy of renunciation, the policy not of peace alone, but of peace at *any* price.

How was Italy to use the situation? Continued German successes had, by this time, considerably reduced her freedom of action and diminished, instead of enhancing, her bargaining power. Even the Spanish war, though by now fast moving to a (for Italy) satisfactory close, was not yet completely liquidated. Was there still time to align herself with the western countries and block the rising German power, whose expansion might in the end be as dangerous to her as to them? Even leaving aside the fundamental lack of propinquity between the Fascist and the western democratic regimes, it must be said in justice that the record of those regimes was not encouraging. There were still many in Britain who, while regretting the crudeness of German methods, found comfort in the fundamental "justice" of the Sudeten claim. Another course was open to Mussolini, the outcome of which, however, was wholly unpredictable at the time: throwing all caution to the winds, he could tie himself more firmly than ever to the Nazi power and seek to promote no longer limited and relatively minor rearrangements of territory and power, but a complete breakdown of the existing framework, in the hope of emerging from the ensuing chaos with unlimited, if unspecified, gains. This, in effect, is the course that he chose to adopt. That it was fraught with incalculable danger must, even in 1938, have been obvious; that it must appeal to the gambling instincts of one who had untiringly stressed the virtue of living dangerously should not be ignored as a factor in the decision.

How then implement such a policy? Central and Eastern Europe were irretrievably a German preserve; Fascist realism would not blink that fact. Italy must look to the Mediterranean. In the section of that sea to the east of herself, including the Balkans, she had consistently maintained her interest. In the Balkans some *modus vivendi* and demarcation of spheres of influence would have to be arranged with Germany. In the western Mediterranean, aside from minor differences over Tunis, French dominance had hitherto been unquestioned by Italy. The extension of Italian influence in the Mediterranean must inevitably impinge upon the interests of Britain and France. However desirous those powers might be to make concessions and avoid an issue, there was yet a difference between concessions at the expense of Austria, Czechoslovakia, or any third party, and concessions the price of which would have to come from their own holdings. It would be most unwise to threaten both powers at once for that would be the best way to elicit common action on their part, and there was still in Italy, for all the talk of decadent democracy, healthy respect for British and French power, whether singly or in combination. It would be best therefore to tackle one at a time, and the weaker and most vulnerable first. All considerations pointed to France, which by this time was militarily encircled with the impending victory of Franco in Spain. The duration and difficuly of the Spanish war and the extent of Italian assistance had made Franco a thorough dependent of the Axis and especially of Italy.

MARE NOSTRUM

As the result of the vicissitudes of the Abyssinian affair, the agreement of 1935 between France and Italy had completely failed of its essential purpose of bringing about a rapprochement between the two countries; it had in fact never been ratified by the latter country despite the fact that France had delivered the publicly acknowledged part of her bargain in the form of colonial territory. The argument was now taken up in Italy that the Laval-Mussolini agreement had never come into force, thus leaving the promises of the Treaty of London of 1915 still unfulfilled—a somewhat specious argument—and, more generally, that the formation of the Italian Empire had given rise to new conditions—which indeed it had—as a result of which the terms of the 1935 agreement were superseded and no longer satisfactory. These arguments were aired at length in the controlled Italian press and at the same time, to give them more point, the newly instituted Chamber of Corporations and Fasci, successor of the old Parliament, indulged in a "spontaneous" manifestation during the course of which was heard the cry: Tunisia, Corsica, and Nice. The timing of this demonstration to coincide with an announced twenty-four-hour general strike in France, the equally "spontaneous" incidents and student manifestations before the French embassy in Rome, the press campaign of vilification, were typical Fascist tactics, components of what came to be known as the war of nerves. More formally, the Italian contention was made the subject of a note presented by Count Ciano, the Italian Foreign Minister, to the French Ambassador in Rome on December 17, 1938. To this communication the French government replied that it was for Italy to state her demands and claims if she had any, but that France would decline to negotiate under pressure. The reply was sound enough, the only one in fact that could be made under the circumstances, yet an evasion in the sense that it pretended to ignore the fact that exploitation of the existing international disturbance in order to exert pressure, test resistance, and win concessions was the very key to Italian diplomacy.

There the matter rested for a time, but not for long. In March, 1939, the last shreds of pretense that Germany had been merely aiming at the incorporation of Germans within the Reich—that convenient and fraudulent appeal to the principle of self-determination—were rudely torn with the establishment of the Protectorate of Bohemia-Moravia and the creation of a completely independent Slovakia. The move was engineered in accordance with a now familiar pattern and should have been little cause for surprise. It had nevertheless considerable repercussions, especially because of the effect in Britain. Negotiations between that country and France on one side and Germany on the other had done little to restore an atmosphere of confidence, and the final appearance of German troops in Prague served to induce a needed, if belated, clarification. Chamberlain would seem to have taken the German action as evidence of fundamental unreasonableness and as something of a personal insult. What was more important, even a reluctant British opinion was forced to recognize the true nature of German aims. It is from this moment that one can speak of the awakening of Britain, whose response was swift and, in the light of the immediately preceding years, perhaps surprising. Abruptly breaking with the tradition of non-involvement in Central and Eastern Europe, forgetting how far away and how little known Czechoslovakia had been less than a year earlier, Britain offered a unilateral guarantee to farther-away and even less-known Poland and Rumania. France, continuing to leave the initiative in British hands, followed suit. It should perhaps be no cause for surprise if this sudden about-face failed to carry conviction in the eyes of many outsiders, especially in Moscow, where British and French approaches looking to the renewal of a firm connection were destined to meet with failure. Britain's willingness to introduce peacetime conscription might have been taken as an earnest of British intentions and changed policy.

To Italy, the German occupation of Prague was a logical step rather than an unexpected move, though not necessarily welcome for that.

The Spanish war was at last concluded at about the same time, and at the end of March, 1939, following up the note of the previous December to France, Mussolini announced publicly that Italian claims against France were of a colonial nature and bore the names of Tunisia, Jibuti, and Suez, without giving more specific indications of the precise nature and extent of the claims associated with these names. Such a statement, at the time, was interpreted as relative moderation; outwardly at least, Italy was still maintaining the fiction that she was retaining an independent policy and her freedom of action. But lest this be mistaken for weakness or fear, she proceeded formally to annex Albania in the middle of April. The size and value of the acquisition, the manner of the performance, and the placing of the Albanian crown on top of the Abyssinian on Victor Emmanuel's head were not devoid of touches of Balkan operetta and did little to enhance Italian prestige in the eyes of the outside world. Lest also the western powers should entertain mistaken ideas about the possibility of Italy joining their camp, a military alliance, the pact of steel, was concluded with Germany in May. This was a repetition of the tactics which had juxtaposed the conclusion of the above-mentioned Anglo-Italian agreement and a triumphal reception for Hitler. Count Ciano, in his apologia, waxes indignant at German duplicity and makes much of the fact that the alliance is said to have stipulated a period of peace. Even if genuine, the complaint is little more than humorous, for Ciano, like his much admired father-in-law, was in effect doing everything possible to tie his country irrevocably to the German chariot and destroy her freedom of action. It can only be a reflection on the intelligence and perspicacity of these men if they really entertained any illusions either about German aims or about the reality of German respect for Italian power or German gratitude for services past rendered. The French response to Mussolini's colonial claims was another *jamais;* to emphasize the determination not to yield under pressure, Premier Daladier undertook a tour of the North African territories and used the occasion to assert that France would not give up an inch of territory.

Events were now fast moving to their logical climax. Following the familiar pattern and tactics, Germany began to raise the issue of Danzig and the Polish Corridor. Having secured the preliminary bases for action, Nazism was now playing for high stakes. The mistaken and doctrinaire "realism" of Moscow, insensitive to the role of public opinion in a country like Britain, gave Germany the signal for action. The wisdom of Moscow's agreement, from the point of view of its own interest, has been and will long continue to be debated. It is extraneous to this discussion; it may here suffice to point out that it was Russia which engineered the fourth partition of Poland with Germany, while Britain and France declared war upon Germany when she invaded Poland.

When the attack on Poland took place on the first of September, 1939, without a declaration of war, Mussolini was willing to play a mediating role, but within narrow limits similar to those which had caused him to proclaim himself the savior of peace at Munich. Since the Anglo-French allies made it a preliminary condition of negotiations that German troops should be withdrawn from Poland, nothing came of the proposed mediation and the Anglo-French ultimatum took effect on September 3. The Second World War had begun. As in 1914, Italy remained neutral at the outset and here also there is humor in Count Ciano's complaint of his ally's highhandedness and disregard for the purported terms of the alliance. The picture of Mussolini painted by Ciano during the interval from September, 1939, to June, 1940, is not a flattering one: indecision, occasional annoyance at the Germans, an urge to participate in the war for the mere sake of action, foolish rantings against the democracies. The picture is very likely unfair to Mussolini, an intelligent man after all; yet his very intelligence may have caused him to realize the impasse into which Italy had been maneuvered and may account for an irritability born of frustration. If the war, like the First World War, should develop into a prolonged stalemate, Italy might conceivably, like Russia, emerge in the position of *tertius gaudens*. At the same time, Mussolini, like the Russians again, was well qualified to understand the revolutionary significance of war and not likely to take a position comparable to that of Sonnino in 1915, who thought in terms of a definite bargain and limited advantages within the framework of prewar Europe. Sonnino had thought to substitute Italy for Austria-Hungary as the dominant power in the Adriatic but never dreamed of, nor desired, the complete disintegration of that country. More was at stake now than a limited reshuffling of the map, or even a thoroughgoing application of the principle of self-determination. Austria-Hungary was after all confined to Europe; Britain and France were world powers. Either Germany would be destroyed, or the two world empires would be. Could Italy aspire to play the role of world power, perhaps displacing France in Africa? This was the order of magnitude of the stakes of the war just begun.

The war itself proceeded in somewhat unexpected fashion. The swift destruction of Poland was a credit to the efficiency of German arms. Russia collected her share of Poland and the world could rub incredulous eyes at the spectacle of Molotov and Ribbentrop exchanging toasts of mutual congratulations and good wishes. Russia indulged also in the not too creditable performance of a separate war against Finland in the following winter. The case of Finland aroused much sympathy in the democratic countries; Britain and France may be thankful that they did not become involved against Russia over Finland as they came near doing at one point; the force of an aroused public opinion which was a potent factor in the case must have been equally incomprehensible in Rome, Berlin, and Moscow. In the west, the world was treated to the spectacle of what came to be known as the "phony" war, a period put to good use by the Nazis—with loyal Communist cooperation—to undermine the morale of their enemies, especially the French. The "phony" war came to an end in the spring of 1940 when the German seizure of Denmark and Norway served as an object lesson of Allied weakness and German technique. This event, which brought about the advent to power of Churchill in Britain and of Reynaud in France, was the curtain raiser to the real war. On May 10 the Germans attacked in force in the west. Success, in an incredibly short time, rewarded the brilliancy of German tactics; by the end of the first week in June the power of French arms had been broken.

ITALY AT WAR

The speedy march of events was a cause for general astonishment. The collapse of France caused many to realize belatedly the place which that country had filled in the structure that had held Europe and the world together. Where Italy was concerned, here was the realization, more sudden and spectacular than could have been foreseen, of a situation that had been envisaged only in the more fanciful flights of Fascist imagination. There was an awkward aspect to this French collapse: it was the work of Germany unaided, not a wholly welcome state of affairs from the Italian point of view. But the German triumph was thorough-going; this certainly was not the time to seek mediation or think of balance of power. There seemed to be no choice but to be in at the kill. On June 10, 1940, Italy declared war upon Britain and France. The fact that the gesture was the logical outcome of a long process and that stabs in the back have not been uncommon occurrences in the history of na-tions did not, nevertheless, enhance Italy's prestige. To those who had been wont to think of Italy as a jackal among nations here was con-clusive evidence of the soundness of their judgment. Nor was the extent of Italy's military activity of any consequence. Save for a few wanton air raids on cities in the interior of France, the Italians did not advance more than a few miles in some places along the French frontier. In the circumstances, the French government of Marshal Pétain sued for an armistice from both Germany and Italy, a request which after some de-lay and a consultation in Munich between the Führer and the Duce, was granted. In effect, the terms of the armistices were the result of German dictation and, in view of the fact that Italy was associated in victory, were little less humiliating for her than for France. Whereas Germany occupied more than half of the defeated country, including the whole Atlantic seacoast, Italy was to occupy a narrow strip of territory along the French frontier; not even Nice was included in it. Tunisia and Jibuti, those much touted Italian claims, were left under French control, al-though their frontiers contiguous to Italian territory were to be demili-tarized and Italy was to have the use of the port of Jibuti.

This was a humiliating victory, good expression of the extent of Italian power and of the degree of German respect for that power. Victorious Italy and defeated France, neutral and subservient Spain, were to be used alike as pawns in Hitler's hands. Some consolation for Mussolini might be found in the fact that this was not a final settlement; such a settlement could not be forthcoming until Britain was conquered or chose to come to terms. But neither of these alternatives came to pass. Effectively protected by the Channel moat—for the last time, perhaps— the quality and skill of her air force and the determination of her people (eloquently given voice by Mr. Churchill) enabled Britain to stand. By standing alone for a year she not only saved herself but the cause of free peoples in general—a service too easily forgotten since. From Italy's standpoint, the fact that the war continued gave added importance to the Mediterranean area and was, or might have been, a last and golden opportunity. The Mediterranean was of vital importance to Britain but, poorly prepared and hard pressed at home, Britain could spare very little at the time for defense of the Mediterranean and the surrounding lands where she was established, especially the approaches of the Suez Canal. Italy had a respectable naval establishment, especially designed for ac- tion in the narrow seas, and relatively countless man power available for use in Africa.

Italy was in the war against the Allies for a little over three years, and her military record during that period was a sorry one indeed. In part it can be accounted for by the meagerness of her resources, on which the Abyssinian followed by the Spanish adventure had placed a severe strain. The lack of popular enthusiasm for the war at home, while important, would not suffice to explain her poor success had it not been combined with the incredible inefficiency of the regime. In August, British Somali- land was overrun—hardly a cause for pride—and in September an attack was launched toward Egypt where it met with limited success, Marshal Graziani deciding to consolidate his lines around Sidi Barrani, some sixty miles beyond the Libyan frontier. A diversion occurred at this point. Mindful that possession is nine points of the law, especially per- haps for systems like his own and Hitler's, Mussolini decided to stake out a claim in Greece. Already in possession of Albania, he launched an attack from that direction on October 28, 1940, fitting celebration of the anniversary of the march on Rome. It has been said that the Greeks had been bribed by the Italians but that they used the bribes instead to strengthen their defenses. Be that as it may, the world could only laugh when the Fascist armies not only failed to emulate the German perform- ance elsewhere but were actually pushed back into Albania. Actually, they were never capable of defeating the Greeks, and the management of that war on the Italian side was a prime illustration of Fascist politics and incompetence.

The attempt against Greece was a useful diversion for the British who, reinforced meantime in Egypt, launched from there in December an attack that reached Bengasi within two months, collecting some 100,000 prisoners on the way. Not only was Italy unable to give a creditable account of herself, but she must now be rescued by her ally. In the spring of 1941, Germany decided to set the Balkan situation in order—prior to her contemplated attack on Russia in June. Despite some miscalculations and *contretemps,* she had little difficulty in disposing of Yugoslavia; Bulgaria repeated her performance of 1915—against both Yugoslavia and Greece this time—and Greece, too, was overrun by April. As a result of the German successes the Greek resistance against the Italians on the Albanian front also collapsed.

The war in Africa was ranging far and wide during this period. Attacking from both Kenya and the Sudan, the British reached Addis Abeba at the beginning of April, bringing back Haile Selassie in their train. By June the Italians were cleared from their short-lived East African empire; that campaign offered one of the few occasions when some Italian forces gave a good account of themselves. But the British meanwhile had diverted some of their Libyan forces to the aid of Greece. Politically desirable as it may have been, the gesture could not prevent the German conquest of the country and even of Crete; it weakened the naval position of the British in the Mediterranean, forcing them to withdraw from Libya before an offensive led and reinforced by the Germans. Even in her own special sphere, Italy was falling ever more deeply into the position of a mere German satellite, one of not even too great consequence.

The North African desert of Egypt and Libya is eminently suited to a war of wide movement. The British, attacking once more in November, reached El Agheila by the end of the year, only to be pushed back once more by the Axis forces under Rommel early in 1942, this time to within sixty miles of Alexandria. But the year 1941 witnessed events of far greater significance than the vicissitudes of war in the desert, events that proved in the end the undoing of the Axis. Unable to destroy Britain and finding their relation with Russia one of growing distrust, the Germans decided to attack the latter country in June. They met with considerable initial success, but the Russians made use of their inexhaustible asset, space, and despite enormous losses and destruction found in retreat salvation. After a difficult winter the Germans resumed their advance the following year, reaching the Volga and the Caucasus. Meanwhile, in 1941 also, America's indecision had been resolved through the agency of the Japanese attack on Pearl Harbor, followed by a German and an Italian declaration of war. As in the First World War, America's open participation in the conflict held the promise of unlimited potential aid for the Allied cause, but American unpreparedness, plus British weakness in the Far East, resulted in spectacular Japanese successes. Axis strategy was developing on a truly global scale in 1942: Rommel's force in Egypt, the Germans at the Caucasus, and the Japanese at the gates of India were the three prongs of a gigantic pincer whose focus was the Near and Middle East. In this grand strategy, the Italian role was increasingly one of effacement.

Allied fortunes began to turn when they were seemingly at their lowest ebb. In the Pacific, the Japanese began to be at least contained; with the failure of Stalingrad, the initiative passed out of German hands on the Russian front as well. The British victory at El Alamein at the end of October was the beginning of the most spectacular of the desert drives; Mussolini need not have gone to Africa in anticipation of his triumphal entry into Alexandria. Simultaneously with the British drive from Egypt, American and British forces landed in French Morocco and Algeria, which were quickly secured. The attempt to reach Tunis was frustrated, but the result was mere delay. With the entrance of the British into Tripoli in January, 1943, nothing was left of the Italian possessions in Africa. In May, the last remnant of Rommel's Afrika Korps surrendered in Tunisia.

THE RECKONING

For Italy the curtain was rising on the last act. The western Allies, disposing still of only limited resources, had decided at Casablanca, in January, to concentrate their effort in the Mediterranean against the weakest link of the Axis. Two months after the clearing of Tunisia, on July 10, 1943, their forces effected a landing near the southeastern corner of Sicily. With the fall of Messina, five weeks later, the whole island was theirs and they stood poised for an invasion of the mainland. Even before they took this step, however, at the beginning of September, political events in Italy had overshadowed the military.

Shortly after the invasion of Sicily, Mussolini and Hitler had had a meeting at which the Führer declined to furnish additional assistance to his now wholly dependent accomplice. The desperateness of the Italian situation was by this time so inescapable that it gave rise to an open clash at the very center of the regime; on July 24, Mussolini's resignation was demanded in the Grand Council and the next day the King, exercising a prerogative of the Crown supposedly fallen into desuetude, dismissed Mussolini, who was thereupon arrested, and appointed Marshal Badoglio Prime Minister. Unlike the Nazis, the Fascists had retained the constitution of the state they had taken over, and the retention of this framework, however much modified and strained in spirit and practice since 1922, proved useful in effecting a smooth transition at this juncture. One of the first acts of the Badoglio government was to decree the dissolution of the Fascist party, an act received in the country with no manifestations of opposition. The artificial bubble that Fascism had been collapsed without even a whimper amid the weary indifference of a people which was now concerned with the sole thought of escaping the consequences of the folly into which it had been led.

For the moment at least—though not permanently—Fascism and its fate were of secondary importance. The dominant factor for the Allies, for the Germans, and for the Italians alike was the military situation. The possibility of Allied exploitation of the war weariness of the Italian people and of the attendant revulsion against the regime was limited by the more immediately relevant consideration of the power available to the various participants in the drama. Badoglio's freedom of action, further limited by the inevitable distrust of which Italy was the object on the part of both ally and foe, was extremely circumscribed. Badoglio was primarily a military man and a patriotic Italian rather than a political figure, no rabid and convinced Fascist, though he had accepted the regime which had dubbed him Duke of Addis Abeba in recognition of his services in the Abyssinian war. He was in most respects the logical candidate to guide the country through a difficult transition. At the same time that he decreed the dissolution of the Fascist party he announced that Italy would continue in the war at the side of her Axis ally; but he also initiated secret approaches to the Allies. These negotiations, very difficult to conduct in the circumstances, were somewhat protracted as a consequence, but finally led to Italy's unqualified surrender on September 3. Italy had to submit to the awkward and humiliating stipulation that the armistice would be kept secret until it suited Allied strategy to announce it publicly. This announcement, which could not have been long deferred in any case, was finally made on September 8 to coincide with the Allied landing at Salerno.

Meanwhile, on September 2, General Montgomery's troops had crossed the Straits of Messina and started moving up the toe of the peninsula. The announcement of the armistice was made simultaneously by General Eisenhower and by Marshal Badoglio who issued instructions to the Italian forces to cease opposition to the Allies everywhere but to resist attack from any other quarter, which, in the circumstances, meant primarily German. There ensued a period of uncertainty and confusion. The Germans seemed to hesitate for a time before taking the decision that a delaying action fought through the length of the Italian peninsula would be a good investment of military power. Had the Allies been bolder and more reckless, it is conceivable that an attempt in the center and the north, exploiting German hesitation, the general breakdown of authority in Italy, and the spontaneous outburst of anti-German resistance in the country, might have given them the whole country at one stroke. This might-have-been will long be argued. Allied resources were limited, the power of Italian resistance was small, and the moment, fleeting at best, was allowed to pass. Upon the announcement of the Italian armistice, the Germans had proceeded to disarm the Italian forces, an operation which offered little difficulty, and they proclaimed the formation of a National Fascist government in the north, whither Mussolini was brought after a dramatic rescue from his place of detention on September 12. The Allies, preferring safety and caution, continued their advance up the peninsula against what resistance the Germans, fighting a delaying action, could offer. On October 1, the combined armies of Generals Montgomery and Clark entered Naples and a front was stabilized shortly thereafter along the Volturno river. On the 13th, the Badoglio government, sheltered behind the Allied lines, formally declared war upon Germany.

Fascism could not have brought the country to a sorrier pass. Not only was Italy thoroughly defeated, but even the final attempt to extricate herself from the war and avoid its physical consequences on her soil was a failure. In the south, the government of Badoglio and the King, recognized by the Allies, was at war with Germany, while in the north, an Italian Social Republic continued as a Nazi ally. Taking the broad view, this worst of all possible solutions from the Italian point of view was the direct consequence of an attempt which stemmed from a wanton disregard of the factor of power, of the relationship between the ends pursued and the means at hand to achieve those same ends.

There was no preordained reason why the appanage of empire in the nineteenth century should have fallen to Britain and France rather than to Italy; there were, however, historic and economic reasons for this development. Nor was there any reason why the existing *status quo* should be irrevocable and everlasting. Power shifts and its changes are bound to cause rearrangements, political and territorial. But the mistake of Fascism was to proceed from false premises. Even assuming that the heyday of French and British power had passed and that the dissolution of those empires was at hand, what prospect could there have been of Italy's substituting herself for these powers? She could only, at best, aid and abet the dissolution by allying herself with a power capable of issuing a real challenge, such as the German. It was inevitable that in the attempt, even had the disruptive part of the program been successful, she should become a mere dependent satellite. The appalling performance of her arms merely accentuated and accelerated a process which it did not create and, in the ridiculous attempt, Mussolini's Fascism came to the same end as the frog of the fable.

But there is even more. Granting that Fascism, like Nazism, is in the last analysis a response to the problems of our time, an attempt to solve problems with which the traditional nineteenth century approach of liberal, democratic, parliamentary capitalism seemed unable to cope, these new totalitarian systems, in their imperial attempt, represented a retrogression rather than a forward step, a sterile effort of nationalism gone mad. If the day of empire is passing, surely the way to a new read-justed order lies in the path of greater freedom rather than renewed coercion. Had Italy succeeded in falling heir to France as a colonial power in Africa, it is conceivable, quite likely indeed, that the Fascist regime would have been capable of organizing effective methods of sup-pression of native movements—its treatment of natives in Libya may be taken as an earnest of this ability. But along that path there is no future. From any point of view, it could only result ultimately in greater blood-shed, misery, and hardship than the bungling and often uninspiring process of retreat of what may by contrast be described as the liberal em-pires of the west. Here also, as on the home theatre, the self-advertised vigor of the "young" countries was a misleading façade concealing retro-gression. By comparison, the "decadent" democracies stood for progress, not ruthlessly suppressing, but allowing some scope, at least, to the live forces of change in the dependent world.

Part IV

EPILOGUE

Chapter IX · ITALY TODAY

WARFARE AND POLITICS

So far, this book has been a survey of the course of Italy's development from the time the impact of the forces unleashed by the French Revolution and carried about Europe by Napoleon fatally shook the structure of the *ancien régime*. For Italy the story has been that of the clearing away of the ruins and building the edifice of a new nation. But the ground whereon to build had not changed, nor were the materials used in the building new; hence the many recognizable aspects of past inheritance in the structure of United Italy. That structure was still incomplete when a major war interrupted the process. In 1919, partly because of this impact of war on the peculiar circumstances of the Italian scene, the Giolittian approach and outlook proved inadequate to cope with a novel set of conditions. Fascism was the answer to the groping search for solution. Fascism, once in power, was shaped quite as much by its adaptation to circumstances as by the varied forces of the past that went into its composition. But certain fundamental vices in the inner core of Fascism plus the peculiar idiosyncracies of its leader eventually involved him, the movement, and the nation in unprecedented disaster. Whatever the future may hold in store, it is clear that this particular experiment has failed, and the year 1943 that witnessed the collapse of Fascism and the surrender of Italy obviously marks the closing of one chapter and the opening of a new.

The six years that have passed since these events took place have not brought to the world as a whole nor to Italy in particular a clear pattern of stability. In the confusion of the aftermath of a war of unprecedented dimensions we can perceive many trends, cherish certain hopes and predilections, avoid or combat other fears, but we cannot discern the outline of the future with clarity. Much that is currently happening is obviously shortly destined for the discard of insignificance, and there would be little point or profit in a detailed recital of the contemporary course of Italian politics, for example. No more will be done, therefore, in these closing pages than to indicate a few major developments which may even now be assumed to have definite and lasting significance —the terms of the peace settlement, for instance—and to mention some obviously important features of the political and social landscape out of which the future will be shaped, though in what manner we cannot tell.

The reason for the overthrow of Fascism on July 25, 1943, and for the subsequent armistice of September 8 was simple: Italy was no longer capable of carrying on the war. By acknowledging defeat, she attempted to withdraw from it. But the choice was hers only within narrow limits. Germany and the Allies were still at war. Her best hope resided in a prompt and complete taking over by the Allies. But events took a different turn and, instead of being able to withdraw from the war, Italy found herself caught in it in the most cruel, if relatively passive, fashion. The legal government of the King and Badoglio, sheltered behind the Allied lines in the south, went to war against its former ally, while the newly organized Neo-Fascist Italian Social Republic in the north continued as a German satellite. But the disruption of all forms of organization, not least the military, which followed the armistice, made the Italian contribution to the war itself, on either side, perhaps significant as a gesture, though of little consequence militarily. The war was fought by the Allies and the Germans, but Italy was the battleground.

Whether Allied strategy was sound in giving the Mediterranean sector priority over a second front in western Europe has been and will continue to be debated on military as well as on political grounds. Be that as it may, there is no question that Mr. Churchill's "soft underbelly of the Axis" turned out to be, as was pointed out after a while, a rather stiff spinal column. For the better part of two years, the Germans fought a skillful delaying action, the details of which do not belong in this treatment. The final act was swift. Mussolini, whose role had been increasingly one of effacement, was captured while trying to escape and was executed by partisans on April 28, 1945; his body was taken to Milan where it was displayed to the accompaniment of gruesome, if understandable, scenes. The prolongation of the war for Italy beyond the armistice of 1943, coming as it did to an already exhausted country, had the effect of intensifying the strains and stresses which she had unsuccessfully sought to escape, most of all perhaps the economic stresses.

It was responsible in great part for the catastrophic condition of Italian finances.

The episode of the Italian Social Republic in the north is an interesting curiosity, but little more. With its collapse upon German defeat it was reduced to the status of a short-lived postscript to the main episode of Fascism. Of more importance were the doings of the legal Italian government and of the advancing Allies. Having declared war upon Germany, Italy was granted by the Allies the somewhat uncertain status of cobelligerent. Depending upon the point of view, this declaration of war could be looked upon as quite in the same category as the original declaration against Britain and France in June, 1940, merely another instance of Italy's "jackal policy"; or alternately, as an earnest of the real passing of Fascism, a token of real intention to "work her passage home." At all events, the granting of cobelligerent status could fairly be taken as an indication that the Allies felt generously disposed toward Italy. This was particularly true in the case of the Anglo-Saxon countries, and it was inevitable that Italy should seek to make the most of this disposition, draw a veil over the past as much as possible, and lay stress on her contribution to Allied victory. It was equally inevitable that those among the Allies who had more directly experienced the effects of the original Italian aggression in their own countries should put first stress on that aggression and look upon the cobelligerent status with unfriendliness and misgivings. Therein lay the basis of a certain amount of future misunderstanding and recrimination.

The result of all this was a provisional situation, and the government of Marshal Badoglio represented no particular political tendency, save that it was not Fascist. It was essentially a caretaker government of technicians and could hardly have been other in the circumstances. With the termination of hostilities, the institutions of pre-Fascist democratic Italy were largely restored, and first and foremost of these, free elections on the basis of universal suffrage, even the sex disability being for the first time removed.

The Italian political scene has presented a familiar shape. The parties are numerous, and their nomenclature may be said to be in large part merely a return to or a continuation of the pre-Fascist pattern. Any hopes that a wholly new leadership or movement would emerge from among those who had played a role in the resistance and liberation have by now been conclusively frustrated. The chief point of interest has been the emergence of three—especially two, if we consider the special difficulties of the Socialists—great mass parties which have come to dominate the scene, and about which a few words should be said.

The Communists need little introduction; whether Italian or of any other country, nationality comes a poor second to ideology for convinced Communists. Communism derives its strength from two sources: first, the enormous discontent born of the misery of the masses to whom it is an easy thing to point out the failures of past regimes; second, among some of the leaders especially, from the power of an idea held with the fervor of religious conviction. These are, in the long run, sounder bases of strength than Russian bayonets, as shown by the fact that, under any free testing of opinion, Communism has shown by far its greatest appeal outside the sphere of physical Russian control. Not without justification perhaps, it has been suggested that the place to look for genuine Communists at the present time is in Paris or Rome rather than in Moscow. Rigidly disciplined, the Communists had played an important and very creditable part in the resistance movement; they are the best-organized and most vigorous of the political parties. They are also liberally financed.

The Socialists derive their support from much the same layer of society as the Communists, the industrial proletariat. They suffer from the handicap of greater mildness, from the fact that, an old party, they have been tested and found wanting, and the great question for them has been the extent to which they should make common cause with the Communists by whom they risk absorption. That is the dilemma which threatens to split, or has split, Socialist parties everywhere. In Italy the split has actually occurred (but not until the beginning of 1947), by far the larger group opting for a policy of collaboration with Communism. For these various reasons, the Socialists find it hard to hold their own in competition with their rivals to the Left and to the Right of them.

The Christian Democrats are the heirs to the *Popolari* whose leader Don Sturzo is one of those exiled Italians who preferred not to return to the fray of political activity. In the political spectrum of postwar Europe, they are a middle party and they also lack the cohesiveness of the Communists. A wide range of emphasis exists among their ranks and they harbor quiescent conservatives. One thing is important, however: the fact that the three mass parties, and the minor ones also for that matter, have considerable common ground in their social outlook, in their acceptance of the role of the mass, and in their consequent advocacy of such matters as state control and the nationalization of industry. Their differences are rather of degree than of kind and, in any event, the still existing emergency determines to a large extent what must or can be done by any government.

The first free consultation of the Italian electorate in a quarter of a century—and the lapse of time must be emphasized—took place in June, 1946. It had the double purpose of electing a constitutional assembly and of serving as a plebiscite on the so-called institutional question (whether or not Italy should retain the monarchy), which had been hotly debated for some time.

King Victor Emmanuel, regarded as no asset to the monarchist cause, had finally abdicated in favor of his son, Prince Humbert, a month before the election—a belated gesture the significance of which seemed too obvious. The poll was fairly close—12,717,923 votes were registered for a republic against 10,719,284 for the monarchy—and served to emphasize once more the division between the North, predominantly republican, and the prevalently monarchist South. On June 10, 1946, Italy was proclaimed a republic, and three days later King Humbert left the country to join the ranks of displaced monarchs. The change was effected smoothly and the Constituent Assembly which had been elected simultaneously with the referendum became the repository of all the power of the state, once the Senate had been abolished.

The returns of the election for the Assembly put the Christian Democrats, with 207 members, well in the lead of all other parties. Next came the Socialists with 115 and the Communists with 104. All the other groups together accounted for the remaining 130 deputies. Following European continental practice, like the French Assembly of 1871 and the German of 1919, the Italian Constituent Assembly had to carry out three main tasks: the current administration of the country, the drafting of a new constitution, and the formal making of peace with the countries with which Italy had been at war.

The job of constitution-making was completed late in 1947. It may suffice to say that, as a result, Italy, now a republic, functions basically in the manner which has come to be that of the western European parliamentary democracies. A bicameral legislature—the Senate, now elective instead of appointive as under the monarchy, has been restored—governs through the instrumentality of a responsible Cabinet headed by a Prime Minister. Despite a tentative encouragement of regionalism, the administration remains centralized as it had been hitherto. The mechanics of government are essentially a return to the pre-Fascist era and therefore need not be examined in greater detail. It will be useful, however, to look a little more closely at the terms of the peace settlement imposed upon Italy, for this instrument creates entirely novel conditions and its effects may be presumed to be of a lasting nature.

THE TREATY OF PEACE WITH ITALY

A knowledge of history, especially an imperfect knowledge, may at times be a dangerous thing. In the awareness of errors in the past, the naive conclusion is sometimes drawn that all that is needed to avoid repetition of these errors is to adopt a diametrically opposite procedure for present or future guidance. At Vienna in 1815 Talleyrand was able to exploit with skill the divergent interests of the members of the coalition that had overthrown Napoleon. Remembering this too well, in Paris in 1919 the Allies arranged a settlement without allowing the enemy a voice in its making. One would hesitate to defend the view that the settlements of 1919 were better than those of Vienna; they certainly proved less enduring. During the interval between the two World Wars, the criticism of the treaties that followed the first was loud and widespread; one aspect of that criticism was to question the precipitateness of the settlement, too concerned with the chief enemy at the expense of the others. That could easily be remedied by reversing the procedure. Accordingly, we have now dealt with the periphery first, leaving the main problems, Germany and Japan, for subsequent settlement. It is clear that we have reversed the procedure of 1919; that the results will be better, it would take boldness to predict. We have also been very leisurely in the task of peacemaking, even in its limited scope;

some may perhaps find consolation in recalling that the Peace of West-
phalia was five years in the making.

But at any rate the treaties of peace with Germany's satellites (except
Austria, if one call her such) have been completed and signed. The
task of reaching agreement over the terms proved to be a laborious, at
times an exasperating, ordeal. This was particularly the case with the
Italian treaty; it took a little over a year for the Allies to agree upon
the final terms. Discussions were begun in London in the autumn of
1945. Departing in this respect also from the procedure of 1919, these
discussions were not conducted by the heads of governments but by
the Foreign Ministers of the countries concerned, who held a number
of meetings at various times and places. The process initiated in London
was continued in Paris during the spring and early summer of 1946,
when a first draft at last emerged. This draft, along with those of the
treaties for the other minor enemies, was then discussed at the Peace
Conference that met in Paris from the end of July to the middle of
October, 1946. The amendments and recommendations there adopted
were in turn taken up in November–December, 1946, at the New York
meeting of the Foreign Ministers, who then entrusted their delegates
with the task of drawing up the final text. This was eventually signed
in Paris on February 10, 1947, and the treaty was subsequently ratified.

The details of these meetings and discussions would alone make the
subject of a substantial volume. They need not concern us here, and it
may suffice to say that final decisions were taken in the main by the
representatives of the Big Four—the United States, Great Britain, the
Soviet Union, and France—and that the difficulties and delays in reaching agreement were, in the last analysis, due to the emergence of two
worlds instead of the hoped for One. The United States and Britain
were usually on one side, the Soviet Union on the other, with France for
the most part in a mediating position, proposing compromises that
finally carried the day. We may therefore confine ourselves to a brief
analysis of the terms of the treaty as it was finally signed.

The treaty opens with a preamble which is significant, for it describes
with accuracy—and fairness—the exact position in which Italy found
herself. On the one hand, states the treaty,

WHEREAS Italy under the Fascist regime became a party to the Tripartite Pact with Germany and Japan, undertook a war of aggression and thereby provoked a state of war with all the Allied and Associated Powers and with other United Nations, and bears her share of responsibility for the war; and

on the other hand, in recognition of Italy's about-face,

WHEREAS in consequence of the victory of the Allied forces, and with the assistance of the democratic elements of the Italian people, the Fascist regime in Italy was overthrown on July 23, 1943, and Italy, having surrendered unconditionally, signed terms of Armistice on September 3 and 29 of the same year; and

WHEREAS after the said Armistice Italian armed forces, both of the Government and of the Resistance Movement, took an active part in the war against Germany as from October 13, 1943, and thereby became a cobelligerent against Germany; . . .

The Italians, understandably seeking to draw a veil on Fascism and the consequent responsibility for its deeds, would have liked to substitute the phrasing "Italy had been led by the Fascist regime . . ." for "Italy under the Fascist regime became a party. . . ." In this attempt they were not successful.

The treaty then proceeds to redefine the frontiers of continental Italy. These involve three of her neighbors, France, Austria, and Yugoslavia.

France claimed and received four very small areas, which may be described as in the nature of minor frontier rectifications. The most significant aspect of these changes lies in the existence of hydroelectric installations in the Mont Cenis and Briga-Tenda regions; these are of importance to Italy and are the object of bilateral arrangements between the two countries whereby France guarantees the power and water supply formerly derived by Italy from these sources. The frontier zone to a depth of 20 kilometers on the Italian side is to be demilitarized.

There was much uncertainty as to what the Allies would decide for the Southern Tyrol. The region is uncontestably of German character, despite the emigration which had taken place as a result of the direct agreement between Hitler and Mussolini in 1939 and a certain amount of Italian immigration. The issue could, or might have been, settled on its local merits, all the more as it was not a case of dealing with an ally on one side and an enemy on the other. The Italian case for the maintenance of the 1939 frontiers was weakest at this point. However, the decision of the Allies was to leave that frontier unchanged. Meantime, the Italian and Austrian Foreign Ministers, Sig. de Gasperi and Dr. Gruber, came to a direct and amicable arrangement insuring cultural rights and a degree of local autonomy to the German-speaking population of the South Tyrol as well as facilities for communications. Despite a certain amount of Russian opposition, the De Gasperi-Gruber agreement was incorporated into the final treaty with Italy.

The frontier with Yugoslavia was by far the greatest stumbling block and the one that held up longest the making of the treaty. The facts in the case were essentially not different from what they had been in 1919 and there is no cause to rehearse them at this point. It was clear from the outset that Italy could not retain her prewar frontier in this region. The situation was complicated by the fact that during the closing phase of the war the Yugoslavs had occupied the whole of Julian Venetia. The western allies claimed the right of occupation within the 1939 frontiers, and there were some hectic days of tension as a consequence. The matter was discussed in Belgrade between Marshal Tito and Field Marshal Alexander, who had gone there for that purpose. Eventually, the western allies took over complete control of Trieste after an agreement had been reached between them and the Yugoslavs, and the so-called Morgan Line was drawn delimiting their respective zones of occupation. There the matter rested, pending final settlement.

When the issue was tackled by the Council of Foreign Ministers there appeared at once wide divergences among them. The Council sent a commission to investigate on the spot in March, 1946. It is a measure of the weight of major power politics that the investigators failed to agree to such an extent that they recommended four different lines. The American line was the most favorable to Italy, leaving her not only Trieste but also about half of the Istrian peninsula. The British line differed little from the American, running slightly to the west of it in the south. The Russians, supporting their Yugoslav protégé, proposed a line not only excluding Trieste but running, in the north, west of the 1914 frontier with Austria-Hungary. The French took a middle position and, after much haggling, the line they had proposed became the basis of agreement. The result is a return to something close to the 1914 frontier but, by way of compromise, Trieste with a small surrounding territory, is to go neither to Italy nor to Yugoslavia, but to be constituted into a Free Territory whose "integrity and independence shall be assured by the Security Council of the United Nations."

The result was disappointing to Italy, who had hoped at one time to obtain the Wilson line of 1919. The quiet and dignified statement of De Gasperi before the Paris Peace Conference was impressive but could make no dent on the effects of power politics. The Yugoslavs professed to be highly indignant and loudly proclaimed that they would not sign the treaty. Moreover, even the compromise just indicated did not end the matter, for the task of agreeing on the details of the statute of the Free Territory proved to be a most troublesome one.

The root of the difficulty lay in the distrust of Yugoslav and Russian intentions on the part of the western allies. Two things are clear beyond dispute: the predominantly Italian character of the city of Trieste itself, and the fact that its significance derives from its being the natural outlet for much of Central European trade. The problem of Trieste, in other words, comes from the fact that the city belongs to Italy ethnographically but economically belongs to Central Europe, not to Yugoslavia alone or especially, but also to Austria, Czechoslovakia, and Hungary. That Yugoslavia should put forward a claim to Trieste was to be expected, but the claim would have been rejected without further ado had Yugoslavia been alone. What gave force to the claim was the support of Russia. In view of the nature of the Yugoslav regime and of Russian policy in Eastern and Central Europe, Trieste was a possible outpost and anchor of Russian influence corresponding to Stettin in the north. It became the testing ground of the two great rivals, the Soviet Union and the Anglo-American combination. Hence the compromise solution at this point where those two forces met and held each other in equilibrium. In this contest, Italy and Yugoslavia had almost become secondary factors. In view also of the techniques and methods used by the Soviet Union in establishing control through amenable puppets, it was felt by the western powers that the statute of the Free Territory should be such as to forestall the possibility of an internal coup which might in effect put it under Yugoslav—hence indirectly Russian—control. That is why the provisions regarding the Free Territory take up so much space—about a quarter of the text of the whole treaty is devoted to them—and why it took so long and proved so difficult to reach agreement on them.

The dispute centered for a long time around the powers of the governor, and there was humor in the fact that it was the Americans and the British who were most insistent on giving him wide latitude while the Russians took the more "democratic"—if perhaps disingenuous in this instance—position that the elected representative body should have the greater powers. The technique of manufacturing elections has been developed into a fine art in Moscow.

Eventually agreement was reached. The Free Territory is to have a governor appointed by the Security Council "after consultation with the Governments of Yugoslavia and Italy." He may not be, however, a citizen of Italy, Yugoslavia, or the Free Territory. The governor may, "in cases which *in his opinion* permit of no delay, threatening the independence or integrity of the Free Territory, public order, or respect of human rights, directly order and require the execution of appropriate measures. . . . In such circumstances the Governor may *himself assume, if he deems it necessary, control of the security services*" (italics added). This is the clause that gave rise to such protracted debate before it was adopted. The significance of it is obvious; it represents the extent of the victory of the western powers, or conversely, the extent of Soviet concessions.

In addition to the governor, the Free Territory is to be ruled by a single-chamber assembly popularly elected according to the system of proportional representation. From this assembly, and responsible to it, will issue the Executive Council of Government. For the transitional period, the governor, upon assuming office, is to organize a Provisional Council of Government in consultation with which elections for a constituent assembly are to be arranged. From the time of the coming into force of the treaty, occupying forces are not to exceed 15,000 men, apportioned equally among Americans, British, and Yugoslavs. These troops are to be at the disposal of the governor for a period of 90 days, after which they are to be withdrawn. There are further detailed provisions dealing with economic and financial matters and, above all, with the organization of the free port. Now that the treaty has come into force the deadlock has been transferred to the choice of a specific individual for the position of governor. Pending agreement on this, the other provisions for the governance of the Free Territory are of necessity held in abeyance.[1]

The rest of the territorial provisions of the treaty did not present too much difficulty. Italy does not retain her foothold in Zara in the Dalmatian mainland, nor any of the islands on the east coast of the Adriatic. Albania regains her sovereignty and is to have the island of Saseno which Italy had acquired as the result of the First World War. The Dodecanese and the small island of Castellorizzo, which are to be demilitarized, are turned over to Greece in accordance with the wishes of their population, despite a momentary Russian objection in this case also.

In regard to the Italian possessions in Africa, no final decisions were reached with the exception of Abyssinia where the effects of the Italian aggression of 1935 are simply undone. For the rest of the older, pre-Fascist, Italian colonies the treaty merely states that the four powers "agree that they will, within one year of the coming into force of the Treaty of Peace with Italy . . . jointly determine the final disposal of Italy's territorial possessions in Africa, to which . . . Italy renounces all right and title." Pending this final decision, which, in their inability to agree, the four powers have turned over to the United Nations, these territories are continuing under their present British administration.[2]

Following the pattern of the post-First World War settlements with the enemy, the treaty with Italy provides for her disarmament. Like the frontier with France, that with Yugoslavia is to be demilitarized, and restrictions are placed on military establishments in the islands of Sicily and Sardinia as well as in some other areas of the mainland. The land, naval, and air establishments are restricted to specified figures.

[1] Following the coming into force of the Italian treaty, the area of the Free Territory has been occupied in part (including the city and the port of Trieste) by Anglo-American forces; the rest, under Yugoslav occupation, is being gradually and quietly integrated into the Yugoslav state.

[2] Throwing the problem of the Italian colonies into the lap of the United Nations has, if anything, made confusion worse confounded, merely increasing the number of influences that have a voice in the problem. In the face of a continuing stalemate, the greater powers, particularly Britain, have endeavored to initiate a variety of (so far unfruitful) proposals. Of the wisdom of the apparently ambiguous British declaration in regard to the Cyrenaican Senussi, time will judge.

Italy is also required to pay reparations to the victims of her aggression, but the painful lesson learned from the failure of the fanciful economics of 1919 seems to have borne some fruit in this case. The amounts due by her are as follows: $100,000,000 to the Soviet Union, $125,000,000 to Yugoslavia, $105,000,000 to Greece, $25,000,000 to Abyssinia, and $5,000,000 to Albania. The western allies (the United States, Britain, and France) renounced like claims, but in all cases Italian property in Allied territory may be used to offset claims and damages. In addition, no part of these reparations is to come from current industrial production for the first two years, and thereafter those countries entitled to reparations are to furnish Italy the raw materials for the manufactures to be used as reparations. The whole account is to be liquidated within seven years.

Italy also undertakes in advance to recognize the peace treaties and other arrangements between the Allies and all the other enemy countries. Following ratification, occupying forces were withdrawn from Italy as provided by the treaty.

It may be worth stopping for a moment to appraise the merits of this peace. Let us examine the territorial clauses first. These are in a sense the most fundamental for, even though economic conditions may be paramount in the immediate aftermath, such conditions are susceptible of far easier change than are frontiers. The history of the treaty of Versailles is a good illustration; after several modifications and revisions, the attempt to collect reparations from Germany was finally abandoned in 1932, but frontiers have seldom been altered save as the result of war. The whole discussion may be prefaced by the remark that, in view of what Italy did to other countries and in the light of the knowledge of what Fascism would have done had it emerged triumphant from the war (and that without serious objection from the Italian people), Italians have a weak case in complaining of retaliation, if retaliation there be, toward their country. Having said this, the fact remains that the Allies stood committed to the principle of justice in general, and more specifically of the self-determination of peoples, just as they were in 1918. This moral obligation is inescapable, having been freely undertaken on their part. Moreover, from the mere standpoint of expediency and practicality, retaliation, however understandable it might be at the moment, if it takes the form of creating territorial grievances, can only serve to impede in the long run the process of reconciliation and the restoration of stability and durable peace.

All these considerations pointed to the desirability of drawing the new frontiers of Italy with fairness, and the case of Italy is among the easiest because of the definiteness of these frontiers. The territories annexed by France are in themselves minute and of little significance, save in the matter of power supply. For that reason, the negligible Italian territorial loss in this case might be said not to be worth discussing. But the argument cuts both ways; if these annexations are so insignificant, they serve little purpose other than that of pinpricks and symbols of defeat. The strategic argument, valid as it may be on the local scale, cannot be entertained seriously, for, in this respect, the French have on the whole the advantage throughout the length of their Italian frontier. While, therefore, it may be said that Italy has cause to congratulate herself in this case at the smallness of her loss, it is equally true that an attitude of generosity on the side of France would also have been one of wisdom. It is of interest that on the occasion of the ratification of the treaty by the Italian Constituent Assembly on July 31, 1947, a unanimous appeal was made to the French people not to annex the territories in question. It would be pleasant if, on the Italian side, there could be an equally unanimous acknowledgment of the aggression of June 10, 1940, for the sort of thing that it was. Of such an attitude, so far, there have been occasional individual instances only.

As to the question of the South Tyrol, it can only be said that an opportunity was missed. There is reason to believe that the loss would have been taken in good part in Italy, and the case is unusually clear. The strategic argument, the only valid one for the Brenner frontier, is insufficient even if one disregard the significance of modern weapons of warfare. Barring change, however, what was done in the form of a direct Austro-Italian agreement is undoubtedly the next best solution.

The frontier with Yugoslavia presented unquestionably the most difficult problem. The whole of Julian Venetia has long been a pressure point of Europe, meeting ground as it is of the three great European ethnic groups, Latin, Slav, and Germanic. Some compromise between ethnic, economic, and strategic considerations is the best that can be done in this case. The frontier drawn in 1920, which gave the advantage to Italy in all three respects, is a good illustration of the point previously made—that a bad frontier is merely a source of future trouble—although in the context of the whole situation at the time it could be considered a not unreasonable compromise.

In 1919, a better solution in this region was suggested in the form of the American or Wilson line. Italy could not be coerced or induced to accept this solution and, in a sense, she may be said to be now reaping the fruits of her earlier intransigeance. For the tables are turned and it is Yugoslavia that has been highly uncompromising. In so far as national sentiment is involved, the feeling of Yugoslavia toward Italy at present is wholly understandable and rather more justified than was the Italian feeling toward the Croats and Slovenes in 1919. But these are not sound bases for the drawing of frontiers. In 1947, as in 1919, the American line would probably have been the best compromise; however, the solution adopted has been different. There is this to be said for the present frontier, and it is a strong argument, that it is closer to the ethnic line than was the Wilson line. On that score the Italians may become reconciled to it, although it will be difficult to forget such things as the voluntary mass migration of the population of Pola. The western coast of Istria is predominantly Italian and certainly Yugoslavia does not need it on any plea of naval strategy, the advantage in this respect being wholly on her side owing to the nature of the Adriatic shores.

The great stumbling block, as indicated before, was Trieste, and the solution adopted in the erection of the Free Territory was the result of extraneous forces greater than the merely Yugoslav and Italian. This is not a good solution. The statute of the Free Territory has been elaborated with great care and in minutest detail. But one can only take a dim view of the prospects of the new creation. There was far more justification for the creation of the Free City of Danzig in 1919 than for that of the Free Territory of Trieste in 1946. We know the fate of Danzig. The fault was not so much with the statute of Danzig; ultimately, Danzig was the pretext, not the cause, for German aggression. If the relations between Italy and Yugoslavia, or rather between the western and the Russian blocks, become tolerable, the Free Territory may prove a viable creation. But in that event it will also be a superfluous one. In the opposite event, it is to be feared that no amount of legal forethought in the form of detailed provisions will be a satisfactory substitute for sincerity of intent; it may be said in fact that the very complexity and elaborateness of the statute will in itself provide all the more grounds for chicanery—if such is the desire. Yugoslavia has it in her power to render the economic as well as the political life of the Free Territory untenable, and the state of affairs in Trieste since the peace has not been a happy one, outside subsidies alone keeping it alive.

To sum up, then, it would have been better if France had eschewed annexations, if the South Tyrol had rejoined Austria, if Trieste had remained unqualifiedly Italian, and if the whole frontier with Yugo-slavia had been drawn somewhat further east. Yet ideal solutions cannot be produced *in vacuo;* it would be merely unrealistic and utopian to ignore the stresses that the war has brought to the surface, and, if it is regrettable that a perhaps transitory relationship of feeling and of power should determine such presumably permanent matters as frontiers, the fact is that it does. Considering all this, it may be said that Italy has not been treated with undue harshness. She may indeed congratulate her-self over the fact that the Allies espoused principles—even though the application of them is at times qualified in practice—so radically differ-ent from those which animated her regime when she made the mistake of abandoning her neutrality.

Italian interests in the Adriatic are bound to remain important, but there is no reason why the Adriatic should be an Italian lake, and it is therefore well, on the whole, that Italy should retain no foothold on the Dalmatian coast or in Albania. The same applies to the Dodecanese, save that perhaps the isolated outpost of Castellorizzo might better have been turned over to Turkey.

The colonial question remains unsettled. That Abyssinia should be restored goes without saying. There is no issue there. That leaves the question of the colonies in existence before the days of Fascism: Eritrea, Somaliland, and Libya. These colonies have never been assets to Italy, though the military significance of Libya in the Second World War was considerable. The simple fact is that Italy cannot aspire to an imperial role. When it is at present a question how far much older, more important, and better-established empires can continue to preserve themselves, it would be a bold but a sensible gesture if the Italian people took the position that they are well rid of their colonies. But it would be unreasonable to look for such reasonableness on the part of national feeling; power, however onerous and futile, seldom abdicates of its own free choice. In all likelihood, the former Italian colonies will become mandates or trusteeships. They could be made joint trusteeships of the United Nations, but condominiums are not, in general, desirable solutions. Taking all factors into account, it might therefore be the part of wisdom to make Italy the trustee of her former possessions. If not Italy, Britain would be the next most logical candidate, at least for the East African possessions. Libya will be more troublesome, for the unrest which pervades the whole Arab world is equally at work there, and Britain, like France, is facing a difficult future in her relations with that world. Libya alone hardly offers the basis for a separate and independent political entity. To be sure, we have only begun to witness the manifestations of Egyptian imperialism. As to the suggestion, made at one time, of a Russian trusteeship for Libya, it does not deserve serious consideration; it has far less foundation than a German establishment in Morocco would have had before 1914.

Taken by themselves, the disarmament clauses are justified, or they would be if one had assurance that none of Italy's neighbors has designs upon her. All depends upon the intentions of Yugoslavia. In view of her claims, her intransigeance, and the position that Yugoslavia has taken with respect to the Free Territory of Trieste, an element of doubt subsists. Yugoslavia maintains an unnecessarily large military establishment. Should untoward developments occur in the Free Territory, Italy is powerless to take action and would have to rely upon the United Nations, or, more immediately and concretely, upon the western allies. This is in reality an issue between the two great blocs in process of crystallization. In many ways, the state of affairs in Trieste is reminiscent of the situation of Fiume after it was erected into a Free State in 1920. One complicating factor has been that of the relations between Yugoslavia on the one hand and the Soviet Union with her satellites on the other. The withdrawal of Russian support is likely to exacerbate Yugoslav nationalism, but the deprival of effective backing force may also make Yugoslavia more amenable in her dealings with the western world. The Yugoslav case is undoubtedly one of the more curious phenomena that the war has produced.

Despite much recrimination in Italy, it may also be said that the total of reparations is not exorbitant, especially when account is taken of the initial two-year moratorium and of the provision for the delivery of raw materials to Italy by the countries entitled to reparations. It may be pointed out that Finland, for example, with a population less than one tenth that of Italy and subject to serious territorial and economic amputations, is required to pay $300,000,000 to the Soviet Union. Taken as a whole, in fact, the Italian treaty, while susceptible of improvement, may be described as a not unreasonable settlement. It is a reflection of the fact that the western countries especially are not fearful of Italian power, actual or potential, and have been inclined to leniency toward Italy. This tendency has increased with the passage of time and with the desire, especially on America's part, to secure Italy for the western European bloc. It is of interest, in this connection, to note former Secretary Marshall's message to Foreign Minister Sforza on the occasion of the ratification of the treaty by the Italian Assembly. This communication implied American sympathy for Italian efforts to secure some revision of the terms of peace, particularly in regard to Trieste, colonies, reparations, and the surrender of naval units.

That the treaty should be welcomed in Italy could hardly be expected. It is difficult to find avowed Fascists in Italy today—just as Nazis are scarce in Germany—and, very understandably, Italians are anxious to draw a veil over the Fascist episode and to be readmitted to the community of democratic nations. It will take more time before Italy has fully and truly worked her passage home.

For that matter, the formal reestablishment of peace, while important, does not solve the pressing problem of either Italy or other European countries. Of necessity, the masses of Europe are less concerned with politics than with the far more immediate difficulty of physical survival. For that reason, it is felt by many that the economic question takes precedence over all others. In varying degrees, the same applies to most

European countries, but the Italian situation is a particularly difficult one. For one thing, it must be remembered that, with few interruptions, Italy had been at war ever since 1935. These wars were a severe strain on the country and have brought out in full the weaknesses of the Italian economy. As a consequence, despite a very substantial measure of recovery, Italy has been living a hand-to-mouth existence, depending to an unusual extent upon American subsidies for survival. Such arrangements are, from their very nature, bound to be temporary. It is a common endeavor of European countries to raise their exports above the prewar level. This is only natural, but even disregarding the difficulties of a purely monetary nature, the fact remains that this endeavor will inevitably encounter the obstacle of competition, both among European countries and between them and the similar urge of a vastly expanded American productivity. The destruction of war in Europe has created a vast demand for American raw materials and manufactures, a demand which will be met so long as America continues to finance it; but any substantial degree of European restoration will again put the stress on competition.

The enforced and traditional frugality and the low standard of living of the Italian masses have the divergent effects of enabling them to subsist on little but also of leaving little margin of safety. If the problem of physical existence is the greatest immediate concern, that does not mean that the role of politics is less, but rather that it is distorted. This is the basis of the great shift to the Left in nearly all European countries and more particularly of the strength of the Communist parties. It is often said that the Italian people, like the French, are not by nature inclined toward Communism. This is in large measure true, and there is little cause to doubt that a substantial part at least of the Communist vote in both countries does not come from Communists by conviction. But, as mentioned before, the Communists in the west of Europe have the double advantage that they represent the promise of something better—a promise which, unlike that of other parties has not been tested in past tenures of office—and that their countries have not been burdened by the presence of Russian troops and had direct contact with Soviet ways and standards. As to Communist leadership in the west, much of it is at once high-minded—in the sense that it is motivated by a deep and sincere desire to organize a new and better society —and at the same time opportunistic and unprincipled—in the sense that it operates on the assumption that the end justifies any means and is not hampered by the tenets of so-called "bourgeois" morality. While the gyrations of the Kremlin have on occasion embarrassed western Communists, these have shown on the whole suppleness and adaptability to circumstances. Italian Communists have shown skillful deference both to national and to religious feeling.

One difficulty lies in the fact that once Communism establishes itself in power it is difficult to dislodge. A Communist regime, like a Nazi or Fascist, knows how to make Giolittian manipulations of the political machine look by contrast urbane, civilized, and amateurish. The possibility cannot be ignored that Communism may be the only way to ultimate survival for Europe. Should that be so, however, the whole war will have been a wasted effort, to be looked upon as in the same category as the blind and irresponsible forces of nature. For, after all, it is also conceivable that, had Germany had her way, in the course of two or three centuries a new Europe would have emerged where human dignity would have been restored. Either solution, in view of what western Europe has been, would be tantamount to a second coming of the barbarians. Future centuries may take a dispassionate view of the historic process and even find good in it, but the duration of human life being what it is, the contemplation of the process has little value as a guide to immediate action. The values and forces that have existed cannot so easily surrender, and, just as the Nazi attempt meant a world conflict, so likewise an attempted dominance of Communism could not be divorced from further warfare, in all likelihood both international and civil.

Italy is one of the major testing grounds of the competing ideologies of our time. The war, distorted in its meaning by the adventitious alliance between the western democracies and Russia, has left the issue unsettled and confused. Reflecting the wartime cooperation among the Allies and the high hopes to which this cooperation gave rise among many, the Communists for a time, in Italy as in France, participated in the government and used their great influence over Labor to enhance the process of recovery. But with the increasingly open clash between

East and West, the Communists have used their best endeavors to impede further recovery. This they have done on the sound (from their point of view) but Machiavellian theory that, once their initial bid for power in the period immediately following the termination of hostilities had failed, their chances can best prosper in the midst of chaos. Since 1947 they have been out of the coalition which had governed the country. Their hostility has been sharpened by the avowed Russian effort to sabotage the Marshall Plan, and the election of 1948 in Italy was an open contest—with few holds barred—between American and Russian influence, with the former carrying the day.

If we assume that Europe will retain something like her former familiar shape, the question presents itself of the role that will fall to that other great force that shaped the nineteenth century, that is nationalism. The settlements that followed the First World War redrew the map of Europe in accordance with the nearest approximation to the principle of self-determination that had ever been attempted. This was wholly proper, but the result in itself served to accentuate the economic difficulties of a continent made up of too many sovereign units. These difficulties in turn had the effect of emphasizing the evils of economic nationalism developed to a degree of suicidal absurdity. Just what the effects of the Second World War will have been on nationalism it is too early to foresee. On the one hand, the motivating force of resistance to German conquest—not excluding Russian resistance—was more national than ideological; on the other, the common misery that prevails at the moment tends to place first emphasis on aspects other than the national. The common man who, in any event, increasingly dominates the scene is not a nationalist by nature. Left to his own devices, he will adapt himself with comparative speed and facility to a milieu other than that of his birth; of this fact America is the living and irrefutable illustration. The old ruling class and financial oligarchies also tend to display a considerable degree of cosmopolitanism, but they stand largely discredited in Europe at present. Nationalism has been the peculiar appanage of the bourgeoisie, highly conscious of its "national" idiosyncrasies. It is this class which has furnished the leadership of nations, in the form of supplying their intelligentsia and their bureaucracy, and, by setting the tone of education, has produced the comparatively recent phenomenon of nationalism as we have known it in our time. That class has been severely injured, inflations are playing havoc with it, and the nationalism of which it has been the prime keeper is certainly out of date. The principle of sovereignty, however much insisted upon and paid lip service to, has in effect become a pious fraud for the majority of nations. Short of chaos and Communism, however, it is difficult to conceive of European nations surrendering their individual identities, especially in the west, where differences have long since crystallized, by contrast with the Slavic east, which presents a much more fluid picture. Europe—and civilization—would indeed be the losers from the obliteration of national differences on the cultural level.

And that is the best that may be hoped for Europe: a degree of economic integration which would make her continued existence possible —indeed, considering her resources and skills, after a time easy and prosperous—combined with the retention of cultural autonomies. In such a Europe it would be folly for Italy not to abandon dreams of political leadership and expansion. But neither need she be degraded to the status of a nation of mandolin players, a playground for more fortunate peoples, strewn with picturesque relics of the past and the attractions of nature. Italy might recall the dream of her Mazzini; intransigeant and aloof though he was, a lover of mankind but not of men, as he put it himself, his vision was yet large and noble. Reverting to her true tradition, after emerging from the costly nightmare of Fascism, she might yet achieve the leadership which would consist in becoming, in the words of a recent writer, "a beacon for all, a thing of beauty."

Olschki, Leonardo, The Genius of Italy. New York, Oxford University Press, 1949.

Prezzolini, Giuseppe, The Legacy of Italy. New York, S. F. Vanni, 1948.

Salandra, Antonio, Italy and the Great War, translated by Zoe Kendrick Pyne. London, Edward Arnold, 1932.

Salomone, A. William, Italian Democracy in the Making, the Political Scene in the Giolittian Era 1900–1914. Philadelphia, University of Pennsylvania Press, 1945.

Salvatorelli, Luigi, A Concise History of Italy, translated by Bernard Miall. New York, Oxford University Press, 1940.

Salvemini, Gaetano, The Fascist Dictatorship in Italy. New York, Henry Holt, 1927.

—— Under the Axe of Fascism. New York, Viking Press, 1936.

Schneider, Herbert W., Making the Fascist State. New York, Oxford University Press, 1928.

—— The Fascist Government of Italy. New York, D. Van Nostrand, 1936.

Schneider, Herbert W., and Shepard B. Clough, Making Fascists. Chicago, University of Chicago Press, 1929.

Shotwell, James T., ed., Governments of Continental Europe. New York, The Macmillan Company, 1940. Section on Italy by Arnold J. Zurcher.

Sprigge, Cecil J. S., The Development of Modern Italy. New Haven, Yale University Press, 1944.

Sturzo, Luigi, Italy and Fascismo. New York, Harcourt Brace, 1926.

Taylor, A. J. P., The Italian Problem in European Diplomacy, 1847–1849. Manchester, Manchester University Press, 1934.

Thayer, William Roscoe, The Life and Times of Cavour. 2 vols., New York, Houghton Mifflin, 1911.

Trevelyan, George Macaulay, Manin and the Venetian Revolution of 1848. London, Longmans Green, 1923.

—— Garibaldi and the Thousand. New York, Longmans Green, 1928.

—— Garibaldi's Defense of the Roman Republic. London, Longmans Green, 1919.

—— Garibaldi and the Making of Italy. New York, Longmans Green, 1928.

Villari, Luigi, The Fascist Experiment. London, Faber and Gwyer, 1926.

—— The Expansion of Italy. London, Faber and Faber, 1930.

Welk, William G., Fascist Economic Policy. Cambridge, Mass., Harvard University Press, 1938.

Wiskemann, Elizabeth, Italy. New York, Oxford University Press, 1947.

—— The Rome-Berlin Axis, a History of the Relations between Hitler and Mussolini. New York, Oxford University Press, 1949.

SUGGESTED READINGS

THE FOLLOWING is a list of books intended for the reader who may be interested in delving further into the whole of the period surveyed in this book or in certain more limited aspects of it. The list is not intended to be either comprehensive or exhaustive, but rather representative; a different one could easily have been made. Unfortunately, for all the traditional English interest in and sympathy for things Italian, English is perhaps not the best language with which to approach the Italian scene. However, to have included literature in other languages would either have resulted in a very lengthy bibliography or presented invidious difficulties of selection. For that reason, the decision was made to confine the list to English titles only.

Albrecht-Carrié, René, Italy at the Paris Peace Conference. New York, Columbia University Press, 1938.

Binchy, Daniel A., Church and State in Fascist Italy. New York, Oxford University Press, 1941.

Borgese, G. A., Goliath, the March of Fascism. New York, Viking Press, 1937.

Crispi, Francesco, The Memoirs of Francesco Crispi, translated by Mary Prichard-Agnetti. 3 vols., London, Hodder and Stoughton, 1912–14.

Croce, Benedetto, A History of Italy, 1871–1915, translated by Cecilia M. Ady. Oxford, England, Clarendon Press, 1929.

Finer, Herman, Mussolini's Italy. New York, Henry Holt, 1935.

Florinsky, Michael T., Fascism and National Socialism. New York, The Macmillan Company, 1936.

Giolitti, Giovanni, Memoirs of My Life, translated by Edward Storer. London, Chapman and Dodd, 1923.

Greenfield, Kent Roberts, Economics and Liberalism in the Risorgimento. Baltimore, The Johns Hopkins Press, 1934.

Hentze, Margot, Pre-Fascist Italy, the Rise and Fall of the Parliamentary Régime. London, Allen and Unwin, 1934.

King, Bolton, A History of Italian Unity, Being a Political History of Italy from 1814 to 1871. 2 vols. London, James Nisbet and Co., 1934.

—— The Life of Mazzini. New York, E. P. Dutton, 1911.

King, Bolton, and Thomas Okey, Italy Today. London, James Nisbet and Co., 1913

Macartney, Maxwell H. H., and Paul Cremona, Italy's Foreign and Colonial Policy, 1914–1937. New York, Oxford University Press, 1938.

Mazzini, Joseph, The Duties of Man and Other Essays. Everyman Ed.

Monroe, Elizabeth, The Mediterranean in Politics. London, Oxford University Press, 1938.